THE REAL JIM HAWKINS

THE REAL JIM HAWKINS

Ships' Boys in the Georgian Navy

by Roland Pietsch

Seaforth
PUBLISHING

Für meine Eltern

Ingrid und Wolfgang

Copyright © Roland Pietsch 2010

First published in Great Britain in 2010 by
Seaforth Publishing,
Pen & Sword Books Ltd,
47 Church Street
Barnsley S70 2AS

www.seaforthpublishing.com

British Library Cataloguing in Publication Data
A catalogue record for this book is available from the British Library

ISBN 978-1-84832-036-9

Designed and typeset by M.A.T.S., Leigh-on-Sea, Essex
Printed and bound by MPG Books Group, UK

Contents

List of Illustrations

Acknowledgements

As does every author, I have an endless list of people to thank. The colleagues who have read, supervised, commented on, or examined the various stages of this study were: Professor Sarah Palmer, who started me on the topic as a doctoral student, Professor David Wootton, my PhD supervisor, Professor Glyn Williams, who went through all my doctoral drafts, even when he complained that my English was increasingly suffering from my allegedly spending too much time with footballers, and Professor John Miller. Furthermore, there were Professor N A M Rodger, who had an answer to almost any naval history question I could think of, and Pat Crimmin, who was also a great support in my search for funding. Grace O'Byrne acted as a tireless publishing adviser over many years, and children's author M E Lehmann proofread the entire manuscript in the shortest time. Dr Dianne Payne provided a challenging and productive exchange in using the Marine Society's boy registers and also allowed me to use her database. Professor Isaac Land was, and is, a unique inspiration when it comes to interpreting the sailors' culture. Professor B R Burg encouraged the debate about homoeroticism on board, and Professor Donna Andrew read what I had to say on eighteenth-century charities in general and gave valuable feedback. Consultant psychiatrist Dr Nikola Kern of Bethlem Royal Hospital speculated with me about the possible mental injuries of the ships' boys. Ian Hunter helped with the photography, took all the photos where my happy-schnapper attitude did not take enough account of aperture and composition, and also helped by exhibiting the parallels between a sailor's life and that of a modern-day touring rock musician. Dr Alan Ross shared the trials of being a PhD student, and provided many inspiring exchanges on youth history as a field of study, while children's author Paul Dowswell helped to reignite a juvenile fascination with maritime adventures. Barry Jones worked through many draft chapters of this book and never lost his enthusiasm. Professor Sir Roderick Floud gave helpful advice on transferring the Marine Society registers into a database, and Dr Peter Earle on archives for merchant seamen.

Furthermore, at the National Maritime Museum in Greenwich, I have to thank particularly Dr Margarette Lincoln and Dr Nigel Rigby, as well as

Professor Roger Knight (formerly at the NMM), for their continuous support over many years. My doctoral research was funded by a Junior Caird Fellowship of the National Maritime Museum, and by a studentship from Queen Mary, University of London. At Queen Mary, I would like to thank the staff and students of the history department and of the International Foundation Programme. At the Marine Society, I would like to thank Samantha Shaw, Brian Thomas, Mark Jackson, Nick Blackmore and Jeremy Howard for their interest in my research, for allowing me to work under Jonas Hanway's watchful portrait, and to reproduce paintings and illustrations. Gavin Wilson helped with identifying historic photos, and kindly allowed me to use photos from his collection. At Wall to Wall Television my thanks go to Debbie Townsend and everyone else, not least for advice on copyright issues, and at the 1805 Club to Dr Huw Lewis-Jones and Anthony Cross.

I am also indebted to the Royal Historical Society for funding me to present my research results at the *Maritime History Beyond 2000* conference in Fremantle (Australia) in 2001. Earlier findings of my studies have been published in the *Journal for Maritime Research* (2000), the *Genealogists' Magazine* (2001), *The Northern Mariner* (2004), *Deutsche Schiffahrt* (2005), *The Seafarer* (2001, 2006), *The Oxford Encyclopedia of Maritime History* (2007), and *The Trafalgar Chronicle* (2009). And they have been presented at, amongst others, the *New Researchers in Maritime History* conference (University of Hull, 1999), the *National Maritime Museum* (2001), the *Neuere Forschungen zur Wirtschafts- und Sozialgeschichte* (Georg-August-Universität Göttingen, 2003), the *British Maritime History Seminar* (National Maritime Museum and Institute of Historical Research, 2009), and the *Economic and Social History Seminar* (University of Oxford, 2010) – I am grateful to all the editors and conference organisers involved for giving me the opportunity to present my research.

Lastly, I would like to thank the helpful staff at the National Maritime Museum, the National Archives, the British Library, the London Guildhall Library, the Institute of Historical Research, the Tower Hamlets Local History Library and Archive, the UK Data Archive in Essex, National Museums Liverpool, the Berlin Staatsbibliothek, the National Portrait Gallery, Westminster Abbey Library, Disney Publishing Worldwide, Random House (for Dell), as well as the bar staff in The Hare, my local pub in Bethnal Green, and various other establishments in the East End of London that allowed me to quietly sit in the corner with my laptop and write, whilst some of their punters demonstrated how Jolly Jack Tar lives on in today's leisure culture. I should also thank one real-life ship's boy, Joseph

Conrad (1857-1924), for showing that it is possible to write books in English even if one has only become fluent in the English language as an adult. And perhaps I should also thank Robinson Crusoe, for inspiring me to believe that a son of German parents, and a dreadful sailor, can still leave his name in English maritime tradition.

As historians are human beings, too, the social support while writing a book is as important as the historical advice from colleagues. Hence I would like to thank my dear friends Rabeya Poppy Sultana, Andrew Robertson, Corrado Di Pisa, Adrian Lewis, Richard Burton, Emma Ringqvist, Ben O'Connor, Tündi Reniers, Emma Mukerjee, Jamie Perera, Carolyn Deacon, Davina Brewster, Ane Rodriguez, Karin Dolk, Jorge Mugica, Rebecca Harrop and Basti Lynn Fox, Feli and Alice, Fab Dal Bello, Martin Wissenberg, Rosa and Nick, everyone from the Spitalfields Arts Project (*The Spitz*, 1996-2007) and TELquel (TU Berlin, 1992-1995), as well as Berit Emma Ott and Fridolin der Pirat, Michiel Dyer, Juan Pedraza and Josune, Jens Hobus, Grand Union Co-op, David Martinez, Ian Reid and everyone from Stocks Court (1997-2000), Carsten Böhme and family with Raphaël le pirate, Marc Wiechmann and Katja, for providing the work soundtrack, mainly Smog, Hayden, Micah P Hinson, Little Sparta, Portishead and Fionn Regan, as well as my family Gerarda, Ingrid and Wolfgang Pietsch, Ingrid Schmidt, Karen and Tom Gerlach, and all the Kraatzs (Bärbel for Schätzinsel record and book) and Wetzels. In memory of Peter Schmidt (1940-2004) and Siegfried Kraatz (1940-2005).

Finally, I would like to thank Julian Mannering, Stephanie Rudgard-Redsell, and Seaforth for making it all possible.

'To the Hesitating Purchaser'[1]

I remember him as if it were yesterday, as he came plodding to the inn door, his sea chest following behind him in a hand-barrow; a tall, strong, heavy, nut-brown man; his tarry pigtail falling over the shoulders of his soiled blue coat; his hands ragged and scarred, with black, broken nails; and the sabre cut across one cheek, a dirty livid white. I remember him looking round the cove and whistling to himself as he did so, and then breaking out in that old sea-song that he sang so often afterwards:-

> 'Fifteen men on the dead man's chest –
> Yo-ho-ho, and a bottle of rum!'[2]

SUCH were young Jim Hawkins' vivid memories of his first encounter with the 'old sea dog', Captain Billy Bones, and his sea chest. When Robert Louis Stevenson wrote Jim Hawkins' *Treasure Island* adventure, he could bank on young readers all over Britain sharing Jim's fascination with sailors and his boyish dreams of going to sea. Yet while the ship's boy in the golden age of sail has become a familiar character in fiction, until now little was known about the real-life seafaring boys of the eighteenth century – this despite the fact that, on average, near ten per cent of the crew of an eighteenth-century British warship were boys. This book, which is based on the study of hitherto unused archival material, aims to close that gap in the historiography. It is the first ever history of boys in the eighteenth-century Royal Navy, the captains' and officers' servants or 'powder monkeys', who were brought up at sea to become seasoned sailors and indispensable pillars of Britain's global empire. These boys' lives were no less hazardous and colourful than the adventures of their famous fictional counterpart Jim Hawkins.

The book also aims to go beyond maritime history by picking up on the boys' lives ashore, exploring their social backgrounds, their previous jobs and apprenticeships, and their peculiar, yet surprisingly familiar, youth culture. It was not only family tradition or purely economic reasons which led these real-life versions of Jim Hawkins into the Navy, but also a catalogue of troubles and desires which surrounded Jim as much as they do today's teenagers – from 'anti-social behaviour orders' to the dream of a sailor's life full of 'sex & grogs & sea shanties'.[3] Finally, this account also looks at the social and emotional challenges Jim faced when settling into life on land after returning from his adventures at sea, amongst other aspects also speculating about the possible legacy of having been what we today might term a 'child soldier'.

Whilst the study attempts to cover the entire eighteenth century, the main focus is on the mid century, the time in which Stevenson had placed his *Treasure Island*, and furthermore, on wartime, particularly the Seven Years War (1756-1763), since at times of war a much greater number of ordinary boys enlisted in the Royal Navy. The spotlight is on the boys growing up on the lower deck, rather than those from privileged families destined to become midshipmen and then officers. A convenient cut-off point might have been the abolition of the Navy's officer-servant system in 1794 yet, because of the wealth of autobiographical sources from the early nineteenth century and general interest in Nelson's Navy, the study has been extended to the final defeat of Napoleon in 1815.

Autobiographical sources were particularly valuable for the investigation in chapter 5 into the fascination for sailors' culture shown by eighteenth-century boys and also when recreating the battle experiences of these boys in chapter 7. Such sources also add essential colour and life to the statistics produced by many years of research in dusty archives, and some of these ships' boys turned writers will accompany us throughout the book. Their autobiographies are being increasingly reprinted in modern editions or made available online, thus providing an exciting opportunity for readers with no access to archives to get their own first-hand experiences of life in the sailing Navy. With sailors being known for telling a good yarn, there are, of course, occasional doubts about the veracity of their memoirs, and readers must keep in mind that memoirs were usually published with a motive, be it to sell a dramatic story or even to expose maltreatment in the Navy, and that the authors were perhaps better educated than the average sailor. Furthermore, we are dealing with boyhood memories written later in life, and these may not always be accurate. On the other hand, official Navy documents, though written at the time, were often equally biased or flawed, and these also must be read with a similarly critical approach.

The main focus of the book is on boys in the Royal Navy, yet occasional references are also made to boys learning the ropes in private shipping. This study aims at both academic and non-academic readers, and furthermore the hope is also to make a small contribution to drawing naval and maritime history out of its former isolation to take its place firmly in general social and cultural history. Even though eighteenth-century sailors were looked upon as exotic creatures apart, there is no reason why maritime historians today should be equally separated from the rest of historical research, when seafaring and related trades played such an important role in the economic, social and cultural history of eighteenth-century Britain. For reasons of accessibility, nautical and academic jargon is avoided as much as possible in this book. The terms 'ships' boys' or 'boys' are preferred to the Navy term 'servant'. One very good reason for a closer integration of history at sea with history on land is, as this book argues, that many Britons took to deep-sea sailing only temporarily, during their youth, that is in their teens and twenties, and then afterwards settled down to a job on land, or to work in coastal and inland shipping. In a novel approach, this study links the sailors' culture with the culture of young people on land and interprets the behaviour of sailors in the light of this youth culture.

With regards to historical sources, one of the pillars on which this book is based is the archive of the London Marine Society, a charity which supported boys willing to join the Royal Navy from the eighteenth century onwards, and chapter 3 delivers a brief, but much-needed, institutional history of the Society's early years. The account will begin with an introduction to the subject of boys in the eighteenth-century Navy in chapter 1. Chapter 2 picks up on the boys ashore and looks at the possible troubles and circumstances that made them wish to bid farewell to their life on land. Chapter 3 tells the story of the Marine Society, whilst chapter 4 musters the typical ship's boy. Chapter 5 explores the motives which drove ships' boys to sea, and interprets the sailors' culture as a youth culture. Chapter 6 welcomes the boys on board and looks at all the potential trouble and enjoyment they faced when trying to settle into their new life in the wooden world. Chapter 7 covers the boys' adventures at sea, their first taste of battle, their encounters with death, and their coming of age and being rated as men. In chapter 8, the boys return from the sea, facing the difficult decision whether to settle down, or remain at sea in their new home. The book finishes with a few thoughts on the history of boy sailors, British maritime culture and youth history in general, followed by a very brief presentation of the main sources and literature.

No history book is a purely neutral account of what happened. In between the lines it can also mirror its author's own story. *Treasure Island* has not only captured the imagination of young readers in Britain but also worldwide, crossing national boundaries and even the hardened ideological borders of the twentieth century; in the case of my own childhood in West Berlin, I grew up with a West German television adaptation of *Treasure Island*, accompanied by the novel itself and a record produced in Communist East Germany, gifts from an aunt on the other side of the wall. Undeniably, there is more than just a breeze of romance to the topic, and I hope a little of this will also blow through these pages. After all, even the real-life Jim Hawkins fell victim to the romance of the sea, as we shall discover.

If there is one lesson that historians can learn from Jim Hawkins and all the other sailors, then it is the importance of telling a good yarn. And so we return to Jim Hawkins and his tale of the terrifying lodger at his parents' inn, the singing and storytelling old sea-dog Billy Bones:

> There were nights when he took a deal more rum and water than his head would carry; and then he would sometimes sit and sing his wicked, old, wild sea-songs, minding nobody; but sometimes he would call for glasses round, and force the trembling company to listen to his stories or bear a chorus to his singing. Often I have heard the house shaking with 'Yo-ho-ho, and a bottle of rum;' all the neighbours joining in for dear life, with the fear of death upon them, and each singing louder than the other, to avoid remark. For in these fits he was the most over-riding companion ever known; he would slap his hand on the table for silence all round; he would fly up in a passion of anger at a question, or sometimes because none was put, and so he judged the company was not following his story.[4]

With this in mind, we had better give the utmost attention to the following tale of the real-life Jim Hawkins.

CHAPTER 1

Seafaring Boys in the Eighteenth Century: Fiction and Reality

THE Battle of Lagos, 1759: this year marked the turning point of the Seven Years War and the Royal Navy's ascent to ruler of the oceans. On board one of the Navy vessels facing the French fleet, Olaudah Equiano, a fourteen-year-old ship's boy originally from Africa, experienced his first naval battle as a 'powder monkey':

> My station during the engagement was on the middle deck, where I was quartered with another boy, to bring powder to the aftermost gun; and here I was a witness of the dreadful fate of many of my companions, who, in the twinkling of an eye, were dashed in pieces, and launched into eternity. Happily I escaped unhurt, though the shot and splinters flew thick about me during the whole fight. . . . We were also, from our employment, very much exposed to the enemy's shots; for we had to go through nearly the whole length of the ship to bring the powder. I expected, therefore, every minute to be my last, especially when I saw our men fall so thick about me; . . . at first I thought it would be safest not to go for the powder till the Frenchmen had fired their broadside; and then, while they were charging, I could go and come with my powder. But immediately afterwards I thought this caution was fruitless; and, cheering myself with the reflection that there was a time allotted for me to die as well as to be born, I instantly cast off all fear or thought whatever of death, and went through the whole of my duty with alacrity.[1]

Olaudah's account is a rare voice, preserved from the thousands of boys who were brought up on board eighteenth-century British warships to become sea-bred sailors and the backbone of Britain's maritime empire. These real-life versions of Jim Hawkins, from Robert L Stevenson's novel *Treasure Island*, faced no lesser dangers than their famous fictional counterpart. Yet the story of these ships' boys has, until now, remained untold. Who were they, why did they enlist in the Navy, and what were the dangers and rewards awaiting them at sea? Stevenson had placed his *Treasure Island* story in the middle of the eighteenth century, over a hundred years before his own time. Hence his ship's boy Jim Hawkins would have gone to sea at exactly the same time as Olaudah Equiano. Ever since *Treasure Island* was first published in book form in 1883, generations of young readers have grown up with Jim

Treasure Island (US, 1950), with Bobby Driscoll as Jim Hawkins.

Walt Disney's *Treasure Island* as a Dell comic.

Hawkins' adventures – through the book itself, as well as through countless radio, stage, television and cinema adaptations in Britain and worldwide. The story of the boy at sea, travelling to exotic places and performing heroics in the adult world, hit a universal chord amongst readers.

Numerous authors followed Stevenson's theme of the ship's boy in the sailing Navy. But Stevenson was not the first to tell stories of boys at sea; others before him had specialised in the genre.[2] Earlier in the nineteenth century, Captain Frederick Marryat (1792-1848) found a wide audience for his stories of *Peter Simple* (1834), *Mr Midshipman Easy* (1836) and *The Pirate* (1836). What makes Marryat so fascinating for the historian is that he had experience of Nelson's Navy at first hand, as he went to sea as a boy, and served as a midshipman with Lord Cochrane during the war against Napoleon. A few other officers of Marryat's time also published stories about Nelson's Navy, perhaps feeling that they were the last witnesses of the 'great war' and the golden days of the sailing Navy; none reached Marryat's fame, though. *Peter Simple* was once the most widely read of his novels, yet today Marryat's best-known, and frequently reprinted, story of a boyhood at sea is that of *Mr Midshipman Easy*.[3]

The adventures of midshipman Jack Easy, and the comical confrontations Jack experiences, as his youthful ideals regarding the equality of men clash with the reality of naval life, are a treasure for anyone curious to discover what it was like to come of age in Nelson's Navy. Though Jack Easy's adventures have to be taken with a pinch of salt, Marryat's hero leads us much closer to the reality of a boyhood at sea than the fantastic story of Jim Hawkins' treasure hunt. If all maritime fiction can indeed be divided into just two classes, the 'Royal Navy yarn' and the 'desert island romance', then Marryat is as soundly settled in the former, as *Treasure Island* is in the latter. Unlike *Treasure Island*, *Midshipman Easy* was also aimed at a more mature audience. However, the great regret for the purpose of our story is that Jack Easy is the privileged son of a gentleman: he enters the Navy with the prospect of becoming an officer rather than a common seaman, and once again we hear little about the numerous boys on the lower deck who were raised to become able seamen.

In the second half of the nineteenth century, amidst the boom of adventure stories published for boys, the ship's boy established himself as a regular character in fiction. Just before Stevenson wrote *Treasure Island*, William H G Kingston (1814-1880) and Robert Michael Ballantyne (1825-1894) captured the imagination of young readers with their stories of seafaring boys. Like Marryat, Kingston's books, such as *From Powder Monkey to Admiral* (1870) or *The Three Midshipmen* (1873), were 'Royal Navy yarns' and tried to stick closer to the reality of a boy's life in the Navy. However, instead of Marryat's mature irony, Kingston's books were juvenile adventure stories. Because the days of the sailing Navy, the drifting sailor and unexplored exotic lands had disappeared with the arrival of steam-power, industrialisation, and uniform-wearing seamen in continuous service, there was now an outpouring of fictional and (pseudo-)autobiographical literature of the romantic sailing days. Robert Ballantyne's *The Coral Island* (1857), telling the adventure of three shipwrecked boys who end up on an uninhabited Polynesian island, would fall into the category of 'desert island romance' and was allegedly one of the main influences for Stevenson's *Treasure Island*. Stevenson mentions both Ballantyne and Kingston in his poem 'To the Hesitating Purchaser', which opens *Treasure Island*.

Stevenson also refers to a third, older author in the poem: James Fenimore Cooper (1789-1851). Cooper was serving in the US Navy as a midshipman around the same time that Frederick Marryat entered the Royal Navy. Although Cooper did not specialise in novels about boys at sea, he was one of the authors who established sea stories as a popular literary genre in the US. Midshipman turned author Cooper thus laid the foundation in the US readers' market for the first cabin boy turned author: Herman Melville (1819-1891), author of the classic whaling adventure *Moby Dick* (1851), but also of

Redburn (1849), a novel based on his own experiences as a cabin boy. Like Marryat's Jack Easy, Melville's young hero in *Redburn* first of all must overcome the culture shock of encountering the rough company to be found at sea. And some years later, so too does the cabin boy of Jack London's (1876-1916) novel *Sea-Wolf* (1904) – all of them stories of boys and youths who come of age at sea.

In the twentieth and twenty-first centuries, the ship's boy theme was continued by, amongst others, Leon Garfield's *Jack Holborn* (1964),[4] and also a string of novels, all sharing the same title *Powder Monkey*, by different authors of children's and juvenile historical fiction: George Manville Fenn (1904), Maureen Rylance (1999), George J Galloway (2001), and the first book in Paul Dowswell's series of the adventures of ship's boy Sam Witchall (2005). Karen Hesse's *Stowaway* (2000) contributed a fictional diary based on the real-life ship's boy Nicholas Young, who sailed on James Cook's *Endeavour*. Boys destined for an officer's career were covered by C S Forester's *Mr Midshipman Hornblower* (1950), the prequel to the Hornblower series, keeping Marryat's title, and aimed at mature readers and naval enthusiasts. Comic strips and television cartoons produced further celebrated ships'

Scene from *The Death of Nelson*, by Daniel Maclise (1859-64).

Detail of the powder boy from
The Death of Nelson.

4

boys, such as the cabin boy Tom in Captain Pugwash's adventures (first televised by the BBC in 1957), with the boy Tom seemingly being the only member of crew on board actually capable of sailing the ship.

Whilst the ordinary ship's boy has become a favourite character among authors of juvenile fiction, historians have so far neglected him. Boys destined to become midshipmen and officers have received some attention,[5] yet those hailing from humbler backgrounds, and not aiming at an officer's career, have until now remained totally anonymous. The paucity of studies can be partly excused by the lack of source material: eighteenth-century records telling us about boys aboard who were training to become ordinary sailors are scarce. Until the 1790s, the documents of the Royal Navy treated boys rather indifferently, the recorded information about the youngsters being often sketchy and time-consuming to collect and interpret. One thankful exception is the archive of the London Marine Society, a private charity which equipped thousands of boys for the Royal Navy, and later also for the merchant service. The Society's historical records regarding ships' boys give a unique insight into the nature of the real-life Jim Hawkins.

There have always been boys working on board ships. The seventeenth-century Spanish Navy had its *pajes*, the medieval German Hansa had its *Jungen*, and eighteenth-century British society was no different from many other societies in believing that a sailor had better start in his boyhood, otherwise he might never become a proper seaman. Marine Society founder and philanthropist Jonas Hanway (1712-1786) reckoned that it was 'beyond all contradiction, that those who are bred to the sea from the earliest part of life, generally become the ablest mariners', and that by 'being inured to hardships, they are not only rendered the more active and intrepid, but they can also bear long voyages, winter cruizes, and change of climate.'[6] Sailors were often described as an oddly distinct group with a separate culture, making it hard for outsiders to enter their community. Many landsmen failed to adapt to this foreign world when they embarked on a life at sea. In order to serve Britain's global political and economic ambitions, which relied so heavily on her ships and sailors, it was vital to nurture this peculiar breed of sailors in sufficient numbers from a very young age. Throughout the history of great navies, the lack of skilled sailors in times of war had always been a much bigger headache than lack of ships – in this respect the eighteenth-century British Navy struggled as much as the Athenian, the sixteenth-century Spanish, or the seventeenth-century Dutch navies, in filling its boats.

There is an assumption that seafaring was largely a hereditary trade, with most boys going to sea simply because that was how their fathers earned their living. However, this assumption has never been proven by a comprehensive study, and we shall see later that in times of war a large number of boys and young men from all sorts of backgrounds, and with no maritime connections at all, found their way into the Navy. In the Royal Navy the 'land-boys' at times even outnumbered the sons of seafarers and boys from coastal communities. Furthermore, we shall also see how throughout the eighteenth century various public and private schemes were devised to encourage more boys from non-seafaring families to go to sea. Hence Jim Hawkins, who only knew the sea through the tales of the guests and drunkards in his parents' inn, was not unusual for a ship's boy in the Royal Navy.

The boys on board the Navy vessels were an essential component in securing the future supply of quality seamen, and within a few years the youths were turned into able seamen. However, there was no continuous service in the eighteenth-century Navy; sailors were hired when needed, and many of these newly-trained boys were likely to go on to work in the merchant service or related trades. Yet they were always available when war dramatically increased the Navy's demand for manpower. The boys appeared in the Navy's muster books as captain's servant or officer's servant, regardless of their social backgrounds, and whether they were aiming at an officer's career or just at becoming able seamen. Although in their life and training the two groups differed greatly, official class differentiations were only intro-

Thomas Rowlandson, *Cabin-Boy* (1799).

duced to the Navy's muster books at the end of the century. The boys were not merely called servants, they were certainly also frequently called upon for personal servant duties by their officer (the term officer will include both captains and officers from now on). Yet despite the title, the boys' main purpose was not to be someone's domestic servant, but to be 'trainee sailors'. The Admiralty wished them to be the Navy's 'nursery' for seamen.[7]

Thirteen was the official minimum age for a servant, with an exception for officers' sons, who were allowed to be as young as eleven – 'Much too young,' Horatio Nelson once muttered in a conversation, without going further into detail, but probably remembering the time when he had to bid farewell to family and home, entering a warship as a tender twelve-year-old.[8] Older boys, aged eighteen to twenty, were usually allowed to omit the servant role and enter the Navy as paid landsmen. The Navy Regulations allowed each captain four servants for every hundred men of his ship's complement. Lieutenants, masters, pursers, surgeons, cooks and chaplains were allowed one servant if the complement was at least sixty. Boatswains, gunners and carpenters were also allowed one servant for a complement of at least sixty, and a second servant when the ship's complement reached a hundred. An admiral, depending on his rank, was entitled to ten to sixteen servants.

For each of his servants an officer received the net monthly pay of an ordinary seaman, whilst only having to spend about a fifth of this wage on the boy for clothing, other necessities or pocket money. However, to say that the officer pocketed the boy's wage, as it is often phrased in the literature, is slightly misleading: the ordinary seaman's wage had less to do with rewarding the boy's work, than being primarily a means of encouraging officers to take boys on board. By thus providing a financial incentive to each individual officer to recruit and look after one or more boys, the Navy hoped to ensure that enough youngsters would make their way to sea. Yet in finding their boys the officers received very little help from the Navy. There was no centrally co-ordinated recruitment and never any bounty payment offered to attract boys into the service. And despite its frequent occurrence in novels, it is unlikely that an officer would have been allowed to have his press gang grab randomly a boy who had never been to sea – under-eighteens with no seafaring experience were no legal target for the press gang.

In accordance with the Navy's servant quotas, between five and ten per cent of the crew of an eighteenth-century man-of-war would have been servants – a remarkably large proportion. Yet if we were allowed to step back into the eighteenth century and muster a few crews ourselves, we would probably be surprised to find that the ships had an even higher number of what we would consider boys, for we should find young recruits rated as men in the muster books: some because they already had significant seafaring experience, some because of preferential treatment, and others who were rated as men simply because no other suitable position was available. Additionally, in peacetime, we might also come across the odd apprentice to an officer, such as the gunner, boatswain or carpenter.[9] Next to them, we would also find the occasional underage son of an officer among the crew, who was not kept on the muster lists, defying the Navy's age regulations. Nicholas Young, for example, the boy who first spotted New Zealand on James Cook's journey, only appeared on the *Endeavour*'s muster list for the first time when he replaced a deceased sailor at Otaheiti (Tahiti). Thus the average Navy ship would have had a remarkably large percentage of boys on board. With that in mind, we may understand the astonishment of the Spanish sailors of the gold galleon *Nuestra Señora de Covadonga*, which was captured on Commodore George Anson's voyage around the world in 1743: upon coming on board Anson's *Centurion* as prisoners and seeing her by then diminished crew for the first time from close-up, they cried out with anger that they had been beaten by a bunch of boys.[10]

Yet the Royal Navy's training scheme had its flaws. In peacetime most servant positions were occupied by the sons of officers and better-off families, who were destined for an officer's career.[11] Only in times of war, when the number of servant placements multiplied with the additional men employed, did more opportunities for boys from humbler backgrounds open up. During the Seven Years War, the Marine Society estimated that there were at the time around 4,500 servant posts in the Royal Navy, of which around a thousand were occupied by the sons of gentlemen and other 'reputable persons'. However, the Society complained that possibly up to a quarter of the servant positions simply remained vacant, despite the financial incentives for the officers.[12] Even worse, not wanting to lose their wage bonus, some captains, who were unable to find or replace a servant, mustered a prisoner of war or a survivor of a shipwrecked merchantman to fill the position.[13] Others enlisted their personal slaves as servants, as was the case with Equiano.

Sometimes young men who could easily have been rated as ordinary seamen or as landsmen had to remain servants until a replacement was found. In all such cases, the original idea of the servant as a trainee sailor in a nursery for new seamen was disregarded. Some captains even invented a servant in the muster books. The 'phantom servant' had the bonus that a relative studying navigation on land could be provided with a falsified history of seafaring experience and thus shorten the six years at sea he needed for a lieutenancy. James Cook was among the culprits committing such fraud.[14]

Ironically, Lord Powlett, who initiated Marine Society member John Fielding's (1721-1780) recruitment scheme for boys, was also once caught mustering his own and his first lieutenant's son without the two boys being on board.[15] The Marine Society, aware of this deceit, suggested that officials in the home ports should check if all those servants for whom the officers asked to be paid their wages were actually present.[16]

In defence of the Navy's officers, it has to be acknowledged that, even with the help of private organisations like the Marine Society, it was sometimes difficult to fill servant positions, particularly when the ships were away from England and had no way of replacing deceased or promoted servants. The Navy finally acted at the end of the century and abolished the officer-servant model altogether in 1794.[17] Instead the categories of first-, second-, and third-class boys were introduced. From then on, the boys received pay from the Navy, instead of an allowance from their officer. The officers in turn received a monetary compensation for their lost servant-pay bonus. The class distinction was then made visible: first-class boys were to consist of 'young gentlemen' or 'volunteers', aged at least eleven and aiming at an officer's career. The second- and third-class boys were those destined for the lower deck. Second-class boys were meant to be between fifteen and seventeen years old and already being divided into the ship's watches with the seamen, while third-class boys were the newcomers aged thirteen to fifteen. Boys of the first class were paid £6 per year, second-class boys £5, and third-class boys £4, approximately double the amount that they previously received on average as an allowance from their officers. The boys' pay even went up by £3 for each class in 1806, during the years of the Bank Restriction and the inflationary paper pound. The only downside to the new system was that the Navy's ships now had fewer spaces for boys, in order to compensate for the increased expenses.

Why was the Navy so slow in improving its training scheme? The absence of a continuous service, only introduced in 1853, may have been the main reason, as it made the problem appear less pressing. It was never planned to keep the newly trained boys in the service for a lifetime. And there was a huge variance between the low manpower demand in peacetime, dictated by the constraints of public finance, and the high demand in wartime. Thus any boys trained in the Navy could be lured away by the often better-paying merchant service, and most of them would anyway have to be discharged at the end of a conflict. It therefore appeared more cost-efficient to let private shipping do the 'nursing', and then take trained sailors from there whenever needed – if not with the promise of bounty payments and prize money, then forcefully with the press warrant.

In private shipping, boys embarked on their seafaring careers in a similar manner to which they would have learned any other trade on land, that is, either as apprentices or paid servants. They began sometime between the ages of twelve to sixteen. An apprenticeship would have been the proper way into the trade, yet it was by no means an essential one, and a large part, possibly even the majority, started their seafaring career as hired servants, or cabin and ships' boys instead.[18] Also, as in most land-based occupations, the quality of the apprenticeships varied greatly, depending on the personal master-apprentice relationship, and on the apprenticeship premium paid for the boy by his parents or sponsors. Premiums ranged from close to £100 at the very top end, where the boys were trained up quickly to become masters or mates, to more commonly between £10 and £20, and down to £5 or less paid for pauper apprentices sponsored by their parish. The lower the premium, the greater was the likelihood that the boy was misused as a cheap labourer without any training being provided. Just as in land-based occupations, pay was only expected in better apprenticeships, and in the latter years of the usual seven years of service, with the pay normally rising with years of service.

Boys with no good family connections, or with parents who could not pay a decent premium, thus had low expectations about the training they would receive in an apprenticeship in private shipping. To many it appeared more convenient to avoid the apprenticeship altogether, and instead to go on board as a paid servant, or a ship's boy or cabin boy (personal servant), who would – after a few unpaid voyages – soon receive a monthly wage. For the ship's master, employing a servant or boy instead of an apprentice had the advantage of yielding fewer obligations, such as not having to guarantee any continuous employment beyond the next voyage or during the winter months. Only in times of war, when press warrants were issued, was the apprentice clearly the more desirable option for a ship's master, as he could obtain a three-year protection from being pressed into naval service for the youth. Accordingly, in times of war the number of apprentices in merchant shipping reached a high point. During the Seven Years War, three to four thousand of such apprentice protections were issued every year.[19] At the same time the Navy would have taken on roughly one or two thousand new servants each year. Furthermore, there would have still been a large, albeit unknown, number of youths newly entering private shipping each year as servants or boys; all in all one senses that in times of war a large number of British boys chose to go to sea, at least temporarily, each year. It is, however, difficult to come up with a meaningful percentage of the total population of roughly 250,000 boys in Britain aged between thirteen and fifteen, as the ages at which these boys first went to sea varied greatly, and so too did the service years and the annual demand.

Yet private shipping and the Royal Navy together still did not train up enough boy sailors to avoid the dangerous shortages of skilled seamen which the Navy faced at the outbreak of hostilities. Thus throughout the eighteenth century various public, as well as private, attempts were undertaken to attract more boys and young men to seafaring. With the Navy's manpower requirement rising in a conflict such as the Seven Years War from 10,000 to over 80,000, and the continuous need to replace losses due to death, sickness and desertions, the recruitment task seemed rather hopeless. In all, there might have been only between 35,000 and 80,000 (between one and two per cent of the total male population) sailors outside the Navy, who could have been attracted or pressed into naval service.[20] The Navy's recruitment task was made more difficult as in times of war wages in the merchant service rose dramatically, and so too did the demand for sailors by privateers. Furthermore, many sailors, worrying about their safety, retreated inland or stayed overseas to avoid the press gangs and the war completely. There was no way that the Navy could fill all its ships without some form of coercion.

Much has been written about the Navy's merciless press gangs, that 'worthless set of body snatchers' as sailor Jack Nastyface cursed them in his memoirs of a life in Nelson's Navy.[21] They roamed the harbour towns and raided merchantmen, with the right to kidnap any sailor, and take him away in an instant from his work, family and home, into an indefinite service of years at sea. Yet impressment could only target sailors, not landsmen and not inexperienced boys. Admittedly the gangs' definition of a seaman could sometimes be rather broad. To the Navy impressment was a necessary evil. Captains disliked it, as it filled their ships with unwilling recruits, who were understandably angry that they had been picked and had to make do with the regular Navy wages. Unlike the more equitable conscription, impressment was simply discriminatory. Only a general naval service for all sailors, or even a national service also including non-sailors, could have avoided the injustice, yet all attempts in setting up such schemes failed.[22] The Navy's press gangs were so unpopular that they sometimes encountered the violent resistance of an entire community, which refused to let its sailors go, or of a whole ship's crew when trying to board a merchantman. In 1760, for example, several hundred people, carrying firearms and other weapons, 'inhumanely treated' (according to the Secretary of the Admiralty) the press gang in Greenock, destroyed the King's boats, and threw the lieutenant and his press gang into gaol.[23] The Navy had asked parish authorities to assist with the recruitment efforts, and offered them rewards. Yet, despite this, the gangs

Children's Games: The Press Gang (1780).

were occasionally even hindered by magistrates. Magistrates were keen on keeping their community content, and were also frequently influenced by bribes or physical threats.[24]

Magistrates and other parish authorities were much more co-operative when it came to sending undesirable members of the community to the Navy, and here an opportunity was taken to channel more boys and young men into a career at sea. At the beginning of the eighteenth century, in Queen Anne's reign, laws were introduced allowing and encouraging magistrates, church-wardens, overseers of the poor, justices of the peace, mayors, aldermen and bailiffs to place boys who were supported by the parish in a maritime apprenticeship.[25] Furthermore, trade masters, who struggled to care for their parish-sponsored apprentices, were also allowed to turn their boys over to a maritime apprenticeship; the parish paid the apprenticeship fee for these boys. In the same legislation, masters of ships were ordered to take on one or more parish boys as apprentices, depending on the tonnage of their ships: one boy for the first thirty to fifty tons, one for the next fifty, and one more for every subsequent one hundred tons. Non-complying masters were threatened with a hefty ten-pound fine. Although these laws were about apprenticing poor boys on merchantmen or other waterborne businesses, and not in the Royal Navy,[26] the thinking behind them was that after their training the youths would be readily available to the Royal Navy in times of war. Historian Peter Earle considers that after the introduction of Queen Anne's acts perhaps thousands of poor boys entered apprenticeships in private shipping.[27] However, by the mid century the acts were widely neglected by parish officers and ships' masters.[28]

An interesting aspect of the acts, which is unclear to us today, is how far pressure could be applied to force boys to take part in the scheme. It is often hard to determine whether a boy himself perceived being sent to sea as a charity and a chance for a better life, or as a punishment and a means of removing him from the community. Charity and (precautionary) disciplinary measures overlapped, and throughout the book we will have to return to the suspicion that His Majesty's ships were occasionally misused as 'floating workhouses'. The debate is, however, by no means confined to seafaring, as parish authorities had the right to order any boy relying on parish support into a compulsory apprenticeship of any kind on land. And such schemes were not confined to Britain: in early seventeenth-century Spain, for example, privately run seminaries had been set up to train orphans as sailors, and the Spanish king had introduced a scheme by which beggars and orphans aged twelve to sixteen were collected, clothed, and assigned to captains and masters of ships. The programmes frequently failed though, because the boys were unmotivated or even delinquent. In Britain, the governors of London's famous Foundling Hospital for orphans, established in 1739, reckoned that their boys had a 'Destination to Navigation'.[29] Maritime employment was often used as a threat to those of their foundlings who made troublesome apprentices, urging that if they would not improve their behaviour they would be sent to sea.[30] Nearly a century later Charles Dickens still had the board of the workhouse threatening the orphan Oliver Twist that, if he would not be a good apprentice, they would send him to sea.[31]

Other institutions trying to channel poor boys to the sea had a more positive approach and were clearly just there to support motivated lads: there was, for example, the Stepney Society, established in London in 1674, which provided apprenticeships in maritime trades for impoverished boys from Stepney. Others focused on the boys' education: some of the charity schools established during the school boom in the first quarter of the eighteenth century instructed their boys in seafaring skills. There were also specialist schools like Christ's Hospital School and the Royal Hospital School, which was part of the pensioners' home in Greenwich, which were meant to prepare impoverished boys for the sea service, in particular the sons of deceased or disabled sailors. However, it seems that these specialist schools in the end always attracted boys from less desperate backgrounds, as being a student required not just a seafaring father, but also the necessary free time, reading abilities and sometimes also costly equipment, as the boys were prepared for higher ranks on board.

Queen Anne's acts promoting maritime apprenticeships also gave authorities the right to force into the Navy any boys and men considered to be petty offenders, rogues, or 'lewd and disorderly' servants, sturdy beggars and vagabonds, the latter including wandering actors of illegal performances, jugglers and other street entertainers,[32] and the Vagrancy Act of 1744 re-emphasised this right. These acts were not directed at proper felons, but were a precautionary measure against boys and young men who appeared likely to be recruited by criminal gangs if nobody else stepped in. Such recruits were, however, regularly rejected by captains; perhaps the captains felt they did not need any more street entertainers and ruffians on board their ship, and certainly not when those being offered were just boys.[33] They wanted sailors. The other side to the story is that the Navy officers often rejected these candidates on physical grounds, as magistrates often sent sick and crippled recruits, unfortunate individuals physically unable to support themselves, hence the reason for their parish being eager to get rid of them. At the end of the century, the Quota Acts of 1795 and 1796 made the problem even worse. The idea of these acts was that each county and port had to deliver a certain number of recruits – in theory a reasonable measure to spread the burden of naval service evenly and recruit suitable landsmen, yet unfortunately it further encouraged the practice of trying to dump onto the Navy undesirable men considered a burden on the community.

Some judges attempted to send genuine criminals into the Navy, either in terms of an offer to those indicted but not yet convicted, or as a condition for being granted a pardon to those already convicted. Those belonging to the former group are sometimes hard to detect in the sources, and we will return to the problem when discussing the motivations of ships' boys. In times of war the Navy was not opposed as a matter of principle to the recruitment of convicts, as long as they were sailors and appeared motivated. In times of extreme manning shortages, the Navy even sent its own officers on tours around prisons to see if they could free any sailors by paying their debts or by providing legal assistance.[34] Contrary to lexicographer Samuel Johnson's (1709-1789) much-quoted sarcastic comment, that the gaol was preferable to being on board one of His Majesty's ships, since in the former one was at least safe from drowning, the prison inmates preferred naval service. Recruited inmates were mostly seamen held for unpaid debts which is not surprising as, apart from debtors, most other offenders in the eighteenth century would only be in prison for the short time until their trial, after which they were either acquitted or hanged, transported, whipped or branded. There were also many smugglers among the recruited convicts, smuggling being a common crime in seafaring communities. On some rare occasions one also finds convicted pirates who had been sentenced to death receiving His Majesty's Pardon conditional on joining the Royal Navy.[35] Yet in relation to the total number of sailors employed in the Navy, the numbers of such convict sailors appear to have been small.

Using condemned men to make up missing numbers on board certainly had a long tradition in European history. It was a lot more popular in the days of the great Mediterranean galleys, as oarsmen are more easily controlled than sailors. The ancient navies were nevertheless still reluctant to use convicts as rowers, and mainly left them to serve in merchant shipping, contrary to the popular image created by the rowing Charlton Heston in the film *Ben Hur* (1959). Only in late medieval times did the rowing navies become less reluctant to use them: in fifteenth-century France, Charles VII allowed privateers to impress so-called *forçats*, idlers and vagabonds, as rowers. Sixteenth-century Venice even took men offered by the Duke of Bavaria from Bavarian prisons. Seventeenth-century Spanish galleys relied solely on slaves and convicts. Yet for the sailing navies things were more difficult, as sailors move freely and need specialist skills. In crucial manoeuvres, inexperience and disobedience could have disastrous consequences for the entire ship. As Samuel Leech, a sailor in Nelson's Navy, put it: 'A ship contains a set of human machinery, in which every man is a wheel, a band, or a crank, all moving with wonderful regularity and precision to the will of its machinist',[36] and each crank and wheel needed to be reliable and professional. Hence the Navy would have accepted inexperienced or unwilling recruits only in emergencies, especially when those on offer were merely boys. Nevertheless, it did happen that boys were pushed into the Navy, as we shall see when exploring the motivations which led our real-life versions of Jim Hawkins to sea.

However, we shall also learn that many of Jim's comrades had positive expectations, both culturally and economically, about what life as a sailor would be like, particularly those who did not come from seafaring families. Whatever the complaints about living on land Jim Hawkins might have had, and which made him desirous of going to sea (or that made the adults around him desirous that he should disappear to sea) will be explored in the next chapter.

CHAPTER 2

Jim's Troublesome Youth on Land: 'The Idle Apprentice Sent to Sea'

W HAT possible difficulties with living or working on land led all those real-life versions of Jim Hawkins, for whom seafaring was not a family calling, to leave their warm dry homes and opt for the unknown life at sea? Or might we ask: what possible troubles had Jim given his family and neighbours on land that made them wish he would opt for a life at sea, far away from them? For at exactly the period in history where Stevenson placed the adventure of Jim Hawkins, London's most

Plate 5: Tom Idle is sent to sea, from William Hogarth's
Industry and Idleness (1747).

popular caricaturist William Hogarth (1697-1764) had created a rather different stereotype of a land-boy gone to sea: the 'Idle Apprentice' Tom. Hogarth's engraving of the Idle Apprentice being sent to sea depicted an all too familiar eighteenth-century stereotype. The illustration was part of Hogarth's series *Industry and Idleness* (1747), a moral tale for apprentices, illustrating the lives of the two fellow weaver apprentices Francis Goodchild and Thomas Idle, with the rise of the former and the simultaneous decline of the latter.

After idle apprentice Tom enraged his apprenticeship master with his laziness, and also shunned Sunday service in favour of gambling in the company of dubious characters, we see him in plate five of the series being 'turned away and sent to sea'. The boatmen delivering Tom to his ship are grinning devilishly. One of them, also just a boy, is showing Tom the cat-o'-nine-tails as a taste of the discipline on board. The other points to the waiting ship and to a hanged pirate or thief, displayed as a warning on Cuckold's Point in Rotherhithe. Tom's mother is weeping for her son, and she is dressed as a widow, suggesting that Tom was fatherless, just like Jim Hawkins. The message of the engraving seems to be that with no father, master or any other authority able to control Tom, sending the troublesome youth away to the sea is the only solution. Meanwhile, Tom himself is still defiant; unmoved by his mother's tears, he responds to the boatman who is pointing to the gallows at Cuckold's Point by showing him the horns, the symbol of cuckoldry, while carelessly dropping his old apprenticeship indenture into the Thames.

Tom is representative of many eighteenth-century youths who failed to settle to any trade on land, or for whom the apprenticeship system or poor relief could not find suitable employment. In London and other big cities people noticed an alarmingly growing presence of unemployed and unsuper-vised youths. The sea service appeared as the most convenient remedy, especially when those concerned about Britain's maritime power felt that not enough boys took up seafaring. As cabin boy Edward Coxere put it: 'I not settling my mind to a trade, my lot fell to the sea.'[1]

This chapter is a chapter for landlubbers: if we want to understand what led the real-life Tom Idle or Jim Hawkins to sea, we first of all have to look at their lives on land, at the culture of their peers, and at the difficulties they encountered as youths, problems with their work masters or even with the law, the kind of trouble that might have made the boys, as well as the authorities, conclude that going to sea was the best solution. Hogarth's Tom Idle is a particularly irredeemable character, who is eventually hanged as a criminal at the Tyburn gallows, yet there were thousands of other youths, who did not follow Tom's criminal path, but went to sea under the influence of the same economic, social and cultural pressures as Tom. While some of their troubles with socialisation on land were specific to the times in which they lived, others will sound rather familiar to young people today.

It would be wrong to stereotype all ships' boys in the Navy as trouble-makers, and even those who were sent to sea by parish overseers and other authorities were definitely not all Tom Idles, yet the prejudice that the sea was the destined career for the juvenile delinquent was deeply rooted in society. Samuel Richardson's *Apprentice's Vade Mecum* (1734), one of many guidebooks for apprentices, finished with the conclusion that for boys who felt no need to adhere to the rules of proper behaviour laid out in the book, the sea service would be the best career choice – and not only for them, but also for everyone else who would otherwise have to endure the 'ill humour' of such boys. Seafaring played an important role in employing, and ulti-mately policing, the children of the working classes and the poor. The acts introduced at the beginning of the century to promote maritime apprentice-ships among parish boys,[2] for example, were not just about securing a sufficient supply of sailors for Britain's emerging empire, they were an additional tool to employ and police youngsters. The logic was simple: seafaring provided the boys with a profession that was generally regarded as requiring hardened individuals, and seafaring kept them away from the community and any negative influences that threatened to divert them from the path of virtue. If the boy had no caring family, then the easier it would be for him to bid farewell to his home.[3]

Complaints about an increasingly unruly youth are to be found in almost any period of history, and the eighteenth century is no exception. The negative impact of urbanisation and modernisation, social alienation, poverty, and the conglomeration of lost youths, became apparent in the cities, particularly in London. The population of London doubled from 1650 to 1750, yet the city still had no proper police force, and many citizens perceived the presence of numerous idle youths as a threat.

When the London Marine Society, a charity that was to send thousands of boys to the Navy, was founded in the mid-eighteenth century, its supporters were initially only thinking of recruiting the unemployed and destitute youngsters they encountered on their daily walks in the streets; they wanted to collect urchins for the sea. Often enough, it appeared that there was no parent, no master, no authority, nor any other adult responsible for these boys, 'distressed orphans, who wander about like forsaken dogs', as the Society's founders described them in rather gloomy language in their publicity material.[4] Indeed, around twenty per cent of the five thousand boys the Society was to recruit during the Seven Years War were not merely orphans, but had no adult at all responsible for them. Jim Hawkins and Tom Idle, who still had mothers, would have been among the better off. Compared to child mortality, parent mortality has received less than its due attention in the historiography of the eighteenth century – losing one or both parents as a child was by no means an exceptional experience. It is estimated that up to a third of eighteenth-century children lost their fathers before they reached the age of twenty; among the children of sailors this share may even have been as high as fifty per cent.

Many other boys were simply abandoned by their parents at an early age. Magistrate John Fielding, who founded London's first police force together with his half-brother, the novelist Henry Fielding (1707-1754), wrote of London being full of 'Shoals of Shop-lifters, Pilferers, and Pickpockets, who, being the deserted Children of Porters, Chairmen, and low Mechanics, were obliged to steal for their Subsistence'.[5] Children were often abandoned when they were illegitimate. As illegitimate children, or foundlings, they not only had to endure poverty, but also the widespread prejudice that they were not worthy of compassion. Henry Fielding reflected the common antagonism against such children in his novel *Tom Jones*, in which Mrs Deborah commented upon the discovery of the foundling Tom that 'it is, perhaps, better for such creatures to die in a state of innocence than to grow up and imitate their mothers, for nothing better can be expected of them'. And Captain Blifil rejected Tom's adoption by stating that 'bastards' like Tom should have to suffer the punishment for the crimes of their parents, and that 'at the best they ought to be brought up to the lowest and vilest offices of the commonwealth.'[6] It was a vicious circle: the lack of provisions and affection for illegitimate children would have led many of them to exhibit criminal or aggressive behaviour, which in turn reinforced negative prejudices against them.

Another group which fell through the poor relief system were boys whose fathers had moved to London and then died. The eighteenth-century Poor Law restricted aid to those with a settlement in a parish, and the surviving mother and children were often incapable of establishing settlement in a London parish. The Poor Law with its Act of Settlement (1662) was not able to deal with the negative effects of rapid urbanisation; in fact, it was not intended to cope, the main reason for introducing the Act of Settlement having been to prevent uncontrolled migration. As a consequence, the children of migrants appeared most frequently in the courts charged with delinquent acts. John Fielding felt that these young offenders had to be rescued not punished. Fielding deplored that 'for want of a seasonable relief, carts full of these unhappy wretches have ended their days in the vigour of their youth, at the dreadful tree',[7] that is the gallows. Ending his life at the

John Fielding (1762), by Nathaniel Hone.

hands of the hangman was not an unlikely encounter for a teenager, the greatest part of those hanged being youths aged between sixteen to twenty-one.[8] Surely, in part the high number of hanged youths stemmed from the fact that the youngsters were often framed by older criminals; some were even seduced into committing a crime by the thief-catchers, the Jonathan Wild types, themselves. Yet this only reinforced the belief of the authorities that the youths needed stricter supervision.

Ideally, boys in their teens and early twenties should have been employed and supervised in an apprenticeship, or working as servants in some business, and not wandering around in the streets. Boys in the care of the parish could even be forced into an apprenticeship,[9] and failure to follow an order into a compulsory apprenticeship could get a boy into a workhouse or even a house of correction.[10] Here again it becomes evident that the apprenticeship was as much about employing the real Jim Hawkins, as it was about policing him. However, parish officers sometimes neglected their duty, or simply could not find a placement, so that a boy remained without employment. And seeing that the apprenticeship was a very long, and usually unpaid, servitude, many poor boys preferred to work in paid jobs instead, as servants or labourers in some business, often on a temporary basis, but earning money that could also supplement the family income.

Once the boys found an apprenticeship, problems did not necessarily cease. Some of the youths 'lurking around' in the alleys, which so upset the Marine Society's members, might have actually been in an apprenticeship, but were either neglected by their masters, or neglecting their duties. Others were former apprentices who had run away from their masters. Eighteenth-century newspapers were full of advertisements by masters offering rewards for finding their runaway apprentice. Some runaway apprentices left because they wanted to sell their acquired skills elsewhere, where they would be paid for their services, yet many runaways just ended up on the streets, not finding employment, being unable to pay the fee for another apprenticeship, and thus roaming through life with no direction. Satirist Ned Ward, deliberately getting lost with a friend while walking through eighteenth-century London, felt like one of those lads: 'Being now quite out of our knowledge, we wandered about like a couple of runaway apprentices, having confined ourselves to no particular port, uncertainty being our course and mere accident our pilot'.[11]

To a great extent, the problem of having these unsupervised apprentices and runaways on the streets arose from the insufficiencies of the eighteenth-century apprenticeship system itself. Jonas Hanway, London magistrates John and Henry Fielding, and Saunders Welch (1711-1784) were all actively involved in projects which attempted to improve the apprenticeship system. A closer look at the faults of the system not only illuminates the problem that many boys had in settling to a trade, but also the reasons why numerous boys from the lower strata felt attracted to the sailor's life, an attraction that often led them to run away to join the Navy. At the same time, investigating the faults inherent in the system of apprenticeship will make apparent why it is difficult to judge whether a boy went voluntarily to sea, or whether he was pushed by social circumstances and authorities. Last but not least, it will also become clear that in order to understand fully the motives for going to sea of these real-life examples of Jim Hawkins and Tom Idle, we have to place the boys within the wider context of youth history and culture.

As with maritime apprenticeships, the quality of apprenticeships on land differed greatly, depending on trade, master and mistress, on the social background of the apprentice's family, and on the fee the parents paid to the master. Apprenticeships were very personal: the master and his wife were parental figures, and rather than just apprenticing the boy, the master was also meant to house, feed and discipline him. Master and apprentice had to get along on a personal level, otherwise one party could quickly lose patience. Wages were paid only in better apprenticeships and in the later years of the boy's service, though this became increasingly common as the century neared its end. The long binding of the apprentice was one major problem of the system: apprentices commonly had to serve seven years, yet poor boys placed by the parish had by law to serve until they reached the age of twenty-four.[12] In most trades the youth was able to fulfil all the tasks of his work long before his apprenticeship was over, which was a reward to the master for training the boy. The apprentice, however, grew impatient in the meantime, longing to work, live, and earn money on his own. For a sixteen-year-old boy, the age of twenty-four appears light-years away. On top, the apprentice also reached sexual maturity before his apprenticeship was over, yet marriage was not only out of the question financially, it was even explicitly forbidden in many apprenticeship indentures. Hanway began to campaign against the long apprenticeship of parish boys after the Seven Years War, until finally, in 1767, the Act for the Better Regulation of the Parish Poor Children,[13] one of the so-called Hanway Acts, included the reduction of the binding time for parish boys to seven years or until the age of twenty-one.

Another problem was that when trade was booming, a master would take on many apprentices, but when recession struck he often found it impossible to provide for all of them. In return, the apprentices would, in view of the bad prospects in their trade, become reluctant to carry on with their apprenticeship. The fee that had to be paid to the master for apprenticing a boy, either paid by the boy's parents or by the parish, was sometimes another source of wrongdoing, as it tempted masters to take on apprentices purely in order to acquire the fee. Such masters would afterwards try to get rid of the boy by ill-treating him, either by encouraging him to run away, or provoking a reaction which would justify the cancellation of the indentures without an order from the magistrate to return part of the fee. Apprenticeship court cases feature regular complaints about masters who had no work with which to occupy the apprentice, or who misused the apprentice as cheap labour without providing any industrial training.

Boys placed by the parish were in particular danger of ending up in such apprenticeships, hence it is not surprising that many pauper children preferred never to embark upon an apprenticeship. Watermen were often said to take on parish boys for a fee and then just leave them idling at the river front with meagre provisions. Furthermore, cases of masters physically abusing apprentices, or even leaving the boys begging in the streets, were among the court complaints. Such cases were surely the bottom end of apprenticeships, yet we cannot say how many incidents never made it to court.[14] Young chimney sweeps were thought to be among the most badly off among apprentices and were frequently left begging during the summer. In 1773, some members of the Marine Society collected nineteen London chimney sweep apprentices. They washed and clothed them, and encouraged them to talk about their background. It turned out that the boys were not parish boys, but mainly poor and illegitimate children who had been sold to their masters – children who had fallen through the system of statutory relief or had not been aware of their entitlement to support.

There were legal ways to end an apprenticeship by appealing to a justice, giving the apprentice the opportunity to regain the fee for another apprenticeship. However, a young apprentice without any adult supporting him, and with little education, was unlikely to make the way to court. He would rather react by running away, or neglecting his duties, and thereby forcing the master to cancel the indentures.[15] The master did not have to be evil-minded to neglect the apprentice; some masters were simply not economically or pedagogically able to take care of all their boys. Furthermore, the structure of the economy was changing in the eighteenth century, making the traditional paternal relationships increasingly unworkable. Businesses grew in personnel; traditional small workshops were replaced by larger ones. Masters began to take on more apprentices and journeymen than they were allowed. The young employees could not all live with the master, thus the paternal influence of the master waned, and so too did the hopes of the increasing number of young employees ever to become masters themselves.[16]

Sometimes apprentice and master or trade were simply not made for each other. Sailor Edward Barlow remembered in his memoirs how he disliked his apprenticeship from day one: he was angry to see that the food at the master's end of the table was of much better quality.[17] And the older apprentice scared Edward with stories of years of hard labour lying ahead of him, with the master and his wife often beating their apprentices. To the older apprentice Edward also began to talk about travelling, and the riches one could acquire if one only dared to venture into the wide world. Seeing that young Edward had dreamed of travelling, and had always enjoyed the stories of those who had seen foreign countries and peoples, as well as having a great aversion to the agricultural toil in which the people in his rural community were employed, it was no wonder that he eventually packed his belongings and made off for the port of London. Barlow's apprenticeship had still been in the initial trial period, which many better apprenticeships included, so there was no need for him to make an illicit escape. His parents' neighbours were not surprised that Edward ended his apprenticeship, asserting that they had always had him down as someone with a wandering mind who would never settle to anything.

Unsurprisingly, misbehaviour on one side in the apprenticeship tended to provoke the other side to act similarly. An idle apprentice played his part in making a master desperate to get rid of him. Boys who had grown up without a father might have found it particularly hard to subordinate to the patriarchal power of the master and his wife. Mary Lacy, who enlisted as a servant in the Navy disguised as a boy, admitted that her mistress had actually been particularly understanding towards her.[18] Yet Mary blamed her own juvenile 'roving disposition', as well as the common foolishness of the young, for the relationship breakdown. Stealing other people's horses for a brief ride was one of Mary's favourite pastimes – perhaps the eighteenth-century equivalent of today's teenagers joyriding in stolen cars. Night after night Mary sneaked out of the house of her mistresses to go to dances, where she eventually fell so unhappily in love that her teenage heart saw no other solution than to run away to sea.

Hogarth's idle apprentice Tom was indeed a familiar eighteenth-century stereotype; the youths were mocked in popular theatre plays such as *The Apprentice*, 'a satire on those young mechanicks, who neglect the business of their trade to attend to the diversions of the stage'.[19] It was not just idleness of which apprentices were commonly accused, but also a tendency to drink, party, gamble or exhibit disorderly behaviour – all rather sailor-like stereotypes. Apprentices seemed to be at the forefront of any riotous disturbance on the streets, from playing football to political demonstrations. It is difficult to say how political the apprentices were; although they sometimes appear as the harbinger of the workers' movements, all too often the border between political protest and a mere expression of adolescent spirits and aggression is blurred. The weaver apprentices, to whom Hogarth's Tom Idle belonged, gave plenty of good examples for such 'semi-political' riotous behaviour.

Guidebooks like Samuel Richardson's *Apprentice's Vade Mecum* (1734) which set out rules of good behaviour, and in reverse read like a catalogue of common misdemeanours among apprentices, show a sometimes amusing resemblance to the antics of today's youth. Incidentally, eighteenth-century literature often used the terms 'the apprentices' or 'prentices' as a synonym for youth in general, regardless of whether the boys were actually proper apprentices or not. Though some historians argue that the concept of youth, as we know it today, did not exist in pre-industrial Europe,[20] there are a number of aspects which would justify describing these eighteenth-century urban apprentices, and also other boys working as servants in a business, as youths in the way that we use the term today. Apprentices formed a distinctive intermediate stage between childhood and adulthood. They had left their family home,[21] yet rather than living on their own they lived under the supervision of the master and his wife; they were still in education, but occasionally already earning wages; they were working with adults, acquiring adult abilities at work but not full responsibilities; they did not own any means of production; they were reaching their sexual maturity but were not married and had no children. Of course, if we define youth as a stage of semi-dependence it could include all the unmarried and those without their own permanent residence, and thus youth could be prolonged to a much higher age. Yet defining youth by such economic and social factors, rather than by age, would seem a reasonable concept, even in relation to contemporary society. Such a definition of youth can still contain different sub-stages of development. Later, when exploring the connection between sailors and youth culture, this concept will be used to interpret the behaviour of eighteenth-century sailors in general and the attraction that sailors' culture exerted on youths living on land.

Evidence of youthful entertainments, fashion and behaviour crop up in abundance in eighteenth-century sources, and such evidence is often found in magistrates' reports, for in their search for the causes of crime, judges identified the various entertainments enjoyed by the young as a major factor. Of course, the attempted suppression of youth entertainments only fostered escapist dreams amongst Jim Hawkins and his peers, dreams of a more liberated life, possibly in exotic places across the sea. In this study, by drawing parallels between modern and eighteenth-century youth, the reasons why boys would leave their work on land, in exchange for a life at sea, uncertain and dangerous in comparison, will become clear. Given that a youthful sector of society, comparable to modern youth, existed in the eighteenth century, then it seems reasonable that the extensively observed mental turbulences of today's teenagers – such as anxiety, search for identity and thrills, questioning of authority, escapism – were also present in the mind of his eighteenth-century equivalent. Magistrate Fielding himself cursed the youthful mind: 'A mind restless, roving and perpetually uneasy, is what brings more young people into these paths of ruin, than even their own wicked inclinations.'[22] Whenever the youth's restless and roving mind clashed with the imperfections of his apprenticeship, or his master's authority, then the sailors' counter-culture became more attractive.

Apprenticeship indentures and company guidelines imposed a multitude of rules of behaviour, which could include forbidding visits to bowling alleys, dances, tennis courts, wearing hair long, or wearing clothes other than those provided by their masters. These rules were restrictive, but they were also often broken. London's justices complained 'that there are very few mechanics or shop-keepers in these vast cities, whose apprentices can be kept at home in the evening'.[23] One of Hanway's proposals to restrain unruly apprentices was to close all taverns at eleven o'clock in the evening, a proposal that only materialised one and a half centuries later to keep munitions factory workers sober, yet which was to curb nightlife in Britain for much longer than in any other European country. Saunders Welch emphasised the importance of suppressing 'the debauchery, excesses and immoralities of the numerous fairs' which took place in summer on Sundays, even during the hours of church service. These fairs, Welch thought, were 'the bane of the youth of both sexes, and a great cause of robberies',[24] as here young people mixed with bad company and became involved in gambling and mischief.

Gambling for money during the hours of church service was also one of Tom Idle's misdemeanours which, combined with his laziness at work, got him sent to sea. Notably, Hogarth's *Industry and Idleness* series does not show that his idle apprentice Tom had committed any serious crime although, admittedly, not observing the Lord's Day was considered by many contemporaries as being the first step towards greater sins. Sending Tom to sea was therefore also a precautionary measure against a boy who seemed alarmingly disobedient. *Industry and Idleness* was mass-produced and sold inexpensively; it was primarily aimed at masters, who would hang the prints as educational tales on the walls of their apprentices' workplaces. Yet

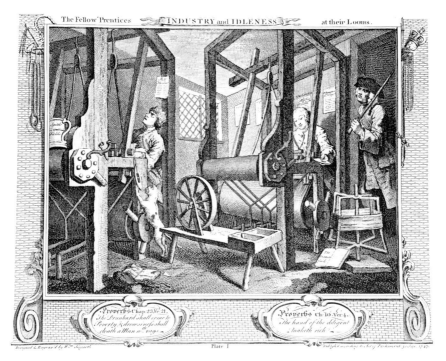

Plate 1, William Hogarth's *Industry and Idleness* (1747).

Plate 3, William Hogarth's *Industry and Idleness* (1747).

Hogarth-expert Ronald Paulson has argued that the one with whom many apprentices sympathised was not the industrious Francis Goodchild, but instead Tom Idle.[25] They perceived Tom as a victim rather than a wrongdoer. To the apprentices, Tom Idle was a 'subculture hero', comparable to the stylised rebels populating the music and movies of modern youth culture.

Indeed, looking at the entire series, one cannot help finding the story of idle Tom a great deal more entertaining than that of sober Francis. On plate one, whilst Francis Goodchild is diligently labouring at his loom, Tom is having a nap, an empty ale measure from 'Spittle Fields' hinting at where Tom spent the previous night. The two apprentices represent the two extremes between which any apprentice would have found himself eternally torn, with rebellious Tom doing what he likes and diligent Francis doing what is expected of him. William Hogarth gave Tom Idle, and not Francis, a face resembling his own, suggesting that even he himself felt pulled between these two extremes; Hogarth had something else in common with Tom, as he too had grown up without a father.

Hogarth might also have chosen Tom Idle to be a weaver's apprentice because weaving was one of the worst-paid crafts and had the worst prospects, unless one had family connections to a master (or married the master's daughter, as Francis Goodchild does later in the series). Being bound to such a trade, possibly until the age of twenty-four, being mostly unpaid and with a fourteen-hour day, could have hardly been motivating for any teenage boy.[26] It is no surprise that restless teenagers like Tom would have longed for some diversion from such a bleak life of toil. Perhaps they looked with envy at sailors, no older than them and sometimes even younger, who were raucously celebrating their shore leave and had money to spend. Many of Tom's mates must have dreamed of escaping from their dull work routine, to an alluringly adventurous imagined life at sea, and quick financial rewards with less drudgery.

Magistrates Fielding and Welch, ever fearing that youthful entertainments contained the seeds of idleness and crime, went on a campaign to stop any youthful diversions in London, albeit with little success. On one occasion the two arrested a great number of persons 'of both Sexes' in a house known as Baron's Hop in Soho's Wardour Street, where, as London's *Public Advertiser* reported on 24 June 1756:

> Music and Dancing was carried on for the Lucre of Gain, contrary to the Statute. They were all examined at Night, and dealt with according to the Law. This Kind of Amusement must certainly appear harmless to the Unwary, otherwise reputable young Women would never be found mix'd with Strangers of the lowest Order at these Hops. Whoever can raise a Shilling gains Admittance here; the Ladies indeed, by Way of Encouragement, pay nothing: but alas, these Hops are the very Seminaries of Debauchery.

The two magistrates asked members of the public to inform them whenever such eighteenth-century illegal raves were held. The magistrates alone could certainly not control all apprentices and youths; to police urban youth, society had to rely on the work masters, since the boys had left the supervision of their parents, and because even a city like mid-century London with more than half a million inhabitants still had no police force.

However, we have already noted that with the development of larger workshops the master's traditional paternal guidance waned. The long binding of parish apprentices, as well as the master's obligation to house the apprentice, had partly been established as an attempt to police young men; masters could fine but also physically punish their apprentices – the boatman was certainly not the first to threaten Tom Idle with a beating. On the first plate of the series, when Tom's apprenticeship master finds him asleep at work, the master already carries a cane in his hand, and so too does the sadistically grinning beadle or churchwarden who catches Tom gambling outside the church. Tom was used to corporal punishment, so while Hogarth's polite audience perceived the boatman's threat as a worrying taste of the brutality of shipboard life, it made much less of an impression on Tom.

Masters could get their apprentices sent to a house of correction for a week, and some even went for a month. Being whipped and put to hard labour were often part of the regime of houses of correction such as London's infamous Bridewell Hospital.[27] Samuel Leech, who enlisted in the Navy as a twelve-year-old, reckoned that he probably would have forgotten his childish dreams of a sailor's life had he not so often been beaten with the rod for any tiny fault he committed and for that reason continued to dream of escaping to a life at sea.[28] In *Kidnapped* (1886), Robert Louis Stevenson had his boy hero David Balfour learn the following from the ship's boy:

> I was thrown for talk on the cabin-boy . . . He had a strange notion of the dry land, picked up from sailor's stories: that it was a place where lads were put to some kind of slavery called a trade, and where apprentices were continually lashed and clapped into foul prisons. . . . To be sure, I would tell him how kindly I had myself been used upon that dry land he was so much afraid of, and how well fed and carefully taught both by my friends and my parents.[29]

It is not surprising that the master always stood at the centre of the apprentice's rage against authority. With the indentures between master and apprentice extending into regulating the apprentice's spare time, a master who demanded that his apprentice stick closely to the rules, perhaps with the good intention of keeping the lad out of trouble, could drive a teenage boy who was experiencing the usual adolescent turbulence to the drastic step of leaving the apprenticeship. It would have been difficult for the youth to pay another apprenticeship fee and so return to a normal life. Instead, making a living as a casual paid servant, or possibly even getting involved in crime, to avoid being trapped in badly paid jobs with no future, were more likely and perhaps even rational choices. So too was going to sea, particularly in times of war when there were people desperately trying to fill ships' complements and luring crew with bounty payments, good wages, prize money and adventure.

John Fielding knew very well from his experience in court that, all too often, a bad master, incapable of providing the guidance a teenage boy needed, and a bleak apprenticeship, provoked the youth to behave restlessly. The conflict between master and apprentice was a regular theme in Fielding's court and nurtured his idea that the best for both sides would be to send such troubled apprentices to sea. One curious case tried by Fielding in 1772 involved an apprentice who had been absent for a number of nights.[30] Fielding sentenced the youth to a month in Bridewell, kept to hard labour; the convict, however, reacted by exclaiming he would go for a year if the magistrate would discharge him from his master. Fielding was aware that sending an apprentice to the house of correction usually made matters worse, as there he mixed with criminals, no attempt was undertaken to reform the boy, and he usually left the institution more morally corrupted than he had entered it.[31] To overcome the defects common in apprenticeships, the Fielding brothers and Saunders Welch set up the Universal Register Office in 1749. The Office acted as an employment agency, for apprentices seeking masters and vice versa, and tried to prevent any improper indentures and protect apprentices from masters who were only tempted by the fee. However, Fielding also discovered another way out for failed apprentices, and that was to send them to the Navy.

Britannia Clothing a Ragged Marine Society Boy, by Samuel Wale.

Fielding began to collect boys for the Royal Navy at the same time as the Marine Society was founded in London as a channel for the children of the poor to enter the Navy. The Society did so with dramatically greater success than Fielding or any other scheme in British history. Moreover, the Society not only recruited boys, it also equipped all of the Navy's ships' boys who applied for help with clothing and bedding. Thus the Society's surviving records provide us with a unique insight into who really was the typical Jim Hawkins in the eighteenth-century Navy. These are reasons enough to take a closer look at the Society in the following chapter.

Having glimpsed Tom Idle's and Jim Hawkins' life on land, it becomes easier to understand what led those troubled youths to sea. Many of them, given the alternatives, would not have objected to a new life as sailors. The boys were used to enduring long working hours and being threatened with corporal punishment, and although Tom Idle – if he joined a Royal Navy vessel – would soon find out that when it came to brutality the Navy easily outdid his old apprenticeship master, the workload on a man-o'-war may have possibly been even less. On top of this, Tom would also be turned into a fully-paid adult in half the time it normally took him on land. What Tom lost, however, was his freedom of movement and the opportunity to skive. In the Navy he had to be constantly on the alert, at least once he took part in the sailing of the ship; the boatswain and his mates were only too eager to swing the ends of their ropes at anyone who did not appear on deck in an instant, be it sunshine or cold storm. And this is why the sea service also seemed such a good idea to the concerned adults around Tom.

Tom Idle was Hogarth's stereotype exaggerated to the state of caricature, yet there were plenty of tamer versions of Tom being influenced by similar pressures and desires. It remains difficult to determine to what extent boys like Tom were just escaping from their life on land, and were helped on and even pushed by their masters and parish overseers, or whether they were keen on experiencing the life at sea as pictured in their juvenile imagination. This is the one important aspect that also remains unclear about the 'Idle Apprentice': Hogarth does not tell us how far Tom himself wanted to go to sea. The dramatic gestures of the depicted characters, and the wording of the title, give us the feeling that Tom did not have much choice, and that his former master or some parish authority must have pushed him. It will remain a tricky question, which we shall attempt to answer in later chapters when exploring Jim Hawkins' motives for going to sea.

CHAPTER 3

Poor Jim: Charity and the Marine Society

C ITY of London, 1758: amidst the hawkers and traders outside the
Royal Exchange, regular passers-by frequently noticed gatherings
of groups of boys, most of them only fourteen years of age, neatly
dressed in blue pea-jackets and canvas trousers supplied by the Marine
Society, the charitable organisation residing above the Royal Exchange. An
attendant, Mr Tyson, was usually with the boys. He told them to line up in

Painting commemorating the Marine Society's incorporation (1772), with Lord
Romney, John Thornton and Jonas Hanway (attributed to Edward Edwards).

pairs to give a better impression to onlookers, and then they would start to march. Mr Tyson led them through the City's busy centre, for every Londoner to see the clean and orderly appearance of these previously rather ragged boys; then he would take them across the Thames via London Bridge. At this point Thomas Tyson might have taken a concerned look at the sky, wondering if bad weather would slow down their intended four-day march to Portsmouth Harbour. Heavy rain would have given him permission to spend some money on covering part of their journey by coach.

The thoughts on the minds of the boys following Tyson, meanwhile, were likely to be a little less mundane. Some of them might have turned their heads to take a last look at the city, just like sixteen-year-old Edward Barlow had done when he first went to sea, looking back to contemplate 'leaving that famous city of London, where many, both rich and poor, have taken a farewell both of their friends and country, little thinking that it would be the last time that they should see them.'[1] For too many boys it would indeed turn out to be the last time, as they embarked on their new life at sea as naval servants on board His Majesty's men-of-war, joining the campaign against France in the Seven Years War.

During the Seven Years War alone, nearly five thousand naval servants from all over Britain were equipped by the London-based Marine Society; at the end of the Napoleonic War in 1815 the total had climbed to over twenty-five thousand boys. The Society began its life in 1756, founded by merchants and philanthropists who were alarmed by the Navy's desperate lack of seamen, and intended to recruit ships' boys and landsmen new to the sea for the Royal Navy. Among the wave of philanthropic societies that were founded in the eighteenth century, the Society was to become one of the most successful. Founding father was Jonas Hanway, an overseas merchant and philanthropist. Unfortunately, popular history merely wants to remember Hanway as the man who introduced the umbrella to the streets of London, thereby overlooking the many charitable projects he established in his lifetime, which saw him rightfully rewarded with a memorial in Westminster Abbey after his death.

The Marine Society initially only thought about targeting impoverished and unemployed boys and men, attracting them with a new set of clothing and other useful items, before handing them over to Navy officers. However, during the Seven Years War the Society soon expanded its clothing gift to almost any Navy boy who applied, including boys already serving on board who had never visited the Society's offices. Thus the Society's surviving registers of supported boys provide a unique picture of the typical Jim Hawkins of the time. The founders of the Society were guided by a mixture of charitable, religious, patriotic and commercial motives. Targeting their efforts primarily at impoverished boys and men ensured that these were rescued from poverty and, no less important, also taken off the streets and prevented from becoming a threat to public safety: intentions of helping and policing went hand in hand.

Recruiting unemployed boys also reduced the likelihood that those who were employed elsewhere could be lured or pressed into the Navy and the private economy thus harmed. Certainly the greatest harm caused by the Navy's shortage of seamen was inflicted upon businesses connected to maritime trade: merchant sailors were pressed into the Navy, and because the demand for sailors increased dramatically, seamen's wages doubled or even tripled. It is no wonder that the Marine Society was primarily the project of overseas merchants, all eager to increase the total number of British seamen for the future by ensuring that more boys chose a life at sea. The Society's credo was that 'as a nation whose chief strength is their ships of war, and whose opulence is derived from commerce', Britain had 'to be more careful and industrious in breeding up a race of mariners.'[2] In the eyes of the Marine Society, charity, patriotism and commerce went hand in hand, aptly summarised by the Society's motto 'Charity and Policy United'.

While the merchant community was competing with the Royal Navy for sailors, it also treasured the Navy as a friend. British naval power and trade

Marine Society Boys Being Clothed, with Britannia and Charity (1758), by Samuel Wale.

reinforced each other. The Navy conquered and secured spheres of influence for British businesses, and British trade in turn benefited from the protectionist Navigation Acts that gave exclusive rights to British merchants, enabling them to produce the wealth necessary to finance the Navy. Hence there was a willingness in the merchant community to co-operate with the Navy. Hanway himself had realised the importance of a powerful Navy right at the start of his career when, as a young merchant in Lisbon, his business suffered from frequent attacks by Spanish privateers. After his time in Lisbon, Hanway returned to London, where he joined the Russia Company, whose members were to become his main supporters in founding the Marine Society. Dealing with a distant empire like Russia involved some years of travelling, which, apart from giving rise to Hanway's fame as the author of travelogues, convinced him even more of the necessity of having a large Navy as a safeguard of British trade. For an overseas trading company such as the Russia Company it was vital to establish a good relationship with the Admiralty; creating a Society which provided the Navy with boys and young men could only improve these relations.

The Marine Society was officially founded at a meeting on 25 June 1756 at the King's Arms tavern in Cornhill, London. Surprisingly, the initial gathering was only about providing the Navy with men who would go on board as paid landsmen, while boys were left out. Perhaps they were omitted because it was known that magistrate Fielding had already established such an initiative. In later years, when the relationship between Fielding and the Society deteriorated, the two parties would quarrel over who could claim to be the originator of the idea to collect boys for the Navy. Undeniably, Fielding had started to recruit boys before the Society was founded. Fielding had received a letter from Lord Harry Powlett in January 1756, asking him if he could collect thirty boys, who would be clothed by Powlett and serve on board his ship, the *Barfleur*. Fielding, who according to some sources had been to sea as a youth before losing his eyesight, was inspired by Powlett's letter to turn the idea into a large subscription-funded operation through which he hoped to find a solution for the 'numberless miserable, deserted, ragged, and iniquitous pilfering Boys that at this Time shamefully infested the Streets of London', as well as for all those troubled apprentices who appeared in his court.[3] Fielding's objectives were clear: his boys were not only to strengthen the Navy, they were more importantly taken off the street, or relieved from a dissatisfying employment, and given a new future.

Fielding's subscription operation had started with a public meeting at the Bedford Coffee House in Covent Garden, and Fielding writing to the Admiralty informing them of the project. The Admiralty was very interested

Change Alley, Cornhill, today.

and showed no concern about the fact that the boys came via the efforts of a magistrate: the assurance that the boys were willing recruits was enough. Fielding was told that one hundred and fifty boys were needed immediately and the sooner he sent them the better – another indication of how desperately the Navy needed an organised recruitment of servants. The boys were provided with clothing and bedding, as well as a Bible and a prayer book. They were welcomed with a hearty meal, and even presented to Lord Anson at the Admiralty. Fielding and his partners clothed around four hundred boys, whereby, as Fielding tells us, 'our Streets were cleared from Swarms of Boys whose Situations made them Thieves from Necessity'.[4] Such comments have a slightly odd connotation, giving the impression of a four hundred-strong army of 'Artful Dodgers' marching on board His Majesty's ships. However, we shall soon see, when looking at the way eighteenth-century charities marketed themselves to potential donors, caution must be exercised in interpreting claims about the nature of the boys' possibly delinquent past.

Fielding and his friends collected over one hundred subscriptions, yet in July 1756 he ran short of funds and approached the newly established Marine Society for financial aid. Fielding later claimed that he always saw Hanway's Society as a project that had sprung directly from his own pioneering work. The Society's own historical account, in contrast, claims that Hanway had developed his idea independently of Fielding's project. Indeed, Hanway had, for example, written previously to the Admiralty about a plan to form a society for fitting out boys from London's workhouses for the Navy.[5] When Fielding asked the Society for financial assistance, it provided what he asked for, but it also, from then on, considered the recruitment of boys as its own business.[6] Fielding joined the Society, in his words, to avoid confusion between the two funds. Thus, both Fielding and Hanway had their share in introducing a scheme, which, although there had been predecessors with similar plans, had never before been undertaken on such a grand scale.

To understand the great support received at the time by the Marine Society regarding the idea of collecting boys, each a potential Jim Hawkins, from across the country, the threat of the war against France is a valid but insufficient explanation. To comprehend fully the enthusiasm that the Society met, we have to look briefly at the wider world of private charities in the mid-eighteenth century, because for many members of the Society donating to the cause was only one of many voluntary activities in which they were involved, in the face of a wave of new philanthropic associations springing up all over the country. Most eighteenth-century philanthropists came from what we would call the middle class today, and were concerned about the way the Poor Law was administered, and how parish officers distributed the funds from the poor rate. There was a need for larger agencies, crossing parish boundaries and being able to cope with the rapid migration into the cities. As the government could not agree on improvements, concerned private individuals took it into their own hands. Moreover, there was the hope that private charities would be more efficient, as it was expected that those running a voluntary charity would be less corrupt than parish officers, and that only effective charities would receive continuous donations. Once such institutions were formed they developed an inner dynamic which dragged the founders further into the cause of the poor. Furthermore, philanthropy became fashionable. Wealthy Londoners would, for example, spend time visiting the Foundling Hospital, where they would watch the Hospital's children at work, walk through William Hogarth's gallery or listen to George Frideric Handel's benefit concert. Though similar philanthropic and patriotic societies were set up all over eighteenth-century Europe, today the tradition of having private charities, instead of relying on state relief, still appears to be stronger in Britain than in any other European country, whether Protestant or Catholic.

Looking at the individuals sitting on the committees of the various associations, we often find the same people, linked through their business activities or even family connections. In the case of the Marine Society, as for the Foundling Hospital and the Magdalen Hospital for Penitent Prostitutes, the Russia Company connected many committee members. Hanway was elected to the Court of Assistants of the Russia Company on 30 July 1756, just a month after he had arranged the initial meeting for the Marine Society. Hanway neither had an impressive family background, nor was he an overly successful merchant, but charity brought him admittance to London's merchant elite. Involvement in charities offered connections and credibility. Equally, charities were aware that one of the best ways of promoting themselves was to publish the names of their donors, the lesser known thus improving their image by being named in the company of well-known personalities. Thus a little self-charity was mixed under the banner of 'Charity and Policy United'. Ultimately, the philanthropists were also not just entering the philanthropic arena, but the political stage, too. Charities provided an entry into politics for men for whom entrance to the traditional centres of power, such as Parliament, was not available.

Setting up large charitable institutions by collecting subscriptions was the great innovation of eighteenth-century philanthropy. Instead of the traditional way of charities being run by wealthy individuals, philanthropists now worked jointly in committees to manage the affairs of the charity, while the main donations were made by subscribers from outside. The task of the committee members was to attract new subscriptions and to invest them in their philanthropic work, which they did with the help of paid employees. Basing charity on permanent financial support from the public directed philanthropy towards a more pragmatic approach, both in the way it was promoted and in the objects it chose. In order to guarantee maximum support, the subscription charities needed to show that their work benefited not only the recipients, but society in general. Playing on fears for personal safety makes a powerful advertising message, and the Marine Society used this to great advantage. Its publications played on the external military and economic threat from France, but even more on the internal threat posed by neglected youths.

When, for example, the Society campaigned for support to help find employment in private businesses for their boys after the Seven Years War, the plan was described to the public as 'precautions' undertaken to 'prevent numerous mischiefs which will otherwise naturally arise, by many of these boys turning thieves & robbers of the very worst & most dangerous kinds.'[7] In December 1757, Hanway echoed Fielding's statements by claiming in a newspaper advertisement that 'at a modest computation' the Society had 'cleared the land of five hundred thieves and robbers'.[8] We should note that by then the Society had already equipped two thousand boys and three thousand landsmen. Portraying recruits as (potential) criminals and idlers, whom one had to deal with anyway, was also a neat way to avoid any possible criticism with regards to how beneficial the sea service really was to the boys. And so, too, was it advantageous to overstate the misery in which their boys had been living previously. However, the Society was to learn that those messages could backfire, as they ruined the reputation of all the Society's boys and hardened negative stereotypes of sailors in general. Furthermore, such descriptions encouraged parish officials to try to dump troublesome boys onto the Marine Society. It took the Society a while to realise that, if they wanted good ships' boys, their messages regarding their recruits needed to change to a more positive tone.

The most important tool for the eighteenth-century philanthropist in educating the children of the poor to become law-abiding subjects, and later responsible parents themselves, was Christianity. Religion was also considered to instil acceptance of the political status quo, and the Society wrote: 'that without a sense of religion, it is not possible that peace and harmony, due subordination, and the happiness of social intercourse, can exist.'[9] London's Foundling Hospital claimed to take care that their:

> children do constantly attend Divine Service in the Chapel on Sundays, to often remind them of the Lowness of their Condition, that they may early imbibe the Principles of Humility and Gratitude to their Benefactors; and to learn to undergo, with Contentment the most servile and laborious Offices.[10]

The boys placed out as apprentices in maritime trades by the charitable Stepney Society were warned that rebelling against their underprivileged position would offend God and Christianity, for 'it is by the wise appointment of God, that some of us are rich, and some are poor; some are appointed to govern, and others to obey'.[11] Christianity was to keep the poor in grateful obedience – a maxim which those institutions concerned with the education of pauper children had to be careful to observe, since they were regularly accused of raising rebellious characters by planting too much ambition into the minds of those who were destined to fill the lower ranks. The Stepney Society offered some philosophical comfort for its boys: 'In the mean while it is very obvious, that as the rich are not always happy, nor the poor miserable, happiness must depend either on opinion, which is very changeable, or on health of body, and contentment of mind.'[12]

For the first three years the Marine Society's committee met in the Merchant Seamen's Office above the Royal Exchange, outside which the 'conductor' Thomas Tyson would assemble the boys. In its third year, the Society began renting a permanent office in Bishopsgate Street, reducing the rent slightly by subletting the room to the Stepney Society. The charities were not just sharing their benefactors, but also their premises, and the personnel, too: the Society's first assistant secretary, for example, was also the Secretary to the Society for the Encouragement of the Arts, Manufactures and Commerce (SEAMC). When the Society eventually elected its first chairman, the choice fell not on an active committee member, but on a man of some fame. As in many similar societies, the middle-class philanthropists chose a member of the aristocracy as their chairman: Lord Robert Romney, who was also the chairman of the SEAMC. In addition to Romney, a treasurer (Russia merchant John Thornton) and eight further deputy chairmen were elected, half of them being active committee members, the other half chosen for their social standing and connections, such as the Lord Mayor. However, the one man who was to chair almost all the Society's weekly meetings was not Romney or Thornton, who both rarely appeared, but a man who until 1772 held no elected post at all: Jonas Hanway. The latter was the Society's driving force and (often anonymous) author of its publications.

While Hanway was an overseas merchant with business interests to promote, his involvement in the Society also had a personal dimension. His father had been a victualling agent for the Navy, and his brother Thomas was a captain in the Navy. Furthermore, like so many Marine Society boys,

Jonas Hanway (*c.*1779), by Edward Edwards.

Hanway had largely grown up without his father, who had died in a horse-riding accident two years after Jonas' birth. Starting with the foundation of the Marine Society, Hanway embarked upon a unique career as a philanthropist, whilst gradually withdrawing from the business world. Next to the Marine Society, he was also the co-founder of the Magdalen Hospital for penitent prostitutes, which was often portrayed as the female counterpart to the Marine Society, as well as of the Misericordia Hospital for venereal diseases, and of the Troop Society to support British soldiers in Germany and North America, providing clothing for men in the armed services.

By the end of the Seven Years War, the Marine Society had already attracted donations of over £20,000 – perhaps around £4 million in today's value, though it is hard to compare such figures. These donations came from a wide variety of subscribers. The largest gifts came early on from the City Companies – from the Company of Grocers to the Company of Weavers, from the Merchant Taylors to the Skinners, numerous 'Worshipful Companies' helped the Society onto its feet and are still supporting it to this present day. On London's stages, David Garrick, the number one 'celebrity' actor of the time, gave benefit performances for the Society, as did composer George Frideric Handel. Just like today, celebrity endorsement was vital for a charity. Roughly seventy-five per cent of the donations came from numerous smaller subscriptions between one guinea and £20. Thus, not only in terms of funding, but also in terms of numbers of subscribers the Society was ahead of other contemporary charities. Among the more modest subscriptions were some donors who donated rather unwillingly: Fielding had passed on the fines several bakers had to pay for selling bread of inferior quality, and a Mr Benjamin De Israeli, the grandfather of the later prime minister Benjamin Disraeli,[13] donated four guineas, 'being so much received as a Composition for an Injury received in a Fray at the Playhouse'. The Society even profited from reckless driving on London's streets, as a hackney coachman had to pay a subscription for damage done to a gentleman's chariot.

As part of the Society's anniversary dinner the latest boy recruits, equipped with banners, marched to the sound of drums and fifes from the Royal Exchange to the Admiralty. Such a show of properly-clothed lads marching off was guaranteed to catch the attention of any bystander and potential donor, and the Stepney Society had used it for years to mark its annual so-called Cockney Feast. The Marine Society, which included some men who also organised the Cockney Feast, was certainly able to equal the spectacle of the Stepney Society, particularly on the day of David Garrick's benefit performance of *The Suspicious Husband* in 1757: seventy-five Marine Society boys and forty young landsmen, all of them bound to march to

Portsmouth the following day, were first assembled on Constitution Hill by John Fielding, to be presented to King George II. His Majesty's coach passed the recruits very slowly, during which, according to a newspaper report, 'a Smile expressive of paternal Delight overspread his Royal Countenance'. Afterwards the recruits marched to the Admiralty to be presented to the Lords, and then went for a roast beef and plum pudding meal, while the members of the Marine Society went to dine separately and were joined by many 'Gentlemen of Fashion'. Cannon salutes concluded the feast, and in the evening recruits and Society members together went to attend Garrick's play. Garrick had arranged some additions to the comedy to ensure that the young recruits were sent off with their heads filled with emotive patriotism. He spoke a prologue dressed as a sailor, and in the epilogue even Britannia herself appeared on stage together with some of the boys.[14]

Fielding's connections to London's artistic scene were certainly valuable, yet his independent recruitment efforts brought him into conflict with the Society. Something was already wrong with the very first boys he had collected: Vice Admiral Henry Osborne in Portsmouth was alarmed to find that many of them were apprentices, who either must have run away from their masters, or wrongly assumed they could just leave without cancelling their indentures. Or perhaps they had felt going to sea was a magistrate's order they had to obey. What Osborne worried about was the danger that their apprenticeship masters could rightfully demand a share of the boys' official wage, that is the wage the officers were normally pocketing.[15] The Admiralty advised Fielding to be more cautious about which boys he took, and not to send any apprentices whose indentures had not been cancelled. Fielding's selection of his recruits, or rather lack of selection, became a crucial point in his breaking up with the Marine Society after only two years of co-operation. Fielding's main aim remained the use of the sea service as an alternative to punishment for young offenders, and as a precautionary measure for those whose circumstances might lead them into crime, to convert 'Thieves in Embryo into useful sailors' as he phrased it.[16]

The Marine Society members shared this intention, and they used these extensively for advertising purposes, yet to them serving the Navy had priority. Initially, everyone involved had assumed that both objectives would go hand in hand, that charity and policy would be united, but they clashed. When the Navy's complaints about runaway apprentices, and more importantly about deserting boys, reached the Society, and it appeared that many of these boys had been sent by Fielding, a rift opened up between the Society and Fielding. Deserters not only harmed relations with the Navy, they were also financially damaging, as the boys ran away with the Society's kit. More than once, the Society's committee reprimanded Fielding, yet in the end they saw no other way than to stop the co-operation. This, however, should not leave us with the impression that the Society entirely distanced itself from the idea of recruitment by magistrates. At the same time as the quarrels with Fielding unfolded, the Society's publications still styled the enterprise as a crime-prevention programme, and Hanway was about to publish a plan for raising additional seamen in which he underlined the importance of magistrates picking up vagabonds and informing the Society about them.[17] Even though the Society preferred well-motivated boys, what counted in the end was that the boys were not apprentices and would not run away.

The Society initially thought its work completed once its boys were safely on board; even more, with the advertising campaign playing so much on the threat of war, the members expected that funds would only flow in as long as the Seven Years War lasted. Yet when the war drew to a close, the Society was positively surprised by the fact that in the immediate post-war years the subscriptions even rose again. This allowed the Society to supply boys, who had returned from the war and wanted to go back to their homes, with new clothing and travel money. Many among these boys were invalids, juvenile war veterans physically incapable of finding future employment at sea. Yet the biggest financial boost of all came when a merchant in Hamburg, William Hick(e)s, who had befriended Hanway on his travels through Germany, bequeathed a legacy of £22,000 to the Society, a sum equivalent to all the Society's previous subscriptions together. Suddenly the Society's office was no longer big enough to accommodate all the philanthropists who wished to attend its meetings. Founding members returned to the gatherings, but also many men who had never been to any meetings previously now turned up. Hickes' bequest came with the condition that the Society would carry on its work.

However, as peace had arrived, demand from the Royal Navy for boys from humbler backgrounds was greatly reduced. The Society had to rethink its programme. Hanway developed the idea to broker and sponsor apprenticeships in the merchant navy and with fishermen, watermen or related trades on land, such as shipwrights or sailmakers. He argued that Queen Anne's laws regarding maritime apprenticeships for parish boys lacked coercive authority and did not fulfil their purpose, that is, to train up more seamen. Hanway's plan was put into practice, but surprisingly there were few applicants for the Society's charity.[18] This, combined with the uncertainty about the legal costs for claiming Hickes' legacy, led the committee to stop their apprenticeship programme completely until the case

THIS GROUP REPRESENTS CHARITY PROTECTING A POOR BOY AND
COMMEMORATES A LARGE BEQUEST MADE TO THE MARINE SOCIETY
IN 1768 BY WILLIAM HICKES. THE WORK WAS COMMISSIONED BY
THOMAS NASH OF LONDON AND EXECUTED BY JOHN FLAXMAN
THE ELDER THE STATUE WAS FIRST ERECTED IN 1772 IN THE ROYAL
EXCHANGE. IN 1818 IT WAS MOVED TO THE GARDEN OF THE MARINE
SOCIETY'S PREMISES IN BISHOPGATE STREET WHERE IT STOOD UNTIL
1854. IT WAS THEN REMOVED TO LLOYD'S AND REMAINED THERE
UNTIL THE COMPLETION OF THIS BUILDING IN 1959

THE MARINE SOCIETY
FOUNDED BY JONAS HANWAY 1756.

Sculpture commemorating W Hickes' bequest, and the Marine Society's
incorporation (1772), by John Flaxman the Elder.

was decided. Furthermore, the Society's activities had lacked the necessary input from its members, for while the meetings concerned with recovering Hickes' bequest were extremely well attended, the normal gatherings to run the Society's business were anything but. Most of the workload was left to Hanway alone. At least Hanway had finally received his eagerly-sought position of a Navy commissioner for victualling, which bound him also professionally with the Navy and made him financially independent.

Early in 1769 a compromise about Hickes' bequest appeared to be finally within reach, and the Society prepared to restart its activities. In the end they had to be satisfied with half of the legacy. The Society now intended to apprentice boys to masters of trading ships, coasting vessels, colliers, fishermen, watermen and lightermen, as well as Navy officers to whom the Navy Regulations allowed apprentices in peacetime.[19] Advertisements asking for interested masters and boys to come forward were put up in the streets. Once again distressed orphans and vagabond boys were to be the prime target, yet once again the boys who were eventually supported came from a wide variety of backgrounds and were by no means all destitute. The Society paid for clothing, bedding, and the apprenticeship fee, as well as for medicines and medical treatment.

Most importantly, the Society acted as the boys' guardian, keeping a close eye on the masters. Disreputable masters, who were only after the fee and hoped to get away with short-changing or maltreating friendless boys, were only too familiar to them. The Society's correspondence shows that they actively investigated any complaints their boys had, checking if the masters provided sufficient food, clothing, housing and training. One boy, for example, complained that his master had left him alone in a harbour town two hundred miles away from home, with just a little pocket money to find his own way back.[20] The master might have got away with treating a friendless boy in this way, but the Society immediately intervened, demanding that he explain his actions and return at least a part of the fee. In other instances, when masters appeared to have valid complaints about their apprentices, the Society apologised, yet indirectly also pleaded for a little patience and understanding for boys who sometimes had endured a difficult childhood.

The Hickes bequest, or the difficulty in obtaining it, was one of the reasons that prompted the members to incorporate the Marine Society, which was completed in July 1772. Romney remained the chairman, and Thornton the treasurer, but Hanway now received for the first time an official position, that of deputy treasurer. It was, however, pointed out that he had already served in that capacity without formal election for the past years.

The problems of the teenage population in the growing and modernising cities appeared to the Society to be more worrying than ever. The first official publication of the newly incorporated Society outdid older publications in its dramatic tone, painting an apocalyptic picture of London's youth: 'We now lie open to a nursery of thieves, bred up in this metropolis, with the effects of blood and rapine, and the untimely death of many victims to the gallows.'[21] One of the most famous children's charities, the Philanthropic Society, founded in 1788, saw no other solution than to take the children away from their parents and environment at an early age, and occupy the children through institutionalised education and vocational training – something which, of course, continues today, even supported by the force of law.

The Marine Society was not to be disheartened; it went on to sponsor boys willing to begin a career at sea, and by 1815 it had equipped twenty-five thousand boys for the Royal Navy, sponsored four thousand apprenticeships

Boardroom of the Marine Society today, with Hanway's portrait and chair.

in commercial shipping and also equipped forty thousand landsmen for the Royal Navy. By 1905 the totals had risen to 33,181 boys for the Royal Navy, 3,760 boys for the Indian Navy, and 27,436 boys for the merchant navy.[22] In the second half of the twentieth century, realising that many of its tasks were now taken over by the state, the Society shifted its focus towards providing educational opportunities to seafarers through charities with which it had merged, such as the Seafarers Education Service and College of the Sea. In 2004, the Marine Society merged with the Sea Cadets, and together they now promote opportunities at sea for young people and ensure that seafarers in Royal Navy and merchant ships can access a wide range of educational options via distance learning. The Society's offices are today situated in Lambeth Road, South London, where in the boardroom the members – in a few cases the direct descendants of the Society's founding fathers – hold their meetings under the watchful eyes of Jonas Hanway's painted portrait, the chair on which he sat for the portrait remaining vacant in the corner.

As servant positions were limited in the eighteenth century, recruiting boys for the Navy was slightly more complicated than recruiting men. Initially there had been some unfortunate cases among Jim Hawkins' comrades when the Marine Society sent boys to the Navy regardless of the numbers needed. Uncertain what to do with the extra boys, the Navy kept them together with the pressed men in the tender for far too long, where some boys had their new clothes stolen and/or became sick and so miserable that no officer would take them as a servant.[23] In the end such boys were then just set ashore, being barely dressed and forced to beg their way back home. When the Society became aware of this, it changed its advertisements and often asked for a specific number of boys – also out of fear of receiving numerous boys sent from faraway towns, for whom they somehow had to find positions. For the response in the rest of the country to the Society's call for boys was great, so much so that the Society was swamped and had to issue advertisements asking that no boy be sent to London without prior consultation.

Over the years the Society always struggled to control the recruitment of youngsters from the country, trying to ensure that only boys who were really needed, fit enough, and who voluntarily enlisted and were not apprentices, would be sent to London. The last thing the Society wanted to happen was that rejected boys would be stranded in London with no support – a problem which John Fielding had already encountered when he had set up the Universal Register Office for boys looking for apprenticeships: suddenly would-be apprentices sent by parish authorities from all over the country had appeared at his doorstep.[24] Initially, the Society had tried to set up branches in other parts of the country, yet only the Dublin Marine Society was a success story, while attempts to found branches in Exeter, Plymouth and Bristol all failed. In the end, the Society was to provide from its London base for boys from all over the country, from Cornwall to Scotland. However, individual supporters from outside London often acted as unofficial branches, such as the Colchester MP Charles Gray, who collected youngsters from his home town, or Francis Grant in Edinburgh, who clothed Scottish boys and had them sent south on board naval vessels.

The main means for reaching the real-life Jim Hawkins directly were advertisements placed in newspapers or put up in public places. The advertisements offered free clothing, relied on the lure of prize money, to which, it was underlined, the boys were entitled as much as the men, and also proclaimed that the boys would be provided with accommodation, good food and clothing until they went to sea. The texts in the early years struck a rather unemotional tone; there was nothing that might have appealed to patriotism or adventurousness. In fact, some of the publications were more likely to offend any upright patriotic volunteer, by portraying them as a burden to society, though these texts were aimed primarily at donors and parish officials. Public relations events, such as the theatre plays, also specifically targeted potential donors.

There is hardly any event recorded in the Society's documents that was directed solely at the volunteers. One of the few exceptions occurred in April 1759, when the Society recognised that there were still many boys 'lurking in and about the environs of this great City' and decided to:

> equip three boys with the distinguishing ornaments of a black ribbon round their necks & a ribbon round their hats & a blue ribbon round their knees, with a rattan in their hands & two shillings & sixpence in their pockets & that one of them be a fife & the other two boys who have been at Sea in the Kings service, who are lively, well satisfied & to be trusted, be commissioned to make a Tour & pick up all the boys they can who are proper for the sea, agreeable to the advertisement.[25]

In July 1760, the Society sent one of their employees together with three boys and two fife-playing boys, dressed in the Society's clothing, to march around in the suburbs, and to collect as many boys as possible. But for the entire Seven Years War this is all that is recorded in the Society's documents. Yet it is perhaps understandable that not too much was done to reach the boys directly. Most of the time, not only were there sufficient numbers of boys willing to enlist, it was also safer to contact local parish overseers, magistrates, mayors and other gentlemen, who would know of any trustworthy and unbound boy, thus avoiding the risk of clothing runaways or thieves. After all, even the Navy was frequently criticised for luring away boys who were needed in the local economy, and the Marine Society, too, had to deal with such accusations.

When the boys arrived at the office, they were checked for their suitability. Those with minor illnesses were sent to a lodging house for treatment. All accepted boys were stripped of their clothes, washed and dressed at the office. Some boys were allowed to retain their old clothes, after these had been thoroughly cleaned. Generally, the Society preferred to give the old clothes to the 'ragman' or destroy them, for it regarded them as a health risk. As we shall see, it was a matter of life or death that a strict policy was maintained in this respect, despite the fact that science and most contemporaries had not yet realised the high risk of infection the boys' ragged clothing carried. The boys were also advised to cut their hair for hygiene reasons; they received caps to protect their heads instead. Boys with nowhere to stay, and those with minor illnesses, were lodged at a private workhouse and well fed until they went to sea, all at the expense of the Society.

In the early decades the boys were sent to sea without any pre-sea training. The Society only became more active in the boys' education after it restarted its operations in the 1770s. Hanway had always been convinced, though, that the Navy's officer-servant model was insufficient in terms of training and educating seamen. The French way of teaching seamanship in academies, perhaps the more enlightened way, appeared more effective. The only comparable schools from which the Royal Navy could profit were institutions such as the Royal Hospital School at the Greenwich pensioners' home and Christ's Hospital School, but they operated on a smaller scale. Even with regards to educating boys who were meant to become officers, the Navy still placed more value on practical sea experience than on schools on land, as is evident by the failures of academies like the Portsmouth Naval Academy. In 1779, Hanway, Thornton and others had set up a Maritime School, which targeted sons of deceased officers and noblemen. The school was never really connected to the Navy and closed due to a lack of subscriptions in 1783.

Directed more at the Society's usual boys, in the same year Hanway proposed a plan for so-called County Naval Free Schools, which were to be set up in every county to take impoverished boys and employ them in agriculture, to enable the schools to be self-sufficient and to distance the boys from the corrupting influence of the city. The schools were to be provided with ships on dry land, so that the children could be taught seamanship. Hanway's model went far beyond the simple concern for an institution to breed new sailors; it was a step towards a nationwide harmonised education and vocational training for the sons of the poor. However, this plan of the then grand old member Hanway appeared far too ambitious for the new

Memorial to Jonas Hanway at Westminster; the memorial was unveiled in 1788,
but reduced in size in the late nineteenth century.

generation of Marine Society members. It was rejected in 1786, the year Hanway died.

Instead, the Society acquired an old merchant ship, the *Beatty*, which was moored between Deptford and Greenwich, and turned into a training ship for boys. The *Beatty*, or *The Marine Society*, as she was renamed, could take between fifty and a hundred boys. The twenty-five boys who were chosen to attend Hanway's funeral procession were the first to be trained on board. From then on, many boys began their new life at sea by spending a few days, weeks or months on the Society's training ship. There was no standardised training period; the ship was more a holding station. Next to sailing and the principles of navigation, the boys were trained in fighting with the cutlass and operating the guns, as well as being instructed in hygiene and religion. Browsing through the training ship's registers, the rather blunt character assessments of the boys stick out. While some are labelled as good or even very good boys, there are also many described by phrases such as 'a very stupid boy, cannot read' or 'a very wicked, bad boy'.[26] The ship remained the cornerstone of the Society's training over the next century. The *Beatty* was replaced by a succession of six other ships, the last one being decommissioned in 1940.[27]

In contrast, the only training the Society's early recruits might have been lucky enough to receive, and only one hundred and seventy did so during the Seven Years War, was being taught to play the fife. In May 1757, the Society began to lodge fife-boys in a house at Tothill Fields, where they were taught to play the instrument.[28] The training lasted up to two months, depending on each boy's progress. A drum major of one of the regiments of guards acted as a fife-master, teaching the boys 'To Arms', the 'Grenadiers March', the 'Reveiller' or 'Ravalle', and the 'Tattoo'. Being trained to play the fife was a reward for boys who were regarded as the better recruits. Usually only boys who could read and write were selected, unless they seemed particularly motivated. The fife-master was reminded that: 'If any boy is of a tender frame, you must not harass him, nor endanger his health.' Furthermore, the boys were later visibly distinguished with a white sleeve and a white cape to their blue jacket. They even received a certificate addressed to their captain, asking him to put the boy under the care of a fife player. Sadly, not all future Marine Society boys were to appreciate the privilege of being taught to play the fife: the boy William Stevens, who went to sea via the Society during the Napoleonic War in 1808,[29] was one of their fife-boys, and according to William's great-great-grandson the amusing family story recounts that young William became an expert in the fife and was often requested by the officers to entertain them. Yet William himself regarded this only as an annoying extra duty, and to free himself from it, he decided to let the fife go overboard. When anchoring next at Malta, the officers bought him a new fife, accompanied with the hint that if this one went overboard too, William would suffer the same fate. William took the warning seriously, and the replacement fife is today still in the possession of his family.

Although in the early decades the rest of the boys went on board without any training, the Society did not allow them to leave entirely uninstructed. After they were clothed at the office a few instructions were read out to them.[30] They were reminded of the great benefit they were receiving, and while the lure of prize money was used in the advertisements, Jim's comrades were now warned not to have too high expectations of gaining any. They were advised to keep themselves clean, for the sake of their health and so that their officers would accept them. They were cautioned not to fall in the habit of drinking excessively, swearing, lying, thieving or whoring – the latter 'certainly brings on pain and diseases; if you do not shun bad women, you will die in misery, or at best, whilst you should be drubbing your enemies, you will be languishing in an hospital.' How many of the boys had a cheeky smile on their face while hearing these warnings, we do not know, nor whether the majority of the boys fully understood, seeing that they were just fourteen and experienced puberty much later and less abruptly than today's teenagers. The Society's instructions also went beyond practical advice:

> You are the sons of Freemen. Though poor, you are the sons of Britons, who are born to liberty; but remember that true Liberty consists in doing well; in defending each other; in obeying your superiors and in fighting for your King and Country to the last drop of your blood. . . . To obey God is the first and greatest duty. . . . [God] will give victory to those who he thinks best to reward, and it generally is given to those who are most ready to obey their Commander, and do their duty best . . . [God] will make you happy in life, and in death, even when your souls shall depart from your bodies.

Evidently the Society thought that 'religion makes the steadiest warriors'.[31] The Society also took the opportunity to tell the boys about the New Testament, even about loving your neighbour as yourself, despite the fact that they were sent to war against Britain's neighbour. The reasons for going to war against France, by the way, were at no point explained to the boys.

Most recruits got their written instructions bound together with Josiah Woodward's *Seaman's Monitor* and Edward Synge's *Essay towards making the Knowledge of Religion easy to the Meanest Capacity*, and also a prayer book and a New Testament provided by the Society for the Promotion of Christian Knowledge. Publications like Woodward's *Monitor* show concern about sailors' discipline and religiousness, and the dangers when they encountered foreign peoples and cultures.[32] Woodward worried about crimes like mutiny and piracy, as well as any kind of misbehaviour by sailors towards foreigners, and the shame these actions brought to the nation and to the Christian faith. Woodward was obviously haunted by the thought that the only Christians, or British people, some foreign communities encountered were sailors behaving like drunken hooligans and pirates. In Woodward's eyes all the misdemeanours committed abroad by British seamen stemmed from a lack of religious instruction which had the potential to restrain them. The *Monitor* encouraged sailors to say their prayers on board, even if confronted by the mockery of shipmates. He also warned them that they should not think themselves safe from prosecution for any crime committed abroad. On the other hand we also find in Woodward the fear that the sailors themselves might be negatively influenced by contact with foreign religions and cultures.

Despite Woodward's complaints and the common stereotype that the strongest profession seamen generally made to God was swearing by his name, we should not write off the Society's donation of literature as a complete waste of paper. Many sailors used books as a source of entertainment on long journeys. And it is also conceivable that, facing hitherto unknown hardships far away from home, combined with the usual insecurities a teenager experiences, many of Jim's fellow ships' boys were searching for psychological support. In that case religion was still the first resource, unless shipmates and alcohol fulfilled that function. Reading skills may have been more widespread than we would imagine, seeing that reading was on the curricula of the numerous charity schools. The Society encouraged those who could not read to ask their comrades to read aloud to them.

Equipped with their literature, clothes, bedding and final instructions, the boys then went off to their ships. Once Jim was in the care of his future master, the Society considered its work completed. The Society's immediate success in supplying boys and landsmen for the Navy has been praised by contemporaries and historians alike. For the Seven Years War alone, the Society equipped about thirteen per cent of the Navy's recruits (men and boys); probably the greatest part of the Navy's servants wore clothing supplied by the Society. However, its success has to be assessed with the rider that we should describe men and boys as being 'equipped' rather than 'recruited'.[33] Often officers brought their own boys to the Society's office and, in fact, the Society even encouraged officers to find servants themselves. Some boys who had already entered the Navy came on their own to claim clothing and bedding, and in other instances captains wrote letters asking for kit to be sent to their ship. Admittedly, the Society occasionally tried to discourage just anyone from applying, certainly once suspicions arose that some applied more than once. Yet, in the end, it generally supplied all applicants.[34] From the Society's registers it appears that particularly among the servants to officers other than captains were many boys who had enlisted earlier than their appearance at the Marine Society, suggesting that they, being their master's sole servant, were recruited by the officer himself and only afterwards presented. From 1770 to 1780, for example, ten per cent of the boys had already been at sea when they received the Society's clothes, which again emphasises that the Society's documents give us a good cross-section of the boys fulfilling Jim Hawkins' role. Ultimately, it was only in the best interests of the war effort that the Society was generous with its clothing gifts. In fact, and nobody was aware of this at the time, it was, without exaggeration, a matter of life or death for the crews in the Navy as we shall see next.

Britannia Clothing Marine Society Boys (1757), by F Hayman and A Walker.

There is one significant contribution made by the Marine Society to the welfare of our real Jim Hawkins, and to the strength of the entire eighteenth-century Navy, that has never received its due recognition, not even by the Society itself. And that is its success in defeating the Navy's deadliest enemy. The French were a minor threat in comparison with the most dangerous killer, which was usually smuggled on board by the boys and men themselves. Lice, together with rats, killed more sailors on both sides than any enemy fire or cutlass. Diseases kill quietly, and perhaps herein lies the reason why naval and military historians tend to focus too much on the navies' action-packed engagements and battle strategies, when in reality the decisive battle was fought on the 'health front'. As the celebrated naval surgeon James Lind remarked in 1762: 'the number of seamen in time of war, who die by shipwreck, capture, famine, fire, or sword, are indeed but inconsiderable, in respect of such as are destroyed by the ship diseases, and by the usual maladies of intemperate climates.'[35] Keeping ships and sailors afloat, healthy and fit for action over a longer period was the greatest challenge faced by all navies.

Naval recruits, boys and men, volunteers or pressed, all entered the Navy with the clothes they happened to be wearing at the time. Frantic wartime recruitment resulted in many impoverished recruits entering the Navy, some of them destitute or even from prisons. Their ragged clothes sometimes carried on board deadly diseases like typhus. Unfortunately, nobody was fully aware of the danger lurking in their clothes. As recruits were often kept first in holding ships and from there distributed to their assigned vessels, theoretically a single person could infect the entire fleet. James Lind complained that the guard ship at the Nore, which received the men taken up in London, had often turned into a 'Seminary of Contagion to the whole Fleet' through a single diseased sailor.[36]

Proposals to hand out free uniforms had never been put into practice, because sailors were not permanent employees, and it also made it easier to camouflage ship and crew as a friendly vessel to an unsuspecting prize. The men could obtain clothes and bedding on board in exchange for a wage deduction, at any time, and as long as the ship's stock lasted. However, the fear that they would desert, or sell their clothes, prevented the Navy from giving away anything for free. Particularly for those boys and landsmen who were driven into the Navy by their destitute situation, and who possessed no sailors' clothes at all, fitting themselves out would have been financially impossible unless their captains were prepared to hand out clothing in exchange for a deduction from future wages. Here the Marine Society helped by offering free sailors' clothing and bedding.

The kit given out by the Society varied over time, dictated by available funds, the testing of various new products, and individual needs. In the Society's early years, the boys usually received a felt hat, two worsted caps, a kersey pea-jacket, a waistcoat, two to four shirts, one to three pairs of drawers, a pair of canvas trousers, two pairs of hose (yarn or worsted), two pairs of shoes, two handkerchiefs, a pair of blue horn buttons, a bag to hold their gear, as well as bedding consisting of a mattress, pillow, blanket and coverlet. Furthermore, some useful tools, such as thread, worsted and needles, and even a knife were added. The Society should have guessed that in view of such valuable equipment some boys would be tempted to collect the kit and then run away. The clothes were usually blue; when the price of indigo rose, brown temporarily became the dominant shade, but from 1758 onwards dark blue was the norm – the Society found that dyeing with indigo made the most weather-resistant colour. A sample of the clothing was kept on show at the Society's office.

The clothes were not just given out for health reasons. The concern about the socialisation of the boys and landsmen on board, as well as trying to lower the temptation for thieves and deserters (uniforms are easily spotted), also made a clothing bounty preferable to the common cash bounty. Sailors were often regarded, and regarded themselves, as different from the rest of society, and aversion against inexperienced landsmen and newcomers was widespread, especially in the Royal Navy. The newcomers on board were easy to detect, not just by their inexperience, but also because they were dressed as people on land normally did. 'Long toggies' was the sailors' slang for the landsmen's clothes, the term probably deriving from the word tog for coat (togeman, Roman toga), since landsmen usually wore long coats and waistcoats over their tight breeches and stockings. In contrast, sailors wore shorter clothes, their (usually blue) jackets and (red) waistcoats only reaching their waist, as this was safer for working aloft. Replacing the long toggies reduced the risk that the long garments might cause an accident.

The bully-boys among the sailors loved to take matters into their own hands and cut the landsmen's clothes to the right length, as landsman Robert Hay recorded in his Navy memoirs:

> I soon became accustomed to the jokes and when any of these nautical punsters brandished their knife and threatened to unbend my ringtail and water sail . . . I calmly tucked up my skirts and tucking them up behind buttoned my coat closely so that they could not accomplish their purpose without coming in front to disengage the button, by which I would have been put upon my guard. I was forced to observe this precaution every night otherwise I would soon have been stumped.[37]

Hanway's brother Thomas, a captain in the Navy, told Jonas of the difficulties he had when commanding a ship with a large number of landsmen.
The sailors just did not mix with the landsmen, so Thomas Hanway bought
sailors' clothing for them from their first prize money and observed that the
distinction between seamen and landsmen immediately ceased. Hanway
thought that his landsmen thereby became seamen in one third of the time
they would have normally needed. The Society's clothing bounty was now
to eradicate this visual difference from the start, and according to an
enthusiastic article in the *Gentleman's Magazine* of April 1757 it indeed did
so, ending a distinction between seamen and landsmen, 'which used to
create animosity, and subject the landmen to some hardships'.[38] The article
was probably the result of a well-aimed public relations initiative by the
Society, yet that should not diminish the genuine benefit accrued by their
clothing gifts.

An additional advantage of the Society's uniform was perhaps that
clothing the recruits uniformly also promoted the subordination of the boys
and landsmen to the discipline of the ship.[39] Uniforms suppress individuality
and resistance, though there is no hint in the Society's sources that its
members were aware of this effect on naval discipline. The committee only
hoped that the proper look and good quality of their clothes would constantly
remind the recruits of the great charity they had received. The most
important aspect of offering new clothing and bedding, however, was the
positive impact it had on the health of the recruits and even further – and
here nobody realised the full benefit of the Society's work – on the health of
the whole ship's company and fleet.

The men and boys applying to the Society were often poorly dressed, and
it was obvious to everyone that their ragged clothing would not give them
sufficient protection against the weather. Experience told the Society that
sailors themselves paid less attention to their clothing than did the Admiralty,
and it did not expect its boys and landsmen to take more care than those 'old
salts'. Being the 'hardy and robust men'[40] Hanway wanted them to be, and
their machismo being formed within a male world of the ship, the chances
were high that sailors would rather spend their money in taverns than on
protective clothes. Hanway observed that British seamen were 'confusedly
brave, but they are apt to be careless; and more lives have been lost for want
of clothing than many imagine', and that the Marine Society 'mean to
preserve this nation, by saving our Seamen from avoidable hardships, and
preserving them from their worst enemies, themselves.'[41] It was perhaps
asking the impossible to encourage sailors to disregard their health when
engaging in combat, or to go on long risky voyages, while at the same time

expecting them to be sober enough to spend a large part of their modest income on proper clothing.

Insufficient clothing in stormy and cold weather cost many men's lives. Rheumatism was, after fevers and scurvy, the third most frequent illness for which sailors were admitted to hospital.[42] But old and ragged clothing and bedding posed a much greater danger to the entire crew, even to the whole fleet, and this was that filthy clothing was likely to carry diseases like typhus on board.[43] Typhus, then known as jail distemper, or gaol, ship, hospital, camp, putrid, malignant or pestilential fever, was one of the greatest killers of naval manpower. Overcrowded, damp, and closed environments like warships provided excellent conditions for lice to thrive – any visitor to HMS *Victory* in Portsmouth today feels amazed how 850 men could live and work in a space little more than 160ft (50m) long, 50ft (15m) broad and 20ft (6m) deep. In peacetime, according to Lind, diseases were no problem, or no more than for people living on land. The trouble only started at the outbreak of war, when the press gang roamed the urban slums and filled the ships with 'such idle fellows as are picked from the Streets or the Prisons'. Such men threatened to bring on board 'a Disease of the most contagious nature', a disease that according to James Lind was 'the Produce of Filth, Poverty, and a polluted Air, which subsists always in a greater or less Degree in crowded Prisons, and in all nasty, low, damp, unventilated Habitations loaded with putrid animal steams'.[44]

The exact causes of ship fever were still a mystery. Bacteriology and the discovery that lice (and fleas) were the main carriers of typhus were still over a century away. Though ragged clothing and bedding had always been considered a danger, the predominant assumption was that foul air in a damp and overcrowded wooden environment was the actual cause of ship fever, as hinted by Lind's preceding quote. Consequently, most efforts of the Admiralty concerned the ventilation of the ship. However, as such measures did not bring the hoped-for improvements, people started to look elsewhere. As with so many health issues, the acknowledgement that personal cleanliness and clothing might be connected to the fevers spread long before a proper scientific explanation was found.

Through the provision of new clothing for those who normally posed the greatest health risk to the fleet, and by taking away and often destroying their old clothes, the Marine Society contributed to the Navy's manpower far beyond the mere number of recruits it supplied. In 1761, five years after the Society's establishment, James Lind could proudly observe that the whole fleet had been in an unparalleled state of good health.[45] Lind did not mention the Society, but the positive effects deriving from the Society's provision of fresh clothing, and the enforcement of personal hygiene could not be overlooked. In 1762, Lind added, in the second edition of his *Essay on the Health of Seamen*, 'Rags' as a possible source to his above-quoted description of the disease, and also that 'the purest Air cannot cleanse Rags from Contagion'. He also added an example of a fever epidemic where the 'fatal Mischief lurked in their tainted Apparel; and Rags, and by these was conveyed into other Ships.'[46]

In the following decades, surgeons, captains and other officers pleaded for a uniform for sailors, but it took another hundred years before a uniform was introduced (together with continuous service). Nevertheless, the recognition grew within the Navy of the importance of new recruits being washed, disinfected and made to buy better clothes. New Navy Regulations reminded captains to enforce cleanliness among the men, and to make sure the men washed and aired their clothing and bedding whenever possible, and also gave captains the right to force men (first the pressed, later also volunteers) to buy new clothing or bedding.[47] The Marine Society thus made sure that our Jim Hawkins strengthened the crews in the Navy, rather than unintentionally depleting them. It is now high time to take a closer look at the identity of the typical ship's boy who would have worn the Society's clothes.

CHAPTER 4

The Typical Jim Hawkins

THE best place to begin our search for the real Jim Hawkins is the Marine Society's office, pictured in J B Cipriani's engraving of 1758. At the table the Society's members are debating,[1] and in the foreground we see the boys as they leave their concerned mothers behind, and are examined and then dressed in the Society's clothes. The historical records of the Marine Society provide a unique opportunity for us to peep through the keyhole of the Society's office door and muster the typical ship's boy. Between 1756 and 1815, over twenty-six thousand boys wore the Society's clothes in the Navy, which provides a huge sample for our investigation.[2]

Marine Society's Office (1758), by **J B Cipriani**.

If we wanted to give the typical ship's boy a more likely name at the start of our search, then John would actually be more accurate than Jim/James. Almost every fourth Navy boy was called John. However, after William and Thomas, James was next in frequency. John, William, Thomas and James together made up the names of more than half the naval servants. There was evidently little variety in names, and the fact that half of the boys carried their father's first name suggests that there was not to be any greater variety in the future. Calling out for John on board an eighteenth-century warship would have had a quarter of the crew turn their heads.

On average our Jim was a mere thirteen or fourteen years old when he enlisted. The Navy would have preferred more mature servants, who could sooner be turned into ordinary seamen, yet only a fifth of the boys clothed by the Society were older than fifteen. It turned out to be more difficult than expected to find older boys who were not employed in any other occupation. Possibly all those dissatisfied apprentices and runaways were harder to recruit than anticipated, or there were simply not that many. On the other hand, from age eighteen upwards the youths could enter as paid landsmen, and thus we would probably encounter many of the unhappy apprentices among the recruited landsmen. There was certainly a temptation for the boys to pretend to be older, at the top end to be accepted as a paid landsman, and at the bottom end to be accepted as a servant rather than being rejected for being too young. The boys' real age would have been hard to prove. Many of Jim's comrades were not even sure about their real age; instead they could only give a guess. These were not just the friendless orphans: eighteenth-century Britons were not as meticulous in keeping track of their age as we are today.

The young age of some of Jim's comrades, and the fact that such young children were sent to war, is disturbing to modern eyes. Despite Navy Regulations forbidding the enlistment of anyone younger than thirteen, there were many boys who were not even thirteen. During the Seven Years War, for example, around eight per cent of the boys were younger than thirteen. It is astonishing how, for example, someone like Richard East, an illegitimate child brought to the Marine Society, could be accepted in the Navy: Richard was ten years old and 3ft 11in (119cm) short.[3] It is to be doubted that the sight of little Richard would have scared off any French boarding party. The Navy Regulations provided the exception that the sons of officers could be as young as eleven. In such cases, with their father on board, one may assume that these young children received the necessary guidance and protection. Yet for someone like Richard, with no evidence of a relative on board, one wonders how well he integrated on ship, and we can only hope that either his officer or someone else took care of him. It

Marine Society's Office: Inspection of the Boys (1758), by J B Cipriani.

seems that in practice the lower age limit for sons of officers was also granted to seamen, as a closer look reveals that in some cases of underaged boys their fathers were seamen serving on board the same ship.[4] Next to having a relative on ship, having a relative with good onboard connections could have been another reason for getting underaged boys accepted. Nine-year-old ship's boy Henry Dayby, for example, went to sea in 1756 after a personal request by Captain Campbell.

As young as these naval servants were, there are plenty of examples of other children in the eighteenth century who went to sea, and some also to war, at the same tender age. The laws providing for compulsory maritime apprenticeships for parish boys, for example, referred to all children above ten years of age.[5] Among the slightly older ships' boys clothed by the Marine Society we find some for whom it was not the first time they went to sea, and who had already made some tough seafaring experiences outside the Navy: thirteen-year-old Joseph Graham, who enlisted in 1760, had been a castaway in the *Marquis of Granby*;[6] fourteen-year-old James Martin had come from a French prison in 1758, where he had ended up after being taken while serving on board the *King of Prussia* privateer, on which he had sailed together with the young revolutionary Thomas Paine.[7] Fourteen-year-old Peter Maquire, who enlisted in 1759, had been paid off by the *Neptune* merchantman from Virginia – a friendless orphan, left to his own devices at a harbour in England.[8] The Society explained that pity for the desperate boys, and not the need for recruits, often led them to accept underaged or undersized candidates.[9]

At the other end of the age scale, a few of Jim's comrades were rather old for a ship's boy. A little over one per cent of the boys were aged nineteen or in their early twenties. This is surprising, as they should have been allowed to enter as paid landsmen rather than as unpaid servants. One of the oldest 'boys' ever to enlist in the Navy was an astonishing twenty-eight years old.[10] His name was Thomas Warwick, and in his case, as in many others, one senses that entering a man as a servant was a discrimination. Thomas' stature does not indicate any physical deficiency, but a note behind his name might provide us with the reason why he had to be content to enter as a servant: Thomas was 'a black' coming from the East Indies. In fact, all 'black' boys equipped by the Marine Society were eighteen and older – perhaps they were not just servants to their officers, but slaves or 'apprentices'.

Many of Jim's comrades would have struggled to live up to Herman Melville's ideal of 'the handsome sailor' Billy Budd: smallpox had left its marks on their young faces – so much so that the boys' smallpox scars were used as a way of identifying them. Those of Jim's comrades who had not yet contracted smallpox were a risk to the Navy's crews, as dangerous as those boys carrying lice and deadly diseases on board in their clothes. The Marine Society, exceptionally alert to the importance of fighting diseases, soon began to inoculate all their ships' boys – a radical step, as inoculation, that is, the deliberate instigation of a controllable outbreak of smallpox, became common in Britain only gradually from the 1760s onwards. The high death toll which accompanied the early techniques had provoked widespread opposition to inoculations.[11] Many of Jim's comrades were also suffering from minor illnesses when they enlisted, such as the highly contagious 'itch', scabies to us today, and 'scal'd heads', a disease of the scalp, usually accompanied by dried discharge of pustules in the form of scales, and hair loss. In the first quarter of 1757, for example, more than ten per cent of the Society's boys had to be cured of such minor illnesses first, before they could be handed over to the Navy.

Even disregarding those very young boys we have seen allowed on board above, what we would find most astonishing about Jim's appearance, particularly if he stood right in front of us, would be his height: he was very small. Jim at age thirteen or fourteen would have measured on average a mere 4ft 5in (135cm). Even when aged sixteen to seventeen, Jim would have only reached around 4ft 10in (147cm). Over the decades, Navy officers occasionally complained that the Marine Society sent boys who were considered too slight, and eventually, to avoid any temptation, the Society set up a rule outside its office door showing the minimum height (usually between 4ft 3in and 4ft 6in), so that the boys could measure themselves before entering and would be spared a later disappointment. Of course, special requests and family connections continued to bring undersized boys on board. Thirteen-year-old John Stone, for example, measured only 4ft 1in (124cm) when he enlisted in 1758, yet his brother was a carpenter on board the ship to which John was heading.[12] The Society also publicly advertised that sons of sailors would be accepted even if below the minimum height.[13]

Entrance to the Marine Society today.

Seeing that the children would still grow, the concern about minimum heights is interesting. Height was associated with strength and fitness. A small stature was also believed to be less resistant to disease, which according to modern research might well be a valid point. The growth rate of children, much more than adult heights, can also provide a useful indicator for nutritional health and standard of living conditions. Paediatricians today use growth rates of children in order to determine whether a child is deprived or abused. Even the eighteenth-century Marine Society was already aware of the connection between height and standard of living, claiming that their boys' growth was often 'checked by the poverty and insufficiency of their diet, and the defect of due warmth, occasioned by the want of such clothing as our climate requires to nourish their limbs'.[14] Many children were apparently 'stinted in their growth; some appear with shrivelled countenances, as if they were born of parents, who had received no other nourishment than Gin'.[15] Compared to a thirteen-year-old boy in England today, these boys were on average one foot (30cm) shorter. If any of Jim's mates would miraculously enter a doctor's surgery today, he would be immediately diagnosed as suffering from malnutrition or child abuse.[16]

Unfortunately, there are not many comparable data sets on heights of other eighteenth-century boys from similar social backgrounds. However, something very interesting becomes apparent when comparing the boys to data from middle- and upper-class children: while a fourteen-year-old Marine Society boy measured around 4ft 5in, a middle- or upper-class fourteen-year-old attending the Royal Military Academy at Sandhurst at the same time reached 5ft 1in on average,[17] which is a difference of eight inches (20cm). Thus, in the eighteenth century, the middle- and upper-class boys were quite literally looking down on Jim Hawkins. A slight comfort was that Jim and his mates would catch up a little later in life, as they experienced their growth spurt later and continued to grow for longer. Nevertheless, the height gap was so large that one wonders how strongly it influenced contemporary views on the hierarchical structure of society.

Though small in stature, once Jim started to take an active part in the sailing of the ship, his shoulders and chest would soon become exceptionally broad, due to the heavy hauling and lifting his work involved, often while being bent over the yards. The purser on board, who sold clothes to the seamen, usually covered the chest ranges from 36 to 40 inches. Considering the men's small stature, those sizes appear rather broad and strong. Today, British men are heading for an average chest size of 42in, but that is perhaps rather the result of a heavy burger diet than of heavy hauling and lifting while bent over the yard.

In contrast to his low stature, Jim's literacy level was surprisingly high. At least sixty per cent of Jim's comrades were able to read, and at least forty per cent were also able to write. Most of them might have been taught in a parish or private charity school; in fact, a small number of boys came straight from school when they enlisted for the Navy. However, the majority of Jim's comrades, even the younger ones, had already been working in some business on land before going to sea. It is hard to say, though, how regular and reliable their employments were. Most of the London boys had earned some money by running errands. This was perhaps a good training for what was to be their most important task from now on: being a 'powder monkey' and running to get the powder from below deck to the cannons as quickly as possible. Jim Hawkins, who worked in his parents' pub, seems to come close to his real-life counterparts, too, as drawing beer and helping a publican was the second most common employment among the boys. Seeing that so many boys started their working life in a pub, the stereotypical career of Long John Silver, a former sailor who settles down as a publican, becomes plausible. Hogarth's failed weaver apprentice, Tom Idle, is also not far away from the real-life ships' boys, as weaving, spinning and quilling follow next as the most common previous employments among the boys. However, unlike Tom Idle, the great majority of the Navy's boys had only been employed as servants and draw-boys in such businesses, rather than as properly indentured apprentices.

Those boys who had been proper apprentices prior to enlisting for the Navy gave a variety of reasons for cancelling their indentures. Some had been unable to settle in the business, others claimed to have been mistreated by their masters, and then there were also many cases where the master had simply died or even disappeared. Some apprentices were understandably fed up with their terrible working conditions. Eighteen-year-old Charles Awbrey, for example, had been an apprentice to a chimney sweep before enlisting as a naval servant in 1759 – his stature of a mere 4ft 7in (140cm) was perhaps the sad proof of a long service under very unhealthy conditions.[18] However harsh and hazardous life in the Navy would turn out to be for Charles, he probably welcomed it as fresh air.

Apart from the most common occupations above, we find that the boys had also been occupied previously in a wide range of other employments. They worked for shoemakers, plasterers, paper stainers, some helped in their fathers' or other relatives' businesses, or earned a living as street vendors selling anything from fruits to matches or hardware. One boy had previously been a servant to a puppet show, and another one sang ballads in the street. Many had tried their luck in a variety of jobs, never finding a permanent

Page in the Marine Society's registers.

employment that suited them – boys like Robert Winroe, who 'was a sort of an errand-boy, one while to a distiller, at another time to a grocer, and then he got to be an understrapper at a brew-house. But none pleased him long, his mind was quite unsettled', so eventually 'when he had tried all methods he could by land, and none would doe, he betook himself to sea'.[19]

Many children were simply destitute. In the 1770s, for example, near twenty per cent of the Society's ships' boys were described as having been destitute, or having been in care of the workhouse and the parish. Yet only a few were labelled as vagabonds, while the majority had some employment recorded, though evidently this was not regular enough to help these boys to survive. From outside the cities, many destitute children formerly working in agriculture and with animals, or labouring in the brickfields, were sent to the London Society to be clothed for the sea service. Notably, among the boys in distress were also many who had already been at sea, but had been discharged from their ships, and had tried unsuccessfully to find any other employment. Evidently, even during wartime the Navy sometimes discharged boys permanently when they were not needed, or when they were sick or ill-disciplined, despite Navy Regulations that forbade such discharges.[20] For the boys as well as the men, seafaring sometimes remained a mere temporary episode in their life – permanent employment was in no way guaranteed, particularly not in peacetime.

Having mustered the typical Jim Hawkins, we will see next if we can find out more about his family background and upbringing. However, there is one fundamental question which has not yet been addressed: when mustering Jim, was he always a boy? What about the colourful stories of girls on board disguised as boys, the famous folk ballad of *The Female Cabin Boy*[21] and similar songs? It would have certainly been impossible for a girl to pass the Marine Society's medical check-up, but anyone else being taken straight on board by their officer would not have faced such a close inspection. Alas, those undetected are unlikely to be found in the official historical records. There are a few real-life stories of disguised girls among the ships' boys, the most famous being the published memoirs of Mary Lacy (1740-1773+) and Mary Anne Talbot (1778-1808).[22] Mary Lacy was, by her own account, a rather lively girl, spending the nights at secret dances rather than at home in bed. After falling unhappily in love during her night-time adventures, her teenage mind could contemplate no course of action but

Mary Anne Talbot (1804), by **G Scott**.

running away. Disguised as a boy, she loitered around the harbour and was eventually recruited as a servant in a Navy vessel; we will occasionally revisit Mary Lacy's adventures as a ship's boy. Less romantic is the story of the way in which Mary Anne Talbot got to sea. An evil Captain Essex Bowen of the marines had become the guardian of the thirteen-year-old orphan and had forced her to accompany him to sea disguised as his footboy. Mary Anne later also became a drummer boy and a captain's servant. While Mary Lacy's story is credible, Mary Anne Talbot's cannot be confirmed by the Navy's muster books, and there are inconsistencies in her battle stories.[23] There are also plenty of other stories of the 'pretty cabin boy' which clearly were just fantastic yarns, spun by commercial authors, dreaming girls and romantics on land, as well as (rather more worrying for Jim) by sexually-starved men at sea.

Most of Jim's comrades who were in distress before coming on board had fallen on hard times because their fathers, or both parents, had died or were nowhere to be found. Once again Jim Hawkins and Tom Idle, who had both lost their fathers, seem quite representative of the real ships' boys. In the 1750s and 1760s, for example, more than half of the naval servants clothed by the Marine Society had no father, and a sixth had no adult at all taking care of them. Of course, a few lying runaways made these statistics look worse – boys like fourteen-year-old Thomas Brown, who ran away from his parents in 1759, assumed the name John Chapman when he presented himself to the Society, claimed to be fatherless, and succeeded in being clothed, placed on board a Navy vessel and off to sea just before anyone found out that he was a runaway.[24]

In many cases the Navy itself was indirectly responsible for making the ships' boys fatherless – not only had a few of Jim's mates lost their fathers at sea, the nature of a sailor's life meant that their sons were without a father figure for long periods while growing up. The problem remains even today, although improved technology enables more frequent home visits and communication. In the eighteenth century, wartime posed a particular difficulty, when shore leave was extremely restricted and press gangs kidnapped sailors on the spot, regardless if they had a family or not. Fourteen-year-old John Wilkinson, for example, enlisted in 1759 as a servant in the Navy, shortly after his father had been impressed and taken on board a tender.[25] If their mother became ill or even died during their father's absence, then sailors' children were in acute danger. The Marine Society rightly observed that one death at sea often ruined more than one life,[26] and hence maritime charities always made helping the sons of sailors one of their prime concerns – the simple charitable solution offered being also to send the sons to sea. Sometimes the Navy had an even more direct responsibility for the ship's boy losing his father: Thomas Tilley, a thirteen-year-old from Bedfordshire, who stood at just 4ft, was taken on board a naval vessel as a servant in 1759, after his father, who had been a sailor in the Navy, was shot when he tried to desert.[27]

Some of Jim's mates had as closest responsible relative an older brother, and it sometimes happened that both enlisted for the Navy together. It appears that in cases of siblings the Navy made an effort to keep them together on board the same ship. Just like allowing boys to join their fathers, keeping the boys together with older siblings was both a humane and practical way to ensure that the young recruits had someone looking after them and an attachment figure. The naval vessel could even be host to a family reunion in miniature: in 1758, the Mitchell brothers Peter and James went on board the *Rippon*, in which their father also served as a sailor.[28] Evidently sailors did what was a common practice among officers, that is, taking their own sons on board. With regards to educating, protecting and disciplining the boys this was something the Navy could only welcome.

Historians usually assume that seafaring was largely a hereditary occupation, and that most boys found their way to sea simply because that is where their fathers or their communities earned their living. Naval historian Michael Lewis, for example, estimates that this was the case for very roughly two-thirds of the sailors in the late eighteenth century.[29] However, a comprehensive study proving this assumption is still not in existence. If we look at the Navy boys clothed by the Marine Society, however, the most astonishing aspect is that the majority of their families had no apparent connection to seafaring. In the 1750s and 1760s, for example, among those boys who still had a father, only ten per cent of these fathers had a seafaring background. Furthermore, most ships' boys in that period came from inland towns and not from coastal communities. Of course, we cannot rule out that some of the publicans, labourers or carpenters among the fathers had in their younger years been to sea, and also that some of the deceased fathers had been sailors. Equally, because of the Society's charitable nature we have to expect numerous boys among them who would not normally have joined the Navy. However, this does not change the fact that in a period such as the Seven Years War, the Society clothed the vast majority of the Navy's ships' boys, and that hence most of the Navy's servants in that period did not come from seafaring families. And this happened despite the fact that the Society even advertised that sons of sailors were given priority. It therefore appears

Nineteenth-century Marine Society boys before ...

... and after (in the first photograph, the boy in the centre
and the boy to the right of him are said to be the same
as the boy on the right and the boy in the
centre of the second photograph.).

that in the eighteenth-century Navy and in times of war, the boys coming from non-seafaring families could at least temporarily outnumber those from seafaring families. Of course, in the peacetime Navy their share would have been smaller. And in the merchant navy, coastal shipping and fishing the percentage was probably also much smaller; here we would instead expect to find all the sons of sailors, possibly serving their apprenticeships and enjoying the protection from impressment.

Those landlubber fathers of ship's boy Jim had a wide variety of occupational backgrounds. They were labourers, weavers, tailors and shoe-makers, but also carpenters and makers of small items like watches, as well as soldiers. Jim's mother often earned money too, by working as a washer-woman, shop assistant, servant, weaver or tailor. Some unfortunate mothers, whose husbands had died, lived in a workhouse. It is difficult to say how well Jim's parents fared in their occupations. The title 'labourer' certainly suggests unskilled and irregular work, while weavers, tailors or shoemakers were often recruited from amongst parish children. One frequently encounters the sons of soldiers, sailors, shoemakers and watchmakers in eighteenth-century courts for having been caught pickpocketing. Yet a wide range of social ranks could hide behind most occupational titles, be it carpenter, alehouse keeper or watchmaker. A carpenter, for example, could theoretically be anything from unemployed, a regular wage-earner, to an independent artisan. Eighteenth-century society was not familiar with the concept of permanent unemployment, thus a sailor was registered in recruitment documents as a sailor, regardless if he was currently employed at sea or ashore without a ship. How well his occupation provided Jim's father with regular employment and a sufficient income is therefore open to interpretation in many cases. Certainly, in trades like weaving and shoemaking there was a growing number of men working in large workshops, already resembling factories, and these men had little chance of ever becoming masters. They might have sent their sons to sea because they could not find or afford any work or apprenticeship in their own trade for their sons. For many it must have already been a great financial relief that the Navy would from then on house and feed their boy. Yet, even among those clothed by the Marine Society, we encounter boys who clearly did not come from struggling families. We find, for example, sons of known mathematical instrument makers in London, who must have gone to sea for personal reasons, or even hoping to learn something about the uses to which their fathers' products were put.

The Navy's ships' boys came from all over Britain, and even those clothed by the London-based Marine Society by no means came only from London. London was nevertheless a focus of the Society, and, although hard to estimate, in peak war years the Society clothed around one per cent of London's teenage population for the sea service.[30] We find boys from the same London streets, some of them friends or even relatives, going to sea via the Society. In the 1770s, for example, more than twenty families from the weaving community around Quaker Street in Spitalfields sent their boys to the Marine Society, and nearly thirty families from Long Alley in Moorfields had their boys join the Navy within a short period of time.[31] Unfortunately, the Society was often not very impressed with the boys from

Gin Lane (1751), by **William Hogarth**.

London, and observed some striking differences between them and those coming from the country and further north.[32] To put it bluntly, they felt the northern children had a much more pleasant character, the more northern the better. The Society's members thought this stemmed largely from the fact that in the northern parts the children were brought up in the fear of God, and were educated by clergymen to obey their superiors. Northern boys were apparently more virtuous and honest, more religious, better dressed and behaved, less prone to swearing, and had better reading abilities than their age peers from London. In a letter published in the *Public Advertiser* in 1757, a visitor to the Society's recruitment day expressed the differences he perceived between urban and country youths in rather uncompromising words:

> And when the Town and Country Boys were mixed together, with their respective Parents, the ingenious Mr. Hogarth's two Prints, of Beer-street and Gin-lane, came strongly to my Mind. The Country Boys were straight, stout, and well-grown, and their Complections clear and ruddy, their Coat patch'd, their Stockings dearn'd, their Shoes cap'd, but all tight; and their Parents modest, and anxious for the Welfare of their Children. The Town Boys puny, pale, seemingly check'd in their Growth, ragged and dirty; their Parents abandon'd, noisy, and lost to paternal Affection: And their Cloaths, or rather Rags, burnt off their Backs with the same poisonous Gin, with which they had destroyed their own Constitutions, and the Growth, Strength, and Vigour of their Offspring; for a Country Boy of twelve Years of Age was larger than many of the Town Boys of sixteen.[33]

Historians critical of eighteenth-century urbanisation and industrialisation will hardly find a more moving observation.

Some of Jim's shipmates had unusual backgrounds. We find a few, though very few, Jewish boys among them, even amongst those supported by the Marine Society; this was despite the fact that founder Jonas Hanway had published pamphlets against the naturalisation of Jews.[34] It is likely that there were a few more Jewish boys hiding among Jim's comrades, doing what John Solomons did, who changed his name to John Smith, fearing that with a name like Solomons he would never be accepted.[35] Sailors were prejudiced against Jews because the only Jews they usually knew were the distrusted traders who came on board when their ship lay in harbour. They strongly suspected that those traders were constantly trying to cheat or overcharge them, in the knowledge that sailors could not return to complain about the items they had bought. Such negative prejudices are even to be found in some of the older naval histories, without the reminder that by being blocked from so many other trades, and by being poor immigrants, Jews were forced into making a living through such one-man trading businesses. Jewish, as well as Roman

Catholic, boys would never be allowed to become officers in the Navy, unless they denounced their faith.

Among Jim's fellow ships' boys were also a few who were born outside Britain. They came from Ireland and from places as far away as Lisbon, Berne and Marseilles, as well as from the North American colonies and the Caribbean, and even from Africa and India. Adventurous and sometimes heartbreaking life stories had led some of these foreign-born boys to end up as servants on board a Royal Navy vessel. Fifteen-year-old 'John' Meyer, for example, who enlisted as a servant in the Navy in 1777, was originally from Germany, but had become a castaway on board a Dutch brig near the coast of Yarmouth and had since then lived as a vagabond in England.[36] The German boy was unable to read or write, at least in English, but he had the smallpox behind him and was considered fit and committed enough from now on to serve Britain on one of His Majesty's ships. Twelve-year-old orphan 'John' Munis, who joined the Navy as a servant in 1778, was born in Lisbon; he had come to England on a Portuguese ship which had, for whatever reason, departed without him, leaving the child alone and destitute in England.[37] He was able to read, and even though he was below the Navy's official age limit, he was taken on board to fight for Britain.

Already in the 1760s the Marine Society had specifically advertised that they would also clothe boys from different parts of the world, as long as they were desirous to become one of the King's subjects by their 'Useful Labours in this Nation',[38] which suggests that at the time there may already have been a larger number of boys from other parts of the world living in Britain's maritime cities. These boys had nothing to expect from the parish poor relief; the sea was their only possible home.

The most famous among the Navy's ships' boys born outside Britain was Olaudah Equiano, whose autobiography and political campaign were later so influential for the British anti-slavery movement.[39] According to his memoirs, Equiano had been kidnapped as a child in the 1750s in Africa and was brought to America as a slave. However, his small stature had made him undesirable in the eyes of those attending the humiliating auctions of human beings in their search for strong slaves to work on the plantations. Olaudah was eventually bought by a Navy officer, who gave him the odd name Gustavus Vassa, perhaps in reference to the Swedish sixteenth-century king or the ship of the same name. Non-Europeans were often burdened with mockingly fancy European names by their British superiors. The officer took him to sea during the Seven Years War as a servant and ship's boy. As with some of the other ships' boys (and girls) previously encountered, we will revisit Equiano's story in the coming chapters.

Equiano's initial decision to enlist as a ship's boy in the Navy was as involuntary as it could possibly be. We shall explore next what usually pulled the typical ship's boy towards the sea, whether there were more boys like Equiano who did not go aboard entirely voluntarily, or whether they were all as eager and excited as Jim Hawkins.

Olaudah Equiano (1789), by **D Orne**.

CHAPTER 5

Jim's Motives: Sailors and Youth Culture

WHAT drove boys into the Georgian Navy? The previous chapters have already given us some ideas. The common explanation that most sailors had simply followed in their fathers' footsteps may have validity, but it does not explain all, considering that among the wartime Royal Navy servants the sons of sailors could be in the minority. So what attracted the youngsters with no family tradition of seafaring to the Navy? There seem to be two different archetypes: one is a bit of a Jim Hawkins, and the other is more of a Tom Idle. Yet, in fact, a closer look will lead us to the conclusion that a boy could be both Jim Hawkins and Tom Idle in one person. Judging by the Marine Society's documents, many seem to have been driven by poverty, unemployment or a dire apprenticeship. Others appear to have been pushed by parish authorities, justices or work masters, as was Hogarth's stereotypical 'Idle Apprentice' Tom. But Jim Hawkins and his longing for adventure and fortunes, with his youthful bravado and belief in a cause, was not entirely fictitious, neither was Robinson Crusoe and his desire to see the world. We shall see that the lure of the sea and the lifestyle of the sailor heavily influenced eighteenth century youth culture, and it may well be appropriate to view the social milieu of eighteenth-century sailors in general as a form of youth subculture.

Before exploring the connection between youth and the culture of the sailor further, perhaps the most important issue to clarify is whether any ships' boys were forced to enlist in the Royal Navy. The Navy itself was primarily after seamen. Inexperienced, unwilling young boys were not interesting prey for the press gang, nor was impressing them legal. The pressure for boys to enlist came from the other end, from the authorities on land. The most obvious cases of this were boys who were convicted in court and had their punishments waived on condition that they enlisted for naval service. Their numbers appear to have been small. In theory, they, too, were volunteers, as naval service was the generous offer suggested by the judge, or by the defendants themselves, in order to be spared the regular punishment. Beyond such cases of 'convict boys', there is a greater number of boys for whom the pressure is less visible. Much about an ordinary boy's future was decided informally, rather than put down in official documents, and particularly with regards to the children of the poor we can assume that parish authorities tried to have a say in their choice of occupation. Even more, parish authorities had the power to force those who were dependent on poor relief into certain apprenticeships.

Once again, the boys clothed by the Marine Society provide a good example of the grey area between volunteering and being coerced. Officially, all the Society's boys were meant to be volunteers. Doubts about this claim arise right from the very beginning of the Society's work in the 1750s, simply from the fact that magistrate Fielding played such an important role. Fielding assured the public that all his boys had enlisted voluntarily, but we do not know how many of his recruits had come to his attention because they had committed petty crimes. Fuelled by Fielding's own comments about their delinquent past, we suspect that many of his lads 'voluntarily' went to sea in order to avoid future conflict with the law. Long before the foundation of the Marine Society, Fielding had already complained in a newspaper article that he had to send young boys to prison, when it would be much more productive if they were sent to sea.[1] In the early years of the Marine Society there were also a few troubles with boys running away after being clothed or immediately after arriving on board their naval vessel. Had they planned to steal the Society's clothes all along, or did they experience a sudden change of mind, or had someone indeed forced them to enlist?

Admittedly, the fact that among Fielding's boys were some who later deserted or behaved badly was one of the main reasons why the Society eventually stopped co-operating with him. To clothe deserters was a waste of money for the Society and damaged their relationship with the Navy. Over the years the Society became increasingly cautious and less willing to accept boys who seemed to have been pushed to volunteer or who did not appear trustworthy. However, if we take an explicitly recorded criminal past in the recruitment records as a hint that a ship's boy may not have enlisted entirely voluntarily, then even in the later decades of the eighteenth century we still find many examples. Among the boys clothed in the 1770s, for example, near one per cent have an explicitly recorded history of delinquency.[2] A further three per cent in the 1770s are recorded as having been sent or recommended by a magistrate, the Lord Mayor or other authorities able to send juvenile convicts. And these were surely not all, as such background information was not always recorded in the registers. When the Society was, for example, accused of luring away from the countryside boys who were needed in agriculture and husbandry, the Society defended itself by claiming that most boys from outside London were sent by parish officials, justices or respectable gentlemen, who would surely only send boys who were a 'nuisance'.[3]

From the 1750s to the 1770s, the Society's publications often ascribed to their boys rather unfortunate characteristics, portraying them not just as being impoverished, but also as threats to public safety. We read, for example, that the 'objects of the Society are the removing of those who are Vagrants, Pilferers, or by extreme poverty and ignorance, are pernicious to the community', and only afterwards the intention is added 'to encourage the industrious poor to send their children to sea'.[4] In a publication of 1772, the Society divided its ships' boys into three categories: first the well-behaved, educated, and religious ones; then those who were active and brave, but had 'little or no guard against temptation'. Finally, there was allegedly by far the most numerous group, those who were described as 'abominably corrupted' due to an early loss of their parents and the misfortune of never having received any instruction, living as vagabonds and in a habit of idleness, and in the 'most wicked company, in the most wicked part of these kingdoms', being 'hardened in iniquity'.[5] Once again, we should keep in mind that the Society was a private charity and needed to attract donors, if necessary by portraying their enterprise as a crime-prevention programme. Nevertheless, such dramatic descriptions make us wonder whether all these 'abominably corrupted' boys really enlisted out of their own will or whether someone had given them a push.

The Society's day-to-day work and advertisements indicate some distrust of the motivation of some of the Navy's ships' boys. The Society's minutes record warnings given to captains about to receive boys who had been thieving in the past, and letters were written to captains begging them to be more careful to prevent desertions by their boys. Such precautions suggest that the percentage of youths with a past which made the Society worry about their commitment was probably higher than the one per cent with a recorded criminal conviction. Yet we still cannot be sure whether the deserting boys were 'Artful Dodgers' who faked their enthusiasm and only wanted to steal the Society's kit, or whether they had been put under pressure to enlist in the Navy.

In its early years the Society was not only troubled by boys immediately deserting, but also by some lads struggling to get off their ship by claiming that they were apprentices to some master on land. The Society advised captains not to discharge any boy pretending to be an apprentice, but to inform its secretary first, who would then make an inquiry. Claiming to be an apprentice was a tempting way for a naval servant to get off the ship, as officers were afraid of losing their wage bonus to the boy's real master. Yet why would any boy try to do this, even falsely pretending to be an apprentice, so shortly after apparently volunteering for the service? In April 1757, for example, the captain of the *Ramillies* informed the Society that a number of his boys claimed to be apprentices, yet an inquiry found that most of their apprenticeship indentures had been delivered up by their old masters to be cancelled. The boys had to stay – with fatal consequences for all of them, as the *Ramillies* was to be their deathbed when first she suffered from an epidemic, and was then wrecked off the coast of Devon. Only one boy, Peter Ryalls, was lucky enough to leave the *Ramillies* just before her terrible fate. Peter was transferred to the *Royal Ann*, from which he was finally discharged for being an apprentice after a total of five months in the Navy.

Such boys struggling to get away by claiming to be apprentices also suggests that the deserters were perhaps not all thieves, who simply wanted to steal the clothing, but that among them were youngsters who had been enlisted in the Navy by their parents, former masters, or some authority, without any enthusiasm on their own part about going to sea. Of course, there is also the possibility that some boys had a sudden change of mind after getting their first taste of life in the Navy as, after all, most of them were very young. The unfortunate ones would have had a long stay in the smelly hull of a tender, mixed with victims of the press gangs and all sorts of ruffians. William Robinson, who enlisted in the Navy in 1805, immediately regretted his decision to volunteer when he was put on board the receiving ship and found himself in the company of 'wretched companions down in the hold and the rats running all over them', some of them suffering from seasickness or fainting from the stench.[6] A grate was put over the hatchway and a guard of marines placed around it, so that William felt as if he were being treated as a felon. This was not how an enthusiastic and patriotic youth expected to be welcomed into the Navy.

In view of all the troubles with boys trying to get away, the Marine Society saw the need to take more care that all its recruits enlisted out of their own free will, and also that they were not just physically but also mentally ready to become seamen. An advertisement campaign was started in 1757, reminding anyone intending to enlist a boy to make sure that the lad really wanted to go to sea. But the campaign turned out to be insufficient. The Society had to run further newspaper advertisements, in which it complained that churchwardens, parish overseers, parents and apprenticeship masters from all over the country kept on sending boys who, upon being interviewed, at their arrival stated that they were unwilling to go to sea. The Society threatened that in future it would simply return such boys to their places of settlement, which in reverse perhaps hints that in the past such boys were sent to the Navy regardless. Furthermore, the Society also asked not to be sent any boys who were capricious and did not know their own minds, or were mentally not ready for the demanding life of a sailor. It was not the last time that the Society had to run such advertisements. Sometimes it was hard to determine what the boy really wanted, when the boys themselves did not grasp that the decision was down to them, or were clearly not aware of what awaited them in their new life. On occasions, the Society gave some of them more time to reconsider their decision. In other cases the Society was outraged to realise that relatives or friends had filled the youth with alcohol when they presented him at the office. The Society was clearly up against the common wisdom amongst parents and authorities that, for a boy incapable of settling in any profession, the sea was the ultimate relief for their troubles, often disregarding whether the boy was prepared and fit for such a commitment.

The attempts of the Society to ensure that all ships' boys went to sea out of their own free will were certainly well meant. However, ultimately the Society's efforts were undermined by eighteenth-century poor laws, apprenticeship laws, and laws against vagabonds and rogues, which all ignored the personal liberty of the children of the poor. Local authorities had the power to order children supported by the parish into an apprentice-ship in merchant shipping or water-related trades. Although being a servant in the Navy was not an apprenticeship, one can imagine that some parish officials felt that they were still acting lawfully. Take the numerous boys sent to the Marine Society from Colchester for example: insufficient workhouse accommodation had often led Colchester's overseers of the poor to send their boys elsewhere to work, and impoverished boys in such a town were used to being sent away for their apprenticeships. They were apprenticed to fishermen, oyster dredgers and mariners close to Colchester and as far away as Southwark, Deptford, and even South Shields or Sunderland. With the foundation of the Marine Society, sending the poor boys to the Navy must have seemed a reasonable alternative solution.

Furthermore, the masters of apprentices sponsored by the parish had the right to turn their boys over into a maritime apprenticeship, given the approval of Justices of the Peace, and they, too, might have assumed that the Navy could count as such. This could explain why some boys still desperately clung on to the claim that they were apprentices when on board, while their former master had already cancelled their indentures. Next to apprenticeship legislation, laws against vagabonds made it legitimate to send anyone considered idle, dissolute, a rogue, vagabond or beggar, regardless whether man or boy, forcibly to the Navy. To a large degree the Marine Society also had only itself to blame for receiving unwilling boys, since its own publications portrayed the undertaking as a crime-prevention programme for troublesome youths. It took the Society a while to realise that its own advertising messages had to change to a more positive tone with regards to the boys, if they wanted to avoid being considered a dumping ground for teenage troublemakers.

There is also evidence that many of the boys, used to being ordered into a workplace, assumed that enlisting as ships' boys was a compulsory order. One night in 1763, for example, three lads jumped over the wall of the Marine Society's lodging house and ran away, leaving the Society wondering why the boys had escaped when they could have left freely at any time, and leading to yet another committee resolution to inform every boy that the decision was up to him alone. In the end, we may also presume that even the Society's members, despite all their assurances, would have regarded a certain amount of pressure as helpful, at least when dealing with troublesome or destitute youths. Hanway wrote that it was up to judges and lawyers how far the above-mentioned laws regarding young vagabonds could be stretched. He himself felt, since it was plain that destitute children often had no way to survive other than to steal, and since they were the 'breeding ground for the most dangerous criminals', the country could only benefit if the Society could be 'a means to render our highways and our streets more secure; and by a gentle or compulsive means remove the wretched crowds who disturb the peace of civil society.'[7] Being poor and without support made Jim a potential criminal.

When at the end of the Seven Years War the Society made plans for the dispersal of the Navy's boys to the merchant navy, Hanway again assured the public that no compulsion would be applied, but also noted that 'persuasion and encouragement will go a great way, and necessity still farther', and that 'neither policy, nor humanity' would permit them to let any boy go who could be expected to end up as a vagabond.[8] Thus there continued to be cases like that of Alderman George Nelson, who wrote to the Society in September 1759, recommending a poor boy named Acteon Jefferys for the Navy. Alderman Nelson did not hide the fact that Acteon had been caught pilfering, but he also took the opportunity to invite the Society's secretary to collect a large donation of £21 from him, and in the very same month Acteon was clothed and on his way to the *Royal Sovereign*.[9] Being caught thieving must have made Acteon a great deal more receptive to the Alderman's proposal to volunteer for the Navy, and perhaps the donation helped to overcome doubts within the Society.

Further research in the court archives is needed to explore the position with regards to those boys who were convicted in court, and had their sentences waived under condition of joining the Navy. The records from London's Old Bailey proceedings, as one example, show that between 1700 and 1815 a little over one per cent of the convicted boys aged nineteen or younger were allowed to enter into naval or military service and thereby avoid punishment. The absolute numbers are small though. The majority of these boys were in their late teens, and it is doubtful that they were new to the sea. Instead, many of them already had seafaring experience and were probably not entering the Navy as servants but as seamen. Most cases are recorded in the last two decades of the period, when the quality of the Old Bailey's records improved, and the wars with Revolutionary France made both Navy and Army desperate for men. Here the percentage of convicted teenagers allowed to join the Navy or Army rose to around five per cent; possibly a few more avoided punishment by having their sentences exchanged with naval service at a later date.

Twelve-year-old William Barrett, in 1804 convicted at the Old Bailey of stealing a watch from the publican for whom he worked, was the youngest among the 'convict-boys', and was probably rather an exception.[10] There was also another younger boy among them, a fourteen-year-old called George Mackay, who had been an accomplice to an eighteen-year-old youth in 1793.[11] Together they had stolen a silk handkerchief, worth a mere sixpence, from Esquire Granville Sharpe, the famous anti-slavery campaigner. In George's case it is noteworthy that he stood at the same height as his eighteen-year-old co-defendant – perhaps an indication that recorded ages in eighteenth-century sources are often guesswork, and also that George might have pretended to be younger, hoping for a more lenient sentence. It is difficult to believe that the Navy would have been keen on completely inexperienced young ships' boys like William Barrett or George Mackay, if they seemed unwilling to become sailors, especially once the officers' servant-pay bonus had been abolished in 1794.

Someone like seventeen-year-old George Renny, convicted at the Old Bailey in 1798, appears a much more plausible case of a teenage defendant sent to the Navy:[12] George had already been to sea on board a Navy vessel, and he had been on shore leave in June that year when he committed his crime. He was actually about to collect prize money owed to him for service in his last ship, and at the time of his trial he had already joined his new ship. George had valuable seafaring experience and he was urgently needed on board his new ship. He was accused of stealing a lump of sugar, worth thirty shillings, from a wagon, and he had apparently used very abusive language towards the wagoner's servant – punishing George with service on board the ship in which he was already serving appears like a curious punishment, in fact, no punishment at all. But what counted to the judge was that George was out of the way and harassing the French rather than Londoners. Similarly, seventeen-year-old Richard Mills, convicted in 1814 of stealing a watch, already had at least a year of seafaring experience when he appeared at the Old Bailey and was sent to sea.[13] In times of manning shortages the Navy welcomed such experienced recruits. Their cases also serve as a reminder that peace and war greatly influenced what recruits the Navy would take: whilst in peacetime His Majesty's ships had plenty of able seamen to choose from, in times of war the manning situation became desperate, and the Navy much more willing to accept men forced by magistrates.

Taking inexperienced and unwilling young boys on board, however, would only sound plausible in times of extreme shortage. And the boys had to demonstrate commitment, because if not they would have been quickly back on land and on the streets. For there is evidence that some captains deliberately gave troublesome recruits an opportunity to desert, and unwanted boys were sometimes just discharged in the nearest British harbour, contrary to the Navy Regulations. In fact, it is even possible that some particularly impudent boys might have tricked their way out of legal punishment by 'volunteering' at court for sea service and then giving their

Portsmouth Point (1811), **by Thomas Rowlandson**.

Navy officer a taste of their worst behaviour. The officer's patience would then quickly run out, and he would rather discharge the boy at the nearest port than undertake any further efforts to turn him into a useful sailor. Indeed, in the Marine Society's records we find a few boys who, within a short period of time, are more than once brought by some authority to the recruitment office. Each time these boys rightfully claimed that they had been properly discharged from their ships after only a few weeks of service.[14] Thus, while the judicial power and parish authorities tried to use the Navy as an alternative legal punishment and a relief valve for juvenile misfits, without the co-operation of the boy and the Navy the idea did not always work. If a young Tom Idle was totally unwilling to become a sailor, then it is likely that he would soon return to land. Then again, the boys were young, so there was a chance that the ship's strict discipline and the long separation from the land eventually combined to make them give in and accept their new life at sea.

Let us now turn our attention to other indicators which suggest that many boys were, like Jim Hawkins, extremely keen on going to sea. Like modern youths, elements such as 'action', music, fashion, and dreams of fame and fortune excited their imagination. One of the best examples showing the attractiveness of the sea service is the large number of runaways among the Navy's ships' boys, who had enlisted without the consent of their parents or apprenticeship masters, just like Robinson Crusoe threatened to do:

> I took my mother at a time when I thought her a little pleasanter than ordinary, and told her that my thoughts were so entirely bent upon seeing the world, that I should never settle to anything with resolution enough to go through it, and my father had better give me his consent than force me to go without it; that I was now eighteen years old, which was too late to go apprentice to a trade, or clerk to an attorney; that I was sure, if I did, I should certainly run away from my master before my time was out, and go to sea.[15]

There were many eighteenth-century boys like the cooper's apprentice John Nicol, who claimed that reading Robinson Crusoe's adventures over and over had made him weary of his apprenticeship and eager to go to sea. John had chosen the cooper's trade to please his father, yet his heart was never in the business: 'while my hands were hooping barrels my mind was at sea, and my imagination in foreign climes.'[16] The Marine Society handed out a copy of *Robinson Crusoe* to all the boys on board its training ship. Daniel Defoe (*c.* 1660-1731) might have presented Crusoe (and also the captains and pirates in his other novels) as a rueful character, who warns his readers not to follow his foolish example, yet the Marine Society, and perhaps everyone else including Defoe himself, knew very well that the book had exactly the opposite effect on many young readers.

Robert Hay from Paisley, who ran away to sea as a thirteen-year-old in 1803, had also read *Robinson Crusoe* over and over again 'with great avidity and delight'.[17] He often wished that he had been Crusoe's companion and regretted that his own life did not provide him with such adventures. Robert's parents struggled to make a living, and from an early age he had to contribute to the family's income by working in a cotton factory. Robert longed for an open and active life, but understandably perceived his worklife as close and sedentary. Hence his efforts at the loom were as modest as those of Tom Idle, earning Robert the occasional beating from his master. One day the thirteen-year-old woke up when everyone else had already left the house for work, ate the breakfast his mother had prepared for him, borrowed a sixpence from the neighbour, and without saying farewell went to Greenock to see if anyone would take him to sea.

Some historians have warned us not to overestimate romance as a motive for going to sea, yet having explored the alternative employment opportunities available, particularly for boys from poorer backgrounds, the lure of the imagined sailor's life becomes understandable. William Robinson, who enlisted in the Navy in 1805, was one of these unsettled boys: from an early age he helped his father, a humble shoemaker, to make a living for the family. Yet he writes in his memoirs that his 'roving mind' could never settle in that business. One day Will left the workshop and went, 'in one of the vagaries of my youth' to enlist at the Navy's rendezvous at Tower Hill.[18] As he still wore his shoemaker's apron, it took some effort to convince the regulating officer that he was not a runaway apprentice.

Fifteen-year-old Edward Barlow, on the other hand, had always threatened his parents that he would never stick to his apprenticeship. Edward considered all the available agricultural work in his home parish as mere drudgery. He looked down upon the people employed therein as narrow-minded folk who never dared venture further away from home, whereby in his view they missed out on the fortunes which could be made abroad.[19] Edward eventually left for London, where he first worked as a servant in a pub, in order to avoid the long binding of an apprentice. He frequently loitered around by the river, watching the ships and hoping that someone would ask him if he wanted to go to sea. This was not the safest approach, for not only did it earn him a few beatings with the stick from his master's wife for being absent from work, he was also once approached by what we call today 'human traffickers': people who persuaded naive and impoverished boys to sign indentures which virtually enslaved them for work in the American colonies.

Mary Lacy, the lively and lovesick girl who dressed as a boy, also began her time as a naval servant in the 1750s by simply hanging around in the harbour until someone approached her and asked if she wanted to become the gunner's servant on board the *Sandwich*.[20] The aforementioned thirteen-year-old runaway Robert Hay from Paisley opted for the same approach, after he had made it to Greenock on foot and by hitching lifts. For the first time alone and away from home, and his money running out, Robert became a little anxious when none of the merchantmen would take him. Luckily for him, Robert did not encounter human traffickers, but two (suspiciously) enthusiastic boys who convinced him to join the Royal Navy with them instead of applying to merchant ships.

The Marine Society was so worried about runaways that it advertised in all newspapers that parents and masters whose boys were missing should come to its office and view its latest recruits, to check whether their boy was among them. Should it be suspected that the boy had already sailed off, the Society offered to let parents and masters have a look at its registers. Usually older lads, hopeful of being able to enter the Navy as paid landsmen, were more likely to run away. Sometimes they were lured away by recruiting officers, to the annoyance of apprenticeship and work masters, who were thus robbed of the reward for the training they had invested in the youth. In 1759, when the war had hugely increased the Navy's demand for recruits, one reader of the *Gentleman's Magazine* angrily complained that just the possibility of enlisting was already enough to make apprentices more idle and insolent, being confident that they could run away from their apprenticeship at any time and would be received with open arms in the Navy.[21] Two years after starting its operation, the Marine Society resolved that for the future no boy would be accepted unless a clergyman, magistrate, churchwarden, overseer of the parish, or some other reputable person testified that the youth was not an apprentice to anyone. Former apprentices had to produce the cancelled indentures from both parties as a proof. The keeper of the Society's lodging house was instructed to report any boy in his care whom he suspected of being an apprentice.

Sometimes it was just the belief that the Navy would certainly offer better food than the meagre meals that they received from their master's wife which led apprentices to take unauthorised leave.[22] Unfortunately, this particular hope was often disappointed. Of course, one can also view cases of abusive apprenticeship masters as an indicator for boys being forced into the Navy, particularly when such masters even tried to encourage their apprentices to run away, so that they could keep the apprenticeship fee without having to provide for the boy any longer. In September 1757, for example, the father of William Newton took his son's master, a maker of watch movements, to court, accusing him of having encouraged William to run away to the Navy a year earlier.[23] William's father claimed that the master had tried to tire William out and had made the boy desirous to leave the apprenticeship. His father was sure that his son would have made a faithful and diligent apprentice, yet William had been beaten many times by his master for not being able to accomplish tasks for which he had not been adequately trained. William Newton had not been placed by the parish, he did not belong to the poorest classes, and he was lucky enough to have a father who made the effort to go to court for him, which is how we know of his case. Another boy with a similar fate, but coming from a poorer background and having no friends, would have ended up on a ship without his story ever being drawn to our attention.

The Marine Society, too, noticed several masters appearing with apprentices who were allegedly not capable of learning their trade and were 'desirous of going to Sea'. The Society felt obliged to remind its staff to check properly for the boys' consent and also for that of their parents, if they had any. Personally interviewing the boy was necessary, as some masters might have given their apprentice the impression that there was no real choice for him. Yet perhaps there was indeed none, for a master who did not want the boy could make his life hell. The surgeon and master of novelist Tobias Smollett's fictional hero *Roderick Random* (1748) opted for a more subtle approach, when he tried to encourage his apprentice Roderick to run away to the Navy (so that he could blame his maid's pregnancy on the disappeared apprentice, something for which he himself was responsible):

> I am surprised, that a young fellow like you, discovers no inclination to push his fortune in the world.-By G-d, before I was of your age, I was broiling on the coast of Guinea.-Damme! what's to hinder you from profiting by the war . . . where you will certainly see a great deal of practice, and stand a good chance of getting prize money.[24]

These arguments were enticing, rather than threatening, and not necessarily illusory. Though the boys' share of a prize was tiny compared to that of the upper ranks, even the great eighteenth-century economist Adam Smith acknowledged that the attractiveness of the 'lottery of the sea' was not unfounded.[25] Naval service still contained a great hope for personal enrichment, even though the eighteenth-century Navy was incomparable to Elizabethan days of ruthless legalised plunderers like Francis Drake and Walter Raleigh. In many youthful eyes, the sea still appeared like a world in which a daring young man, even if he came from humble origins, could get rich without having to work a lifetime for it, or at least gloriously die trying. In a way it is akin to the theories of Gary Becker which won him the Nobel Prize in economics, when he explained the phenomenon of modern-day

Chicago teenagers turning to crime as rational choice: to many boys the possible benefits simply seemed to outweigh the risks when considering their alternative options for making a living.

Even youngsters who made more realistic calculations realised that, as servants in the Navy, they could bank on being rated as fully-paid seamen around the age of eighteen, which meant that it would take them a shorter time than in any land-based or maritime apprenticeship to become a wage earner. The Navy's 24 shillings per month for able seamen and 19s for ordinary seamen did not compare badly with land-based occupations.[26] On land, a weaver, for example, would sometimes only earn around 15s, and labourers' wages could be as low as 12s. On top the Navy offered free accommodation and food. Occasionally, seafarers also had some opportunities to do a little private import business, although this was more the case for merchant sailors. In commercial shipping the boys were not confronted with naval rule and warfare, yet on the other hand the workload for a naval servant was lower than what would be expected of a youth when working on a commercial vessel with a master trying to get the most out of his cheap labourer.

And in comparison to the bleak economic prospects of some trades on land, seafaring promised, at least in times of war, better employment opportunities. The parish-supported boys sent to the Navy by MP and Marine Society member Charles Gray from Colchester, for example, could normally expect to be apprenticed to a weaver, bound until the age of twenty-four, misused as cheap labour, and with meagre employment opportunities afterwards in trades swamped with pauper apprentices. Or they were placed in a maritime apprenticeship, where they received between sixty shillings down to nothing each year, and sometimes not even any clothing, before their service was finished.[27] To such pauper boys, the Royal Navy offering a free set of clothing and bedding from the Marine Society, a yearly (though not guaranteed) allowance of around forty to fifty shillings, the prospect of becoming a wage earner around the age of eighteen, and the possibility of earning prize money, could all appear very attractive, at least to those who ignored the occupational hazards of naval service.

Considering that the Navy offered a faster route to independence than any apprenticeship on land, it would also be no contradiction if boys with a history of troubles with authority volunteered for the Navy – ironically, the very same institution others were sent to, in order to be taught stricter discipline. The threat of a cat-o'-nine-tails was no great deterrent to Hogarth's character Tom Idle. Tom thought he was already used to brutality and being forced to work, be it from his apprenticeship or from his spell in the house of correction. Samuel Richardson, in his *Apprentice's Vade Mecum: or Young Man's Pocket-Companion* (1734), a guide setting out rules of proper behaviour for apprentices, advised that for boys who could not obey the rules laid out therein, going to sea was a much better career choice, and also:

> a happy Relief to the honest Tradesman, to whom the Youth might otherwise be bound; a great Ease to his Relations, who would thereby spar'd the Mortification and Disappointment of a fruitless Tryal, and Time and Money lost to no Purpose, and a Benefit to the young Man, and perhaps to the Publick, which can be so well serv'd, in such a maritime Kingdom as this by such bold and daring Spirits, as would think themselves above being confin'd to the necessary Rules of an orderly Family.[28]

Thus the restless boys' 'bold and daring Spirits' and the interests of the Empire could profit from each other. The sea service could be a way out for the authorities as well as for the troubled youth. Whilst adolescent aggressiveness – often fuelled by being neglected by society – might have brought many of Jim's comrades into conflict with society on land, at sea and at war that very same character trait was expected of them. Being troublesome youths did not rule out that they could be patriotic, xenophobic or sectarian enough to go to war for their country, certainly not when further encouraged by prize money for each ship preyed upon. Hanway had complained that some London youths had even learned to laugh at the gallows, but exactly such a daredevil attitude could be turned into an advantage for Britain's fighting power. The Marine Society advertised that they were looking for 'Boys of a daring Temper whose genius leads them to try their fortune at Sea', 'those who are of too volatile a disposition for their trade, or too bold to live on shore with sober masters', those 'whose Heads are turned to War'.[29] The boys cheering on the fighting ships in Hayman's and Walker's engraving of 1757 appear eager to join in the fight of their heroes. The earlier finding that many of Jim's comrades had been in trouble with the authorities does not necessarily mean that these boys had to be forced to enlist in the Navy.

One thing that the Navy offered was what modern youth would call 'action', the deep sea as the epitome of adventure. When analysing the attraction of deep-sea sailing it is important to take the viewpoint of an eighteenth-century poor boy, not that of an educated contemporary like Samuel Johnson, who called the lure of the sea a perversion of the imagination.[30] The tales of adventure, the travelling, and the test of manliness undoubtedly made an impression on youths. Edward Barlow, writing in his memoirs about his motivations, asserted that he always had the desire to see 'strange countries and fashions', which made him bear the hardships of the sailor's life with more patience.[31] In the days before mass tourism, seafaring was still the only way for an ordinary youth to see the

Detail of engraving with Marine Society boys cheering
on the fighting ships (1757), by F Hayman and A Walker.

world. Edward Barlow's uncle had advised him that, if he really wanted to
go to sea, being properly apprenticed to a waterman would be a much wiser
career choice. Yet young Edward rejected the proposal, wrongly assuming
that watermen would never leave the Thames – Edward did not know that
the Navy's pressing wartime demand made sure that many watermen saw
more 'action' than they would have liked.[32]

When sailor William Robinson looked back at what had initially attracted
him to the Navy, he contemplated that 'To the youth possessing anything of

a roving disposition it is attractive, nay, it is seducing; for it has its allurements, and when steadily pursued and with success, it ennobles the mind, and the seaman feels himself a man.'[33] The famous naval surgeon Thomas Trotter (1760-1832) wrote about this youthful enthusiasm for the sea:

> The love of adventure and enterprize, that so soon discovers itself in an active boy, seems to prompt the first inclination for sea; a longing curiosity keeps it alive, and nothing but a voyage will at last satisfy the youthful Argonaut; to which the parent consents, in the hope that a life of danger and toil will soon sicken the inexperienced sailor, and make him wish to live at home. This, however, seldom happens, and the first cruize or voyage casts the die for a future sea life to the young adventurer. It is somewhat remarkable, that boys in inland towns should so often show this early desire of going to sea. I have, however, seen it discover itself there in a very romantic manner, and terminate in an elopement purposely to embark.[34]

Eighteenth-century popular culture was full of tales of seafaring adventures. Since the days of the defeat of the Spanish Armada in the late sixteenth century, stories of heroics at sea were passed on from generation to generation in the evenings of storytelling that disappeared with the arrival of television. Books delivered fictional, real and pseudo-real seafaring adventures. At the start of the century, Daniel Defoe had not only captured many boys' imaginations with *Robinson Crusoe*, but also with *Captain Singleton* (1720) and (presumably written by Defoe) *The King of Pirates* (1720). Travelogues by explorers and privateers enjoyed a particularly large readership. Pirate stories like Defoe's were very popular, too, usually in the form of autobiographies and confessions written before the pirate's execution. As with today's gangster biographies, these confessions had a ostensible moral, condemning the pirates' crimes while at the same time glorifying these outlaws and devoting little space to their victims. W H G Kingston's fictional Navy boy Tom Fletcher, in *From Powder Monkey to Admiral* (1870), had enthusiastically read the voyages of Drake, Cavendish and Dampier, and the adventures of pirate captains like Kidd, Lowther, Davis and Teach, as well as the lives of admirals like Benbow, Hawke, Keppel and Rodney.[35] Tom's naval icons were objects of widespread adulation, the 'celebrities' of their day, and none more so than Horatio Nelson. They fed the public's hunger for battle heroics, love stories and hero worship beyond reason, particularly towards the end of the eighteenth century during the wars of the French Revolution. In those days naval surgeon Thomas Trotter observed that among British youths:

> the history of a broken sailor is accounted the finest piece of eloquence; and whenever he appears, the narration of his voyages, battles, and shipwrecks, are listened to with rapture. The voyages of Drake and Anson round the world, are famous in this way, and

eagerly read by school boys; but Robinson Crusoe has made more proselytes to these kinds of adventures, than all other mariners: his story, from first to last, is so full of incident . . . that the young reader fancies himself the discoverer of some great kingdom, and his imagination wanders for ever in quest of an island. Even the English newspapers, now so generally circulated, have a wonderful effect in spreading this enthusiasm for a sea-life: the number of well-fought actions, between single ships, during the present war, will cherish it, and shape the fortune of succeeding warriors.[36]

Eighteenth-century theatres featured numerous plays with nautical themes. Many patriotic plays re-enacted famous naval engagements, and also on stage pirate stories were particularly popular, beginning with Charles Johnson's *The Successful Pirate* in 1713. In view of the repression of their social lives by apprenticeship masters and magistrates as explored earlier, distant harbour towns and the open sea could only appear liberating to their youthful mind. And then there was the public image of the sailors themselves, the behaviour that 'Jolly Jack Tar' displayed when on land, which was also colourfully represented in contemporary popular culture. If there happened to be a large contingent of sailors in the audience of those nautical theatre plays, for example, visitors could expect the added spectacle of a stage invasion by partying sailors when naval engagements were portrayed. Press and popular art recounted the sailors' excesses in the manner that today's tabloid press revels in the escapades of rock musicians and football fans.

Sailors Carousing, or a Peep in the Long Room (1825), by George Cruikshank.

Regardless of whether this image was an accurate representation of the average sailor, to many restless youths the drinking, singing, raucously partying and womanising sailor in the taverns, making the harbour district synonymous with the amusement district, was probably the best possible advertisement for the sea service.

Undoubtedly, those of a more sober mind, and boys who had grown up with seafaring fathers, knew of the hardships and the dangers at sea. They understood the hard work to which sailors were referring when they sang 'with grog and our lasses, because jolly sailors are free, that money we squander like asses, which like horses we earned when at sea.'[37] Yet among those clothed by the Marine Society for the Royal Navy these boys were the minority. A 'land-boy' like William Spavens, who first went to sea in 1754, only remembered how he looked at the sailors with envy, and never considered any of the perils and hardships they were exposed to: 'I thought sailors must be happy men to have such opportunities of visiting foreign countries.'[38] Sailor turned author John Nicol even recollected that his 'youthful mind could not separate the life of a sailor from dangers and storms, and I looked upon them as an interesting part of the adventures I panted after.'[39]

The economist Adam Smith remarked in his famous *Inquiry into the Nature and Causes of the Wealth of Nations* (1776) that 'the dangers and hairbreadth escapes of a life of adventures, instead of disheartening young people, seem frequently to recommend a trade to them.'[40] The opening of one eighteenth-century sailor's ballad went:

> When I grew up they asked me,
> 'What trade must we prepare for thee?'
> My answer was to them again,
> 'I mean to range the roaring sea;'
> My whimsic brain did falsely show
> The pleasures men enjoy at sea,
> But oh, the sorrow, grief, and woe,
> They suffer in extremity.[41]

Boys and young men with no family connection to seafarers knew only the sailor ashore, who, dressed in his fancy shoregoing clothes, enjoyed the time in between voyages with his recently earned pay. Samuel Leech, who enlisted in the Navy in 1810 as a twelve-year-old, likened the sailor ashore to an uncaged bird, 'as gay and quite as thoughtless', who would 'follow out dictates of passions and appetites, let them lead him wither they may.'[42] Moreover, the boys probably identified only those who lived up to this stereotype as being sailors. Perhaps in most cases these were young deep-sea sailors, sailors who had stories to tell of distant places, foreign cultures and women, easy fortunes allegedly made, and with the odd episode from wartime exploits on board a naval vessel, a private man-of-war, or an armed trading vessel furnished with a letter of marque. Adam Smith observed that 'a tender mother, among the inferior ranks of people, is often afraid to send her son to school at a seaport town, lest the sight of the ships and the conversation and adventures of the sailors should entice him to go to sea.'[43] Those numerous ships' boys who, like Jim Hawkins, had previously worked for a publican, had plenty of opportunities to listen to colourful stories from sailors. Daniel Defoe used the same medium to gather material for his stories, when he spent time in inns and coffee houses, and listened in on the alleged adventures of sea rovers and pirates.

Young Samuel Leech first caught the fire when he moved into the house of his aunt and twenty-two cousins, most of them being sailors:

> some of them were constantly returning home, bringing, with true sailors' munificence, the pleasing and curious productions of distant climes as presents to their parents and friends; then, seated round the bright hearth-side, they used to tell of wild adventures and hairbreadth escapes, spinning out the winter evening's tale to the infinite delight of their willing listeners.[44]

In his published memoirs, Leech added with the sobering benefit of hindsight that five of his cousins later died at sea. There were further episodes in young Samuel's life, though, when sailors caught his envy, such as his journey in a stagecoach when a sailor amongst the passengers entertained them:

> We had another source of relief in the antics of a wild, hairbrained sailor. From spinning yarns, which looked amazingly like new inventions, he would take to dancing on the roof of the coach; at the foot of a hill he would leap off, and then spring up again with the agility of a monkey, to the no small amusement of the passengers. The more I saw of this reckless, thoughtless tar, the more enamored I became with the idea of a sea life.[45]

The warning words of some of the adults around Samuel, that life in the Navy would be harsh, fell on deaf ears. Here lies another reason why the Navy needed to 'nurse' its recruits from an early age: the naivety of a twelve-year-old Sam Leech might have eventually faded in the later years of his life, but by that time he was already at sea and bound to the Navy till it had no more use for him. Sam was to be shocked by the reality of naval life. Then again, he had never experienced the drudgery in which other boys had been employed before they went to sea. After his time in the early nineteenth-century Navy, Leech looked back very critically at the jolly tars who had once enticed him to become a sailor. He wondered whether their entire joyous act was not simply adopted to distract themselves from the tough reality of life in the Navy.[46]

Leech felt that in this self-deception the sailor was even encouraged by the Navy, who found the jolly, merrymaking, devil-may-care type of seaman easier to handle, as he kept up morale.

> Bold Jack, the sailor, here I come;
> Pray how d'ye like my nib,
> My trowsers wide, my trampers rum,
> My nab, and flowing jib?
> I sails the seas from end to end
> And leads a joyous life;
> In ev'ry mess I finds a friend,
> In ev'ry port a wife.[47]

So sang Charles Dibdin (1745-1814), travelling entertainer and composer of many popular songs celebrating the sailor's wild life and fashion. Dibdin's songs were performed everywhere, sold in every music shop, reprinted in newspapers, and reproduced on jugs decorated with illustrations of sailors. Dibdin boasted that his songs produced more recruits for the Navy than all the press gangs that swept through the streets of London. During the wars of the French Revolution Dibdin and other performers were even paid by the government to write songs to excite the young audience to enlist for the sea service. Dibdin dressed and acted like a sailor, but he had never been one. Twentieth-century philosophers of popular culture, such as those of the renowned Frankfurt School, who view the modern music industry primarily as an exploitation of its young and naive consumers, might be equally critical of Dibdin: he seems a pre-industrial harbinger of rock music rebels with a manufactured personal history aimed at gaining credibility with their teenage audiences. But at least Dibdin did not hide the fact that he was merely acting a part. Dibdin's audience was on land: how the sailors themselves viewed Dibdin appears to require more research; some adored his songs, and those who did could make an Oscar Wilde wonder whether art was imitating life or vice versa. That Dibdin did partake of an existing culture is shown by the fact that verses similar to his already graced musical plays in the mid-eighteenth century:

> How happy is the sailor's life,
> From coast to coast to roam;
> In every port he finds a wife,

In every land a home.
He loves to range,
He's nowhere strange;
He never will turn his back
To friend or foe;
No, masters, no;
My life for honest Jack.[48]

Dibdin is, however, just one element of many that make it worth spending a little more time exploring the lifestyles of eighteenth-century sailors in the light of modern popular youth culture which may aid our understanding of what attracted the real Jim Hawkins to life at sea. Additionally, this approach can also illuminate sailors' culture in general. Deep-sea sailing in the eighteenth century was a profession for young men, and for men who kept elements of youthfulness. It is true that the hardships and dangers at sea rushed Jim Hawkins from being a child into coming of age and meeting the demands of a man. Yet in many other ways the sailor's way of life fostered a quality of youthfulness which lasted much later in life than was usual in society on land.

Contemporaries frequently described seamen as being boyish and immature in their behaviour. Even the Navy's captains often used paternal

Sailors Carousing (1807), by Julius Caesar Ibbetson.

language when talking about their sailors. The Navy's crews were indeed young: most of them were around the age of twenty-five, and often younger. Admittedly, the factor of promotion to petty officer rank also kept the average age of the crew low. Yet instead of moving up in the ranks, many deep-sea sailors settled down in the later years of their life (if they survived long enough) with shore-based occupations or worked in the coastal trade and on rivers. Roderick Random's master, as we saw, alleges that it was natural for 'a young fellow' to try his fortunes at sea, before settling down on land. In fact, staying on at sea as an able seaman was by some considered as a failure in life, as ship's boy Edward Barlow was advised by his uncle: 'for he that is but a common seaman that goes to sea when he is past forty years of age, that man earns his living with more pain and sorrow than he that endures a hard imprisonment.'[49] Climbing around in the rigging like a monkey was perhaps indeed not to be desired for a forty-year-old.

Various work-related factors promoted the sailors' youthfulness and prolonged it into higher ages. Marriage, for example, one of the key moments in the transition from youth to adulthood in Western Europe, was difficult to achieve for a deep-sea sailor. Only around a quarter of eighteenth-century seamen were married.[50] Popular art usually portrayed the sailor as unmarried and thus open for sexual adventures. Naturally, not having any dependants also increased the sailor's readiness to take risks. Setting up his own permanent home, another key moment in the move from youth to adulthood in Western Europe, was also difficult for a sailor. Generally, saving any money or investing it in anything more lasting was complicated, as the sailor needed a trustworthy place to deposit it. Taking it on the voyage yielded the danger that the possessions would go down when the ship had an accident, or would have to be left behind when the sailor deserted. Also the threat of the press gang taking him with no chance to settle his affairs did not encourage investments more solid than the next bottle of rum. Furthermore, similar to apprentices, sailors were sometimes forced to work, and corporal punishment was common in disciplining them. And, like youths, they were housed and fed, living like students in a large, and close, male-only community, their movements being strictly controlled. Sailors also did not own their means of production; employers and workplaces could be changed at the end of each voyage, or by running away. All these work-related factors created a more unsettled, much more youthful workforce than that to which pre-industrial European society was accustomed.

The sailors' youthfulness was supplemented by a general feeling of otherness among frequent deep-sea sailors. They had seen distant places and cultures, and as a close-knit group they had mastered extremely dangerous situations. Many seafarers felt the need to express this otherness, be it by bullying the landsmen on board, or by their boisterous actions and fashion when on land. Educated people on land were often appalled by the behaviour of sailors ashore. Novelist Daniel Defoe wrote that 'they swear violently, whore violently, drink punch violently, spend their money when they have it violently', they were simply violent fellows in every respect, who should be encouraged to go to sea, as they were ungovernable at home.[51] What the observers on land tended to forget is that these sailors celebrating their shore leave had spent months imprisoned in a small wooden world, living under a strict regime, with limited availability of alcohol and women. As contemporary satirist Ned Ward observed, the sailor is:

> the greatest prisoner, and the greatest rambler in Christendom; there is not a corner in the world but he visits, and yet the poor slave very rarely makes one step beyond the sight of his old habitation; but when he does get ashore, he pays it off with a vengeance; for knowing his time to be short, he crowds much in a little room, and lives as fast as possible.[52]

Ned Ward, however, shows rather too much understanding for the sailor ashore when he goes on to explain that the sailor is so used 'to reeling at sea, that when he is reeling drunk ashore, he takes it for granted to be a storm aboard, and falls to throwing every thing out at the windows, to save the vessel of a bawdy-house.'[53] The sailor ashore was certainly encouraged by the

Wapping (1807), by Thomas Rowlandson.

fact that he was a 'tourist', a visitor, who usually set sail again before he could be held accountable for any damages, thefts or unwanted pregnancies caused on land.

Even when not raucously enjoying their shore leave, seafaring communities on land often appeared curious and exotic to others. John Fielding recorded in his *Brief Description of the Cities of London and Westminster* (1776):

> The seamen here are a generation differing from all the world. When one goes into Rotherhithe and Wapping, which places are chiefly inhabited by sailors, but that somewhat of the same language is spoken, a man would be apt to suspect himself in another country. Their manner of living, speaking, acting, dressing, and behaving, are so very peculiar to themselves.[54]

There may be an element of dramatisation in this guidebook written by a blind man. Yet part of the reason why, for example, impressment worked was because sailors were so easily identified by the press gang through their appearance 'both in Manners and person'; although if not that then at least the battered hands 'accustomed to handling Ropes', the traces of tar, as well as his weathered face, could act to expose the mariner.[55]

One would have thought that the threat of the press gang, and its network of informers, would have encouraged the merchant sailor to conform a little more to the fashion and manners on land. Yet sailor Robert Hay observed that even this failed to deter some of them in their public display of sailor culture. Hay thought this foolishness was down to the effects of alcohol. Even more irrational was that towards the end of the century tattoos became fashionable among sailors – surely press gangs looking for recruits and worse, the Navy looking for deserters, could not ask for a more obvious identification mark. Clearly the desire to express their sailor culture outweighed any concerns about being recognised by the wrong people. Historian Isaac Land even argues that many seamen actually relished the mad chases and clashes with the press gang, and that these were another rite of passage into the maritime fraternity. They enjoyed putting on a show for their 'audience' on land, often getting them to assist in their escape. Land concluded that sailors 'drew attention to themselves not because they could not help looking and sounding different, but because they set out deliberately to impress the denizens of sailortown with their courage.'[56] To those with no family to support, no good job to lose, and anyway employed in deep-sea sailing, it might have indeed been a bit of a game. Other, more settled, sailors would have failed to see the funny side.

Like most contemporaries, the naval surgeon Thomas Trotter reckoned that all the sailor's 'peculiarities are the offspring of a sea-life, from the little communication it affords with the common manners of society.'[57] However, considering that even frequent deep-sea sailors would still spend large parts of the year in the harbour, particularly in peacetime, or employed in trades near the coast and even on land, the behaviour of these sailors should not be seen as solely the natural result of their work environment. It must have also been a conscious attempt to distinguish themselves from society on land, as Isaac Land suggested. The best sailor's clothes were, after all, reserved for the shore leave. As one observer wrote at the end of the century: 'When left to himself at sea, [the sailor] becomes careless to his person, dirty and indolent. When on shore, however, few like to appear smarter.-A blue jacket, silk handkerchief round the neck, white trousers, and silver buckles, shew him off to the best advantage.'[58]

Cultural historians like Isaac Land, Cheryl Fury and Peter Burke have therefore proposed viewing the sailors' culture not as a specific maritime culture, but rather as a subculture. Burke described it as a culture which was 'partly autonomous rather than wholly autonomous, distinct yet not completely severed from the rest of popular culture.'[59] In line with Isaac Land, I think we can go further and draw a parallel to those subculture models used by sociologists to describe youth cultures in twentieth-century Britain.[60] If we count such groups as youth subcultures which show a conspicuous, intentional distinction from society's norms in dress, hairstyle, jewellery (later also tattoos), language, music, behaviour, religious beliefs (with superstition thriving in stressful situations), and plenty more provocative and hedonistic elements, then the behaviour of many sailors could fit well into such a model. Like modern youths, instead of conforming to society, sailors conformed to the peers amongst whom they spent every day on board. Endless further parallels can be drawn to modern youths, such as loyalty to group members and rejection of outsiders, 'tribal' gathering for rituals and entertainment around the mainmast, the search for excitement, the understatement or glorification of danger and death, machismo, and acts of bravado and deliberate ignoring of safety precautions. The latter appear even more immature when considering the limited medical support and disability provisions. The sailor's life was full of follies which adults with a dependant family were unlikely to commit. Pirate crews even rejected married men, fearing they would not be able to cope with the pirate lifestyle.

> Soon or late death will take us in tow;
> Each bullet has got its commission,
> And when our time's come we must go.
> Then, drink, and sing – hang pain and sorrow,
> The halter was made for the neck;

> He that's now alive and lusty – to-morrow
> Perhaps may be stretched on the deck.[61]

This being another one of Charles Dibdin's songs, we are indirectly reminded how much the Empire could profit from the sailor's bravado and machismo.

Yet perhaps there had also been a change of attitudes towards sailors by the time Dibdin sang his songs. Maybe Dibdin himself had greatly contributed to this change to a more positive image. At the beginning of the century Daniel Defoe, though perfectly aware of the sailor's value at sea, still saw the sailor as a savage when ashore. By the end of the century men like Dibdin had turned the raucous sailor into the more positive Jolly Jack Tar. Jolly Jack Tar's exaggerated masculinity and wildness 'protected' the country from the French. He protected the country not just physically, but also culturally: contemporaries on land feared not only France's military threat, but also the perceived effeminacy which seemed to have entered British high culture from Catholic European countries. Jack Tar's hooliganism now appeared a price worth paying. Even his heterosexual promiscuity, detested as 'violent whoring' by Defoe, made jolly appearances in Dibdin's songs (see the song on page 107), an assurance of Jack's heterosexuality, whilst ignoring any concerns about the sexual exploitation of women or sailors spreading diseases abroad.

Songs and music, books and plays, and the fact that sailors were in constant contact with sailors from other regions were the 'mass-media' for this eighteenth-century subculture. During the long voyages there was enough idle time for chatting and storytelling in the closely confined community on board, a time when the older shipmates could pass down the myths and characters of their sea stories to the next generation. Private Wheeler described how two evenings each week were reserved for amusement when:

> the Boatswain's mates, with their pipes summons 'All hands to play.' In a moment the scene is truly animating. The crew instantly distribute themselves, some dancing to a fiddle, others to a fife. Those who are fond of the marvellous, group together between two guns and listen to some frightful tale of Ghost and gobblin, another party listens to some weather beaten tar who 'spins a yarn' of past events, until his hearers sides are almost cracked with laughter. Again is to be found a select party immortalizing the heroes of gone by days by singing songs to the memory of Duncan, Howe, Vincent, and the immortal Nelson, while others whose souls are more refined are singing praises to the God of Battles.[62]

Wisdoms and sayings, music and dances from all over the world were exchanged on board. Merchant crews were often international, but in times of war even the Royal Navy vessels were quite a multicultural community.

Saturday Night at Sea (1820s), by George Cruikshank.

Near ten per cent of the crew of Lord Nelson's flagship HMS *Victory* were not British when Nelson famously signalled 'England expects that every man will do his duty' when going into the battle of Trafalgar in 1805. Apparently, this share was below average. Nelson's crew included Americans, Dutch, Swedes, Germans, even Frenchmen, as well as men from the West Indies and Africa. Ship's boy Robert Hay was amazed at the Babel-like mixture of languages that was spoken on board his ship: 'Irish, Welsh, Dutch, Portuguese, Spanish, French, Swedish, Italian, and all the provincial dialects which prevail between Land's End and John O'Groats'. This international exchange is the basis for the thought-provoking theories of historians Markus Rediker and Peter Linebaugh of the sailor as transatlantic communicator between lower-class cultures.[63]

Although the multicultural wooden world was not free of prejudices or even outright discrimination against foreigners, cultural exchange was unavoidable. There were people performing all sorts of poetry, songs, and anything from spontaneous raucous comic acts to dances and proper theatre plays.[64] In doing so they were often encouraged by their officers to boost morale and defeat the constant threat of boredom and claustrophobia. Many men brought musical instruments to sea. On board Robert Hay's ship there was 'Black Bob', a fiddler who was almost constantly in demand to provide music for those longing to dance. When there were more dancers than within the sound of Bob's fiddle, then the Admiral's band was ordered up in support.

What to the captain was a sensible exercise for the men's spirits and legs, sounds to us today like a wonderful mixing and enhancing of European and African music and dance. Dancing within the constraints of a limited space and without female partners was, incidentally, one of the things that needed to be cultivated on board.

Song lyrics were a highly important medium as in modern subcultures. The sailors' shanties were full of stories of battles, adventures, pirates, mysteries and in most cases, just like today, of women. Unfortunately, those lyrics which have been preserved were morally cleansed by the Victorians, hence we will never know how they compare to today's popular lyrics, and whether some of them would earn a 'parental advisory' label for explicit content, the 'badge of honour' for any modern music act wanting to sell rebellion to its young audience. While at work, the Royal Navy curbed the singing of shanties, worrying that it would make it difficult to hear commands, and in general give the ship a disorderly appearance. Only the men at the capstan were encouraged by the fiddle or the flute. But there were still instances elsewhere at sea when music was mixed with work, when foremen and crew communicated and encouraged each other with 'calling-and-answering' songs. And here, too, sailors were willing to be inspired by other cultures. Robert Hay described in detail how the steersman and rowers in the rowing crews of the Madras coast communicated via song: the steersman singing a stanza, and then pausing every eight to ten words when all the rest of the crew joined their voices in a short chorus that to Robert sounded like 'ey-yaw'. Anytime we switch on our popular music radio stations today, we still hear the same elements, albeit not performed by Madras rowers. The constant cultural exchange could provide an open-minded sailor with many skills to impress a land-boy. Robert's favourite crew member and protector on board gained his admiration for having learned, amongst other things, to play the German flute, to speak French, to alter his clothes and create fancy straw hats, to make ship models, to do tattoos, and for knowing an endless amount of board and card games.

The apparently colourful milieu of the sailor fascinated boys and young men living on land, and perhaps particularly those with the 'restless and roving mind'. Even Jim Hawkins was in awe of Long John Silver and could not help feeling drawn to him. Sailors had kept many youthful desires, but unlike younger boys they possessed physical and sexual maturity, and unlike apprentices, who were often of the same age, they possessed the money to fulfil all these desires and were willing to spend it all in their short time ashore. On shore leave, sailors hired expensive horse-drawn coaches, packed all of their companions into them, and caroused up and down the town just as do today's

Sailors on a Cruise (1825), by **George Cruikshank.**

youths at weekends in sports cars on the streets of London and elsewhere. It was easy for the sailors to impress their peers on land while on shore leave.

The sailor subculture was made up of a multitude of components of style, language and behaviour. Many of the elements show that sailors were very aware of their audience on land: when, for example, towards the end of the century the predominant fashion on land had shifted to darker and more subdued colours, and to a reduction in decoration, the bright colours with gold and silver ornaments in which the sailor paraded through the streets, the striped trousers, hats, ribbons, decorations and pigtails were all worn to be noticed.[65] And Jolly Jack walked with a swagger, as his contemporaries on land always noted, a swagger that was said to be the result of the sailor being used to walking on a rocking deck. In part this was true, but did it really take that long to get used to a steady walking surface? No. In reality, the sailor was also putting on a show, just like the almost choreographed walk with which some groups of youths walk along our high streets today. Robert Hay observed the sailor parading along the street, in his swagger and his carefully selected and altered clothes:

with his white demity trowsers fringed at the bottom, his fine scarlet waistcoat bound with black ribbon, his dark blue broadcloth jacket studded with pearl buttons, his black silk neckcloth thrown carelessly about his sunburnt neck. An elegant hat of straw, indicative of his recent return from a foreign station, cocked on one side; a head of hair reaching to his waistband; a smart switch made from the back bone of a shark under one arm, his doxy under the other, a huge chew of tobacco in his cheek . . . he strides along with all the importance of an Indian Nabob.[66]

Sailors held on to their fashionable pigtail, even in the face of valid criticism that long hair risked accidents while at work, and also provided a more welcoming home to lice.

As with modern youthful affiliations, we could also accuse the eighteenth-century sailor of not really dressing and acting as rebelliously as he pretended, but instead merely conforming to the dress sense and behaviour of those with whom he spent most of the day. Note, for example, Charles McPherson proudly remembering how he and his shipmates paraded through the streets in similar fashion to Hay's 'Indian Nabob': 'we sallied through the town in a body, all dressed in white trowsers, white shirts or frocks, and straw hats with black ribbons on them.'[67] Cynics might say the young men had created a uniform, the exact opposite of rebellion and individuality.

There is an argument that youth culture allegedly only emerged with the arrival of the 'teenage consumer' in the mid-twentieth century, when the young received a hitherto unexperienced buying power, and the markets were flooded with affordable mass-produced fashion. Yet eighteenth-century sailors were artists in creating and altering their own clothes and expressive fashion, in a way that would have impressed any modern youth. And sailor slogans such as 'a Rowling Stone never gathers Moss', or the praise of a 'Short life and Merry one', as seaman 'Rambling Jack' John Cremer proclaimed them in the 1760s,[68] are also something that even today are characteristic of icons of youth culture. Many other sailor maxims were unquotable, as seamen were champions in swearing – again something attractive to young men for its anti-authoritarian tone. And so, too, is the excessive use of slang among sailors, and of (international) sign language and rituals – language and communication which excludes and impresses outsiders, language that contains a conspiratorial or subversive touch, an audible otherness. The sailor's language was as mysterious to the rest of society on land as the slang of modern youth can be to their parents.

Modern youth cultures also like to borrow from eighteenth-century sailors' culture, be it with an earring referring back to the freedom of the pirate, or by using tattoos as a sign of belonging, or to emphasise masculinity and body. Tattooing became popular amongst sailors who took part in late eighteenth-century Pacific explorations.[69] At that time, a proper Polynesian tattoo would have been a strong reference to a different culture, or even a counter-culture. Perhaps William Bligh of the *Bounty* should have been alerted when young

Fletcher Christian, and several other men who were later amongst the mutineers, had their bodies tattooed during their long stay at Tahiti. The heavy drinking culture of sailors, which prompted sober parents to forbid their sons to go to sea, was another element that was attractive to some of Jim Hawkins' comrades. And so was the sailors' boisterous promiscuity – to return to the songs of Charles Dibdin for one last time:

> I've a spanking wife at Portsmouth gates,
> A pigmy at Goree,
> An orange-tawny up the Streights,
> A black at St. Lucie;
> Thus, whatsomdever course I bend,
> I leads a jovial life:
> In ev'ry mess I finds a friend,
> In ev'ry port a wife.[70]

Dispatch, or Jack Preparing for Sea (c.1800), by **Thomas Rowlandson.**

The list of elements in the lifestyle of the sailor which were attractive to teenage boys, and which can be found even in those of today's youth could be continued for much longer. It appears hard to summarise the common denominator of all such youth cultures and subcultures. Perhaps essentially they are about creating a separated colourful dream-world, away from the mundane realities of life; a parallel universe with its myths, iconic characters, saints and martyrs, with its music, language, codes and fashions, and with dreams of fortunes, spiritual enlightenment or adventures, and all with restricted access, entry having to be earned by dressing, speaking and acting like a member. Of course, this subculture model has limits, and we have to be careful not to fall victim of a later romanticisation of seafarers (or pirates) and their iconisation in many subsequent epochs. While some eighteenth-century sailors would have fitted perfectly into this model, for the mass of them, particularly those working most of the time in coastal shipping or fishing, the image goes a little far.

However, it is important to remember that this model is also about public perception and boys' imaginations encouraging them to become servants in the Navy, more than about the reality at sea. Furthermore, even the subculture models applied to twentieth-century youths emphasise that the core of a subculture is made up of only a few, whilst the majority of young people remain somewhere in the middle between conformity to society and sympathy with the subculture, just as most eighteenth-century youths stayed somewhere in the middle between Tom Idle and Francis Goodchild. Generations of young eighteenth-century fishermen, for example, were probably never influenced by the image of the sailor as a subcultural icon. Instead they went to sea because that was the livelihood of their fathers and their communities; they knew that the reality of the fisherman's life was nothing glamorous, it was just the only available means of making a living – but then again, the sons of fishermen were not the boys who appeared at the Marine Society's office to enlist in the Navy.

Trying to unearth the motivations which drove the average Jim Hawkins to the Royal Navy involves a large element of speculation. For many boys seafaring was simply in their family blood. Others went to sea hoping for a quick route to earning their own wages, and possibly even becoming rich. Often unemployment, the death of one or both parents, or the need to relieve the family, had led adults or authorities to suggest that Jim should try his luck at sea. Sometimes it was also Jim's troublesome behaviour which prompted parents and authorities to action. The extent to which Jim's decision to go to sea was voluntary is debatable. Officially, Jim went out of his own free will. However, this was sometimes affected by the laws and practice of poor relief, which frequently ignored Jim's own wishes, and also by the fact that Jim's comrades were very young and impressionable.

Nevertheless, there were many among his fellow ships' boys who were willing to join the Navy even without the permission of their parents or masters. When considering the alternative options in life for those from poorer backgrounds, we can easily imagine how the sea could appear as a materialisation of escapist dreams in young Jim's head; the dangerous reality which awaited Jim at sea will be explored in the next chapter. For the children of the labouring classes and the poor, the Navy and seafaring thus had a curious dual character: it could appear almost like the 'floating workhouse' for youths for whom the community could not provide, and at the same time it could appear as the escape route for youths who did not want to conform to society's norms. By taking on these youths, by creating and imposing a particular culture on board, as well as in consequence of his work environment, and fuelled by the way in which popular culture loved to alight on the most colourful amongst his companions when they were off-duty ashore, the eighteenth-century deep-sea sailor acquired many of the features of a youth-cultural icon.

CHAPTER 6

Jim's Life on Board

HAVING met Jim Hawkins on land and looked at his appearance, his social background, his dreams and motivations, it is now time to leave the safe base of land and follow him into the wooden world at sea. When sixteen-year-old Edward Barlow stepped on board for the first time he was slightly overwhelmed by the bustle going on.[1] Like most boys, Ed had received no pre-sea training and was at a loss as to where he was meant to stand or what to do. He eventually joined the men at the capstan. Pushing the wooden bars in a circle seemed like a straightforward task, but before long poor Ed was accidentally hit on the back of his head by the bar behind him. To make matters worse, he fell head first through the open hatchway into the hold. Everyone watching the scene was sure that Edward's first day as a ship's boy had also been his last. But miraculously Ed survived, although he suffered from a constant headache for some time. 'Ship's boy' Mary Lacy had a slightly lighter fall into her first day at sea: as she attempted to get into bed on her first night, she clambered into her hammock on one side and immediately fell out on the other, to the great amusement of the seamen present.[2] Learning how to get into their new bed was just one of many skills Jim and his mates had to acquire.

The Navy hoped the boys would learn 'on the job', by taking part in the sailing of the ship and being instructed by other sailors. The Marine Society was worried about the boys' general and moral education, fearing that according to 'vulgar opinion' boys on board a naval vessel would receive no moral instruction at all.[3] But at least in public the Society expressed its faith that the Navy's officers would guide the lads properly, since it would be in their own interest to ensure that each boy became a reliable seaman and not a nuisance.[4] Hanway, who had never served at sea, stated that under a good officer, who would treat the boy as if he were his own son, the youngster would be taught about the duties of a Christian and a seaman by the schoolmaster on board, or an officer who acted as such.[5] Fielding claimed that the boys he sent to sea would even be instructed in navigation by the schoolmaster (although he probably merely meant the duties of a seaman), and furthermore that they would be instructed in the art of rigging by the boatswain, and in the basic principles of Christianity by the chaplain.[6]

However, such statements have the ring of dealing in ideals rather than realities. Schoolmasters were only occasionally on board, although in their absence others were supposed to fulfil their duties. Unfortunately, these schoolmasters frequently crop up in seafarers' memoirs as disillusioned drunks, but perhaps this had something to do with sailors regarding any 'idler' on board with mistrust. Nevertheless, the Navy Regulations ruled that no schoolmaster, nor any chaplain, should be paid without a certificate from their captain testifying 'his Diligence in his Business'. The chaplain was to teach all of the boys, not just the young gentlemen, in the principles of Christianity. It seems that the Navy's main guard ships often held schools for bigger groups,[7] thus perhaps making up for the fact that not all ships had a schoolmaster. Many of the new ships' boys in the mid century spent a few months on board these guard ships, waiting to be distributed to their next servant placement. The benefit of any teaching on board, however, should not be overestimated. Boys with ambitions to become officers were better advised to learn their mathematics and navigation in schools on land.

Officially, the onboard teaching was to take place on a daily basis, and idle pupils had to be reported in order to be corrected. The schoolmaster's orders were to instruct the 'volunteers', that is those destined for an officer's career, in writing, arithmetic and navigation, and the other youths of the ship 'according to such Orders as he shall receive from the Captain, and with regard to their several Capacities, whether in Reading, Writing, or otherwise'. Hence, in theory, and if he happened to be on the right ship, there seem to have been some schooling opportunities for our Jim Hawkins. However, even Hanway clarified that he did not expect boys like Jim to be taught navigation.[8] Fielding even thought that teaching the lower-class boys to read and write was already slightly dangerous, as it would only raise their expectations and make them reluctant to become ordinary sailors.[9] Hanway, nevertheless, considered that 'if there is any boy of uncommon genius, it is but justice to the Community to give him fair opportunities of improvement, as it is constantly practised in such cases by the French',[10] but he did not specify, though, how far this 'improvement' should be allowed to go.

The question about how much education was beneficial for the children of the poor was much debated in the eighteenth century. It was feared that too much education would make them rebellious and unsatisfied with their servile work. There were too many laborious jobs to do in the centuries before industrialisation, modernisation and computerisation, for which education was seen as more of a hindrance than an advantage. On the other hand, men like Hanway thought that religious education was necessary to teach the children of the lower classes virtue and 'due subordination'. These were the two lines of debate, one considering further education of the poor as dangerous, the other as necessary; they argued over means, but in their aims both positions were essentially similar, in that they favoured the preservation of the hierarchical order of society to which they were accustomed, and which was regarded as the most natural and solid.[11]

For the Navy, the priority was that the boys learned the duties of a seaman as quickly as possible. There was no centrally organised system of training. In peacetime there was also no need for this, as there were few openings for boys with no family connections to the Navy, and only a few landsmen on board; the Navy largely profited from the training provided by merchant shipping. In times of war things changed dramatically. A great number of boys enlisted, and the Navy's ships also had to sail with a dangerously high ratio of inexperienced landsmen. At the start of the Seven Years War, the Admiralty finally saw the need to lay down official instructions for training landsmen and boys.[12] The men were to practise sailing and operating the great guns while the ships lay in harbour. They were also introduced to the use of firearms, cutlasses and half-pikes when boarding another ship or repelling a boarding attempt; whether landsman or fisherman, this was the first reminder that sailing in the Navy also meant preparing for combat. All ships lying together at anchor were supposed to perform their exercises simultaneously, and captains were to encourage a competitive spirit by aiming to outdo the other ships.

For the boys similar training orders were introduced. Although Jim was not trained to use the guns or small arms, he, too, was meant to practise sail handling whilst in harbour, also simultaneously with the boys on board other ships in order to instil a spirit of competitiveness. Once the ship was on its way, the boys were supposed to learn everything simply by taking part in the sailing and operation of the ship. On so-called 'cruises', chasing defenceless merchantmen, there was still plenty of space for some practical training, as lieutenant's servant Olaudah Equiano remembered:

> All this time we had never come to an engagement, though we were frequently cruising off the coast of France; during which we chased many vessels, and took in all seventeen prizes. I had been learning many of the manoeuvres of the ship during our cruise; and I was several times made to fire the guns.[13]

There were some tasks for which Jim did not need much training, duties where Jim had physical advantages. Good eyesight as a lookout was one of them: twelve-year-old Nicholas Young was the first on board Cook's

Endeavour to spot New Zealand in 1769, and was rewarded with the headland being named Young Nick's Head (and also with a gallon of rum). The other physical advantage Jim had was that he was quick on his feet and adept at manoeuvring through the narrow spaces of the ship. This was made best use of during combat, when the boys were employed as 'powder monkeys'. In the heat of battle Jim had to run to and fro between the guns and below decks, where the powder was kept for safety reasons. Every boy was assigned to a particular gun and its crew. He might only have had to run to the hatchway, though, where the cartridges were passed up to him. Usually there would have not been enough boys on board, so some men (and women) must have done Jim's job, too. Jim's numerous mates who had spent years of running errands through London's packed streets must have felt as if on almost familiar territory. There was a brutal difference and greater sense of urgency, though, for shot and splinters would fly thick around young Jim's head as he hurried past men dashed to pieces by the enemy's broadsides. Seeing that in most cases the ships fought on one side only, it is, however, conceivable that Jim often had a free runway on the other side of the deck.

As Jim's official 'rank' on the muster lists was that of a captain's or any other commissioned or warrant officer's servant, he also had to expect to be called upon for personal duties for his officer (including captains and other officers, as well as admirals). Even after the officer-servant model was abolished in 1794 and replaced by the categories of first-, second- and third-class boys, Jim's mates still had to act as personal servants to officers. His tasks might have included anything from cleaning the officer's cabin or his shoes, to washing clothes, waiting on officers at dinner, cleaning cutlery and dishes for the wardroom, or fetching water. When Mary Lacy dressed up as a boy and became the servant to the *Sandwich*'s carpenter, her new master instructed her in the most important duties right away:

> Now; said he, you must learn to make a can of flip, and to broil me a beef steak, and to make my bed against I come to live on onboard. Come, said he, I will show you how to make my bed. So we went to his cabin, in which there was a bed that turned up, and he began to take the bed-cloaths off one by one. Now, said he, you must shake them one by one, you must tumble and shake the bed about, then you must lay the sheets on one at a time, and lastly the blankets. I replied, Yes, Sir; Well said he, you will soon learn to make a bed, that I see already.[14]

Mary, or William, as she called herself on board, pretended to appear as ignorant as possible of her new tasks, but soon the carpenter realised that William made an excellent naval servant. While the numerous captains' servants had few opportunities for being close to their master, those serving other officers, who had only one or two boys, were more likely to be used as personal servants. Being closer to the master could not only mean closer supervision and more servant duties, but also a greater likelihood of protection and possibly even education. Mary Lacy was told that she had better remain serving the carpenter, in order to avoid ending up as one of the many captain's servants, which was allegedly the worst place in the ship.[15] Her master even promised that he would arrange an apprenticeship for her after the war was over and pay for all her clothing, though sadly Mary soon realised that he made no attempt to fulfil his promise. In fact, he only ever made these promises when he was drunk and concerned that Mary would, when interrogated by his suspicious wife back in the harbour, reveal how often he stayed up late drinking with the gunner and the boatswain.

Those boys who were rarely needed as personal servants might still have been ordered to perform services for a particular mess or even for the entire ship, anything from fetching food, or shaving the men in exchange for some pocket money, to the unpleasant task of emptying the crew's excreta. As captains and admirals had a considerably larger allowance of servants, Jim was most likely to start as a servant to either one of them. Some boys did not have a master right away and were kept as supernumeraries until a servant placement was found. The remaining boys began as servants to lieutenants, boatswains, carpenters, gunners, masters, surgeons, pursers, or even to the cook or the chaplain.

Linking the trainee-sailor Jim, at least on paper, to an individual officer, rather than to the Navy or the ship as a whole, gave the Navy's 'nursery for seamen' a personal dimension, similar to that which was customary in eighteenth-century apprenticeships. Like a master in an apprenticeship, the officer had to provide his servant with clothing and bedding, for which purpose he had to allow the boy around forty to fifty shillings a year in the mid century. Food, of which the boys received the same rations as the men, was provided by the Navy. It was also very convenient for the officers that those of Jim's mates who had been equipped by the Marine Society came on board with a new set of clothing and bedding. While the Society thought that any unused funds of the boys' yearly allowance would be paid in cash to the servants,[16] it is doubtful whether the officers spent that much on their boys. Some tried to pay as little as possible to pauper boys to whom they were not obliged by any family or friendly connection. As the boys changed their masters frequently before a year was over, it was also impossible to ensure that the officers shared between them the payment of a steady yearly allowance. Mary Lacy, for example, claims never to have received any money at all from her master, although she was able to make some money on the side by selling her wine rations or washing clothes for others.[17] When Mary was temporarily serving a captain on board another ship, her master even warned her not to accept any clothes from her captain, presumably because he feared that this would be deducted from her wage, which he was pocketing. Her master's tightness with money when it came to providing protective clothes proved to be fatal: later in life, Mary was to suffer badly from painful rheumatism, eventually making it impossible for her to work when she was only thirty-three.

In the mid century, the majority of Jim's mates did not remain long with their officers; within a year or two they changed their master or their ship, suggesting that relationships with officers were not usually that close. As they also changed between different types of officers, in most cases they were not learning many specialised skills beyond sailing, that is, any skills which might be useful on land, otherwise a surgeon or carpenter, for example, would have been keen to hold on to a boy. There were exceptions though: the Marine Society boy Martin Hoffmann from London, for example, a son of a silver chaser in the Strand, stuck with the same surgeon for his entire career as a Navy servant in the 1750s.[18] Boys like Martin might have had their servant-placement arranged for them by parents or friends, perhaps with the view of gaining some specialised knowledge. We also have to be careful with reading too much into the boys' muster book entries: the categories in which the boys were mustered appear occasionally rather curious and as if they were governed more by attempts to fulfil the officer-servant quotas rather than expressing anything meaningful about how the boys were actually employed.

The main difference between a Navy servant and an apprentice was the training and supervision. While an apprentice would be instructed by his master, it is questionable how far servants commonly received individual instruction from their officers. Since the officer received his wage bonus as long as the servant was on board, regardless of how much progress the boy made, there was no financial incentive for him to supervise the boy. Things were only different when the boy was a son of a relative, friend, someone from whom favours could be expected, or if the officer developed a genuine liking to the boy. The Navy's 'nursery' lacked a control mechanism which could assess and reward the training efforts undertaken by each officer. A naval servant could also be replaced easily, since he was not personally bound to his master by an indenture. Thus those of Jim's fellow servants who had no family connections would have received their training and supervision by working and living with the crew, rather than through personal instruction by their officer. With regards to the captain, with his entourage of servants, this was also the only practical way, as he would not

115

have had the time to monitor the progress of all of them. Furthermore, we have to remember that we are still within the relative immobility of eighteenth-century society and its ideas about appropriate education: Jim was expected to become an able seaman, not an officer, and hence he was learning among the crew. Nevertheless, there was still space for the personal dimension. Lieutenant John Ides of the *Assistance*, for example, rather enthusiastically wrote to the Marine Society in 1762 that if the next boy they sent to him were as good as the one he had had before, he would turn the lad into an officer.[19]

So, in practice, the quality of the training Jim received would have varied a lot, depending upon his ship, the care of his officers, the crew and ultimately also on Jim himself. Both the atmosphere and the size of his warship played a big part in Jim's training. On smaller vessels it was likely that Jim would be more involved in the sailing of the ship than in one of those huge floating fortresses. It also depended on the care officers took to train the boys. Robert Hay fondly remembered that when Rear Admiral Collingwood took over his ship in 1804, he brought a breath of fresh air for the boys. He inspected the boys every morning and organised little races around the rigging for them, encouraging a competitive and sometimes almost foolhardy spirit.

Collingwood did what perhaps other good captains did too, and that was to place each boy in charge of a trustworthy seaman of the mess, making this seaman responsible for the boy. From his 'seaman-buddy' Jim was to be taught not only the duties of a sailor, but the necessary arts of survival such as making his own jackets, shirts and trousers, as well as washing, repairing and mending them. Such a mentor might also arise quite naturally, for example, if the boy had a relative, friend, or other connection on board, or anyone else who was willing to take an interest in him out of purely benevolent motives. Olaudah Equiano, for example, befriended the captain's clerk, who taught him to write and do some arithmetic in his spare time. He also became very good friends with an older seaman in his mess, from whom he learned things like shaving and cutting hair, as well as reading the Bible.[20] Mathew Barker called his older buddy 'my nautical father', hinting that between boy and mentor strong bonds were sometimes established, even tighter than between some masters and apprentices on land, as theirs was a less formal, more voluntary relationship.[21] Scottish runaway Daniel Goodall was placed in a mess with seven men, whom he instantly liked and who were all very willing to instruct him in the duties of his new profession.[22] At the same time they also acted indirectly as his protectors against any mistreatment.

The boy Robert Hay appears to have been a good example of how much also depended on Jim's individual upbringing and motivation. The thirteen-year-old presented, by his own account, the kind of ideal rural child from the north that the Marine Society compared so favourably to London urchins. His parents, though poor, had always taken care that Robert looked clean and was dressed neatly. They had sent him to a charity school where he had learned to read, as well as some writing and arithmetic. Such a boy was likely to end up with a more caring master when the boys were chosen by the officers according to rank, and also more likely to be shown the kind of paternal care the captain displayed when one day he sent for Robert. The latter was terrified at the thought of what he might have done wrong and the consequent punishment, but as it turned out, it had come to the captain's attention that Robert's father was concerned about not having heard from his son in a while; thus the captain now ordered him immediately to write a letter to his parents with the assistance of the captain's clerk. Another 'ship's boy' who made a very good impression when the servants lined up to be picked by the officers was the disguised Mary Anne Talbot. Mary Anne claims that Captain Harvey of HMS *Brunswick* immediately noticed her clean appearance, much cleaner than all the other lads, and so he made her his cabin boy.[23]

Much depended also on Jim's willingness to learn. After he gathered some seafaring experience, Robert Hay was getting a little frustrated at still being just the 'shoe boy', having to clean his officer's shoes, coat and cabin, and serving him at dinner, rather than learning the duties of a sailor. Clearly, being treasured too much by his officer could backfire, as there was the danger that Jim would be trained as a personal servant rather than a sailor. One day Mary Lacy, who had so impressed her master with her household skills, was ordered by the lieutenant to put a hand to the staysail braces. This was a classic case of how they were meant to learn by taking part in the operating of the ship. Yet Mary's master was furious when he saw this.[24] He ordered her to stop immediately and reminded her in the firmest terms that she was only serving him and nobody else. On the other hand, Robert Hay's officer even allowed Robert to play with the mathematical instruments in his cabin, which Robert put to good use, trying to teach himself navigation. There was only one problem: Robert had to stay in the cabin with the instruments, as he was stuck in the eighteenth-century hierarchical order of society and naval discipline. He knew that, as an ordinary servant, being caught walking around with a quadrant on the upper deck would have earned him four to five dozen lashes. So instead young Robert hid in his master's cabin with the quadrant and had to make do with a candle to simulate the sun.

Trying to settle into their new surrogate family could be slightly daunting for the young boys, especially when there was no particular crew member looking after them. It was an abrupt change of circumstances for a young mind, as Basil Hall, who enlisted in 1802, remembered:

> In most other professions, the transition from the old to the new mode of life is more or less gradual, but in that of the sea, it is so totally abrupt, and without intervening preparation, that a boy must be either very much of a philosopher or very much of a goose, not to feel, at first, well-nigh overwhelmed with the change of circumstances.[25]

Those boys who had first spent some time in a tender had already undergone the biggest culture shock. Daniel Goodall, a Scottish boy who ran away to enlist in the Navy in 1801, was scared by the absolute darkness in the hold into which he had been thrown. Even worse, the ruffians entertained themselves by pushing and kicking him around in the darkness until he was about to have a few bones broken. His ordeal only stopped when one of the bullies had mercy and told the others that Daniel was only a small boy. This alone did not discourage the others until his newly found protector, who was over six feet tall, declared that the next one to lay hands upon Daniel would be up against him. Daniel remembered:

> A more ruffianly, villainous-looking set of scamps I have rarely had the ill-fortune to fall amongst. True, they were seen to the very worst advantage, for they were dirty, ragged and reckless. Many bore marks of violence received in resistance to the press-gang . . . Traces of deep debauchery were visible on the faces of the majority; and altogether the picture was such that I had a strong feeling of having made a very serious mistake in the choice of a vocation. This impression did not, however, last long, and a more careful survey of my companions showed a few honest men amongst them.[26]

Ship's boy Robert Hay, who also grew up in rural Scotland, had never seen anything like this motley crew he encountered in the tender:

> To the eye were presented complexions of very varied hue, and features of every cast . . . People of every profession and of the most contrasted manners, from the Bawny ploughman to the delicate fop. The decayed Author and Bankrupt Merchant who eluded their creditors. The Apprentice who had eloped servitude. The improvident and impoverished father who had abandoned his family and the smuggler and swindler who had escaped by flight vengeance of the laws. Costumes of the most various hues presented themselves from the Kilted Highlander to the quadruple breeched sons of Holland. From the shirtless sons of the British prison-house to the knuckle ruffles of the haughty Spaniard. From the gaudy and tinseled trappings of the dismissed footman to the rags and tatter of the city mendicant. Here, a group of half-starved and squalid wretches, not eating but devouring with rapacity their whole day's provisions at a single meal. There, a gang of sharpers at cards or dice swindling some unsuspecting booby out of his remaining few pence.[27]

After some time in the tender, Jim's future ship's company would surely appear more welcoming. Yet that does not mean it was going to be an easy integration. The wooden world of eighteenth-century sailors was a world apart to any newcomer. Jim had to learn its language, rituals and duties as quickly as possible, and to find some new friends and protectors, amongst the men or his fellow ship's boys. Those boys who had enjoyed a sheltered upbringing found their new company rather rough. But if they made an effort they would eventually become one of them and earn the loyalty and friendship for which sailors were equally famous. There were, however, a few characters of whom Jim had to beware, among the sailors as well as his superiors, individuals who could turn his young life in this isolated world into a nightmare: the excessive disciplinarians and the bullies. Before taking a good look at them, Samuel Leech will serve a reminder that Jim was not always the totally innocent victim, and that some of the troubles he encountered were partly brought upon him by himself:

> Many boys complain of ill usage at sea. I know they are subjected to it in many instances; yet, in most cases, they owe it to their own boldness. A boy on shipboard, who is habitually saucy, will be kicked and cuffed by all with whom he has to do; he will be made miserable. The reason is, I imagine, that sailors, being treated as inferiors themselves, love to find opportunity to act the superior over some one. They do this over the boys, and if they find a saucy, insolent one, they show him no mercy.[28]

The bullies could be merciless, and naval discipline, too, could hit Jim in its full force, with no regard for his young age. Samuel Leech soon had to witness the first flogging with the infamous cat-o'-nine-tails. He thought that no community on land would tolerate it if anyone would use such an instrument against a horse, and here it was used against a human being:

> The boatswain's mate is ready, with coat off and whip in hand. The captain gives the word. Carefully spreading the cords with the fingers of his left hand, the executioner throws the cat over his right shoulder; it is brought down upon the now uncovered herculean shoulders of the MAN. His flesh creeps – it reddens as if blushing at the indignity; the sufferer groans; lash follows lash, until the first mate, wearied with the cruel employment, gives place to a second. Now two dozen of these dreadful lashes have been inflicted: the lacerated back looks inhuman; it resembles roasted meat burnt nearly black before a scorching fire; yet still the lashes fall; the captain continues merciless. . . . Four dozen strokes have cut up his flesh and robbed him of all self-respect; there he hangs, a pitied, self-despised, groaning, bleeding wretch.[29]

This dreadful spectacle was enough incentive for two of Sam's fellow ship's boys to desert at the next opportunity. A third boy was at one point so scared of being flogged that he hid in the cable tier for several days, only to receive his punishment when he was eventually discovered. Although the boys were

The Point of Honor (1825), by George Cruikshank: a flogging witnessed
by a boy standing at the cannons and two young midshipmen on the left.

used to corporal punishment from civil society on land, even the Tom Idles
now realised that all this was a step more brutal than their master's cane and
even the house of correction.

As Jim's mates stood and witnessed the punishment with sheer terror, those
youngsters who were prepared for an officer's career had a different perspective.
Ten-year-old William Dillon, later Vice Admiral of the Red, recollected:

> My next trial was to witness the punishment of one of the crew for some act of
> insubordination, with a cat of nine tails over his bare shoulders. My feelings were touched
> to the quick in that instance, but in the course of time I became used to it, knowing that
> there was no controlling the bad characters without resorting to such measures.[30]

The boys were by no means safe from the lash. On board Horatio Nelson's
HMS *Agamemnon* the youngest boy to receive a flogging had probably not
even reached his fourteenth birthday:[31] Walter Holmes, the son of a smith
from London's Smithfield, was given a dozen lashes on the orders of
England's most celebrated naval hero. He had been accused of stealing. If he
had stolen from another sailor, he probably received little more sympathy
from his fellow crew members than from Nelson himself. Walter had
apparently fallen under the influence of a particularly disruptive sailor in the

crew, who was punished together with him. Walter eventually deserted a year later, during the siege of Calvi in 1794. Another and more severe flogging would have been the least the young deserter could expect. Being hanged from the yardarm was more likely. But Walter managed a successful escape. Nevertheless, he was a long way from home for a young lad – unfortunately the rest of Walter's boyhood adventure is a mystery to us, as it is unknown whether Walter ever made it back from Corsica to Smithfield and his parents.

Other boys received floggings for a lot less, though it is possible that they were often lucky not to experience the proper cat-o'-nine tails. Instead slightly less bloody whips might have been used, such as a cat-o'-five-tails, also known as the 'boys' cat' or 'pussy cat', or the cane administered un-ceremoniously on the spot, something that boys on land knew equally well from their apprenticeship masters. John Wilcott had received several floggings before he even turned thirteen, once for not having boiled his master's kettle, and another time for 'skylarking or playing about at marbles'. Twelve-year-old Richard Hopkins on board John Wilcott's ship had already been flogged twice for breaking his master's possessions.[32] Perhaps more understandably, after the previous discussion of deadly diseases, in 1799 Joseph Hilliar had his bare behind flogged and his head shaved for having scabby and lousy hair.[33] The backside as a target, rather than the back, seems to have been another mitigation of punishing the boys, made more famous in later years when boys were flogged with the cat-o'-five tails while bent over a gun, a procedure known to the boys as 'kissing the gunner's daughter'. In the older days, the boatswain punishing the ships' boys with the rod for 'knaveries' had allegedly on some ships been such a regular Monday morning institution that seamen superstitiously believed it necessary in order to get a fair wind for sailing.[34] It is sometimes forgotten that corporal punishment has only very recently been outlawed as a regular part of educating children.

It was not just the flogging Jim had to beware of, but also the casual everyday violence on board. If Jim, like any other sailor, was too slow in performing his tasks, the rope's end was quickly swung at his head or shoulder by the boatswain and his mates, by the midshipman or sometimes by the officer he was serving. The boatswain and his mates also demonstrated little respect for Jim's dignity verbally. Mary Lacy was frequently violently kicked by her master for minor offences, such as not cleaning his shoes properly.[35] Even the pleasant country boy Robert Hay once ended up serving an officer who gave him plenty of beatings with the rope's end, yet it is noteworthy that Robert successfully complained about the harsh treatment to his captain, who then reprimanded the officer and took Robert away from him. In 1814, the Marine Society had to deal with the angry mother of David

Bale, who claimed that Lieutenant Cooke had kicked her son so badly that she feared David was now permanently disabled.[36] Cooke was in trouble, for not only did the boy have a mother standing up for her son, David had initially also been recommended by a well-respected member of the Marine Society. Cooke had kicked the wrong boy.

This book is not a general study of violence and discipline in the eighteenth-century Navy, but the topic remains one of the most troubling aspects. While historians in the old days used to paint a picture of a floating hell, with British sailors being flogged around the oceans, many current historians favour a more moderate view, or point out that the disciplinary procedures were to a degree accepted as necessary by seamen. As with any academic debate, it appears that the way in which arguments and evidence are presented is also dependent on the personal background and history of the individual historian. The argument for the more positive view of Navy discipline is that the Navy could never have been so successful if it had in reality treated its sailors so cruelly. Nevertheless, it is difficult to read examples of naval discipline in practice without being horrified about the inhumanity. Much depended on the individual ship, the individual captain and the influence of his officers. Some captains managed to run a perfectly happy ship without any floggings, others always found enough room to swing a cat and made the bloody spectacle an almost daily ritual. Ship's boy Edward Coxere remembered that the very thought of his captain's severity brought tears to his eyes, yet the captain never ever struck him nor allowed anyone else to strike him.[37] Daniel Goodall remembered an instance when his captain left it up to the crew if and how stragglers, that is, those returning late from shore leave, were to be punished. As shore leave was taken in turns, and everyone aboard Daniel's ship was keen to have his equal share of time ashore, the crew was no less severe with those who overstayed their visit than any captain would have been.[38]

Of course much also depended on the crew. Whilst in peacetime the Navy's ships were filled with volunteers, in times of war there was a large share of men brought on board against their will. These men felt bitterly about having been pressed to fight for their country, while their fellow seamen enjoyed triple wages in merchant shipping; in this situation there was always the danger of excessive discipline.

Take, for example, sailor William Robinson complaining particularly about the young officers having too much power for their age.[39] He remembered a midshipman, merely twelve or thirteen years old, whose sole delight it was to insult the feelings of the seamen, looking for any excuse to get them flogged, and casually kicking and punching their heads and bodies while they worked. To explain such excesses one has to imagine a teenage boy, being given the power to direct grown men, having been brought up in the belief that he is of a superior class to the men he is commanding. Add to this the separation from the restraints of civil society on land, being a little shocked about the rough culture of these men, possibly also feeling threatened or disrespected by them, and wanting to impress his superiors that he can impose his authority over these men, and thus he might feel safer when feared rather than loved by the crew. Yet brutal behaviour on one side tends to engender the same on the other.

While the arrogant young midshipman's case hints at a good class-war tale, there were also sailors like Charles Pemberton who felt that 'Men who have been promoted from the ranks, or from the mast, are generally the most harsh disciplinarians and industrious of tyrants . . . *it is their turn now*.'[40] So perhaps the system was also to blame for the excesses. It remains hard to judge how regular was the violence against sailors, particularly the casual violence, in the absence of a large-scale statistical analysis of the Navy's sources. Equally, it is difficult to say whether the violence was more representative of the wartime Navy and of the turn of the century; possibly the severity of discipline was increasing towards the end of the eighteenth century. The American (1775-1783) and the French (1789-1799) Revolutions, as well as the mutinies of sailors in the Royal Navy at Spithead and the Nore in 1797, kept the British upper and middle classes eager to quell any signs of social revolution on the lower deck.

At least one of Jim's mates violently resisted his officer's authority. In 1797, fourteen-year-old James Allen took part in the bloodiest mutiny the Navy had ever experienced. James had been a servant to the second lieutenant of HMS *Hermione*, a ship under the command of the notorious Captain Hugh Pigot.[41] Pigot, then twenty-seven years old, was a 'flogging captain', running his ship with a daily reign of terror, particularly when drunk, which he was frequently. One day, when Pigot threatened to flog the last sailor coming down from working aloft, three sailors, in a desperate hurry not to be the last, fell to their deaths. One of them was fifteen-year-old William Johnson. Pigot ordered the immediate casting of the bodies of all three uncere-moniously over board, spitefully calling them 'landlubbers', and additionally a flogging for those crew members who appeared to be complaining about the heartless treatment.

Hermione was far away from Britain, in the unhealthy West Indies, and the patience of some of her crew members now snapped. Not wanting to be Pigot's next victims, the men gathered at night. In a way, the boy James Allen indirectly played a crucial part, because it was the bucket of rum that he had stolen from the officers which the men now used to bolster their courage. But the effect was more than courage, as the men became furious. They slaughtered the captain, then they ran below to the gun room to look for James' master, the equally despised Lieutenant Archibald Douglas. Douglas hid underneath the bed of a sick man, and the raging mutineers did not spot him, but unfortunately his boy James Allen did a little later. 'Here he is! Here he is!' shouted the fourteen-year-old. Douglas begged for mercy, but about twenty men began hacking into his body with their tomahawks, axes and boarding pikes, shouting 'You bugger, we will show you mercy!' Among them was James, also yielding a tomahawk and screaming 'Let me have a chop at him: he shan't make me jump about in the gunroom anymore!' All of this came out in the later trials of the mutineers. Yet nobody at the trial enquired why young James had such anger towards Douglas. When Douglas still showed signs of life, the men from the main deck above shouted down the hatchways: 'Hand the buggers up!', and they continued hacking into him and then threw him overboard like the other officers. The British public was horrified by the savage behaviour of the crew, but the question may be asked: what else should we expect? These men had been trained from a very tender age ferociously to hack their way on board enemy ships with their pikes and axes until any resistance was broken, so why should they show a more genteel side to someone who had driven them over the edge and carelessly killed and dishonoured their fellows?

Young James was later seen swaggering about the deck, wearing one of his master's rings, some of his shirts, and his half-boots, which he had cut down to shoes. The crew, in the meantime, was mainly concerned with helping themselves to the alcohol stores. Still, they were sober enough to realise that they had few options other than becoming 'traitors' and handing the ship over to the Spanish governor at La Guaira. Even though Captain Pigot's excesses were known in the Navy, such a violent mutiny at such a crucial time in history, when Britain tried to stop the spread of the French Revolution, was never to remain unpunished. Examples needed to be made. The mutineers were hunted down over the following years. Captured, brought back to England, and confronted with the charges, the former ship's boy James pleaded that he had been very young at the time, and that he surely would have not been capable of such atrocities. He had indeed been very young, but that did not help his defence. He was hanged in August 1800.

Nearly two years later a trip to the West Indies entangled another ship's boy in a mutiny: Daniel Goodall had a miserable time in the tender and was happy finally to be taken on board HMS *Téméraire*, where the seamen in his mess instantly became his good friends. Daniel's crew had been delighted by news of the Peace of Amiens and expected to be paid off at last. Yet instead of returning to Britain they had to stay on board, as HMS *Téméraire* was ordered towards an undisclosed destination, which later turned out to be a long journey to the West Indies.[42] Anger was brewing, the men, desperate for the shores of home wanted to sail nowhere apart from Britain, and eventually a mutiny erupted. The ringleaders were none other than Daniel's friendly messmates, although they had excluded Daniel from their conspiracy. It was lucky for Daniel, for his little mess not only included the ringleaders of the mutiny, but also an informer who later betrayed them all. After a brief stand-off, the marines quelled the mutiny. The mutineers probably hoped for a lighter treatment, but once HMS *Téméraire* was back in Portsmouth more than a dozen of Daniel's crew were hanged. Also on trial were those who had taken no active part in the mutiny but were suspected of having heard of the mutineers' plans, and failing to inform their superiors. Young Daniel had to be grateful indeed that his mess had excluded him from their conspiracy talks, so he escaped unpunished. Unfortunately, though, he had now lost all his new-found friends, with the exception of the informer.

In any case, Jim was well advised to be on his guard not to act in a way that might bring upon him the harshness of naval discipline. Equally, he also had to watch out for falling victim to maltreatment without having done anything wrong. Apparently, in larger ships, to supervise and protect the boys, they were often berthed in the gun room with the gunner, and the gunner was encouraged to take his wife with him to sea, who could then take care of the boys.[43] Yet this did not protect Jim from the occasional hardship. Stealing from fellow sailors was allegedly considered the greatest sin on board, but many of Jim's mates still somehow lost their brand new Marine Society clothes immediately after coming aboard. There was clearly a good reason why sailors kept their belongings in a chest with a solid lock although, to be fair, most thefts occurred on tenders rather than on the ships with settled crews.

However, nothing could have saved Jim from enduring the sailors' beloved rituals of more or less light-hearted bullying with which they treated the landsmen, such as being ducked into water (or even the ocean) when they passed the equator for the first time. Merchant captain John Newton wrote that this was such a 'fine sport' for the seamen that they would rather lose their forfeiture than allow anyone to escape the ducking: 'in many vessels, they single out some poor helpless boy or landsman, to be half drowned for the diversion of his shipmates.'[44] Bullying would always remain a problem, when so many men worked and lived for such a long time in such a small space, lacking any privacy and with boredom constantly

Crossing the Line (1825), **by George Cruikshank**.

gnawing at the men's nerves. Hierarchies had to be fought out and maintained; and claustrophobia, unused energies and frustrations had to find their release valve – hence the Admiralty's instructions to keep the men constantly at work.

The main problem for us today is that we have to rely primarily on official documents of the time, and there we find only a few hints of the troubles young Jim Hawkins faced in his socialisation on board. To avoid a flogging, sailors preferred to settle their quarrels without the involvement of superiors. Those of Jim's mates who had some of their Marine Society kit stolen would have realised that their complaints tended to fall on deaf ears, if they dared at all to say something.[45] Jim had thus to learn to take matters in his own hands, possibly even to pick a fight with the suspect. He had to assert himself, otherwise there was the danger that he would become the victim of all kinds of bullying; he had to show toughness, but also to form reliable alliances. Some of Jim's mates were already trained in this challenge – we only have to remember the rude boys from London's rough neighbourhoods encountered earlier among the Marine Society boys. They were better prepared for this than the well-mannered country boy arriving alone on board, although the latter might have a height advantage, and was more likely to be favoured by his superiors.

Boys fighting on board: midshipmen Prince William and Charles Sturt (1780s).

It must have been particularly daunting for a ship's boy who was in reality a girl: Mary Lacy, too, had to establish her authority, or be forever the victim.[46] Remarkably, Mary thought that the boys sent by magistrate Fielding and the Marine Society on board her ship, most of them coming from Spitalfields and other deprived areas of London, were very friendly. She had no reason to be afraid, as none of them ever harassed her or wanted to fight with her. Trouble only began when Admiral Geary came aboard: he brought with him a great number of sturdy boys, very wicked and mischievous lads, in Mary's eyes. The Admiral's lads were constantly looking to pick a quarrel with Mary and the Marine Society boys. One boy, William Severy, was a particular nuisance, bullying and slapping Mary in the face without any reason. Mary was outraged, and asked the lieutenant for advice. In a classic example of eighteenth-century naval education, the lieutenant, unaware that Mary was a girl, advised her that the best solution was to start a fight with William. Mary followed his advice. As they squared up to each other, Mary understandably refused to pull her shirt off. Bully-boy William was confident, but he clearly underestimated Mary's fury. Mary emerged as the winner of the fight. In defence of William losing to a girl, Mary was probably a few years older than him. From that day on the boys left Mary in peace, and William even became a good friend of Mary.

Olaudah Equiano and his companions were occasionally encouraged to fight each other for the entertainment of the officers, who afterwards paid the boys between five and nine shillings as a reward.[47] The boys had to fight for over an hour, no bloody nose stopping them. We would consider this as a great maltreatment today, but for eighteenth-century contemporaries and in the light of the aggressive fighting spirit of the Navy this was unfortunately considered rather educational. Equiano probably even relished the fact that he was allowed to fight (and beat) white boys. In the Marine Society's records there are very few hints of bullying. Once a collection was organised by members in 1757 in support of a boy who had been 'accidentally disabled by a blow from a seaman', but no more was recorded of the affair.[48]

Due to their young age, the boys' ability to testify at a court martial was often in dispute and this made them more vulnerable to mistreatment than the landsmen. When, for example, in 1760 the Navy investigated the case of the boy Alexander Nairn, who had been thrown overboard, there were doubts in the Admiralty whether the two prime witnesses, two thirteen-year-old boys, could be allowed to testify against the man charged with killing Alexander.[49] Perhaps cases like Alexander's death were extreme ones, preserved in the Admiralty's records for being exactly that. Yet unfortunately it is difficult to assess how much happened but remained unrecorded. Both the Navy's and the Marine Society's records avoided controversial issues. In March 1758, for example, the Society's minutes mention a complaint of several boys being 'used ill' on board the *Active*, and one of the boys was ordered to attend the committee. Yet that is all the minutes recorded about the case, and nothing is ever mentioned of it again, nor is there anything in the records of the Admiralty.[50]

An extreme example of the difficulties of assessing the bullying, based solely on the surviving official documents, is the question of how great the danger was that Jim was subjected to rape and other sexual acts. Homoeroticism and rape in the Georgian Navy in general are controversial topics. The Articles of War of 1749, which stipulated that anal intercourse with another man was a capital offence even if both parties were consenting, referred to it as 'the unnatural and detestable Sin of Buggery or Sodomy with Man or Beast'.[51] Hanging was the fate of those caught in the act, and several hundred lashes for those who could only be convicted of attempting it. Buggery was classed as an offence against God and religion. Towards the end of the century it additionally acquired a political dimension: homoeroticism was equated with effeminacy, homosexuality and flamboyance, and in Britain all were together branded as the subversive fruits of the cultural influence of the Catholic countries with whom Britain was at war. To be the bulwark against the Catholic forces, the public wanted to see Jolly Jack Tar as staunchly heterosexual as possible – suddenly even his whoring started to appear slightly more light-hearted in popular culture, while his flamboyant dress sense raised a few eyebrows. Socratic notions of lovers being more highly motivated fighters in defending each other seemed never to cross the mind of the British public, nor that of any other society since the ancient Greeks. Homoerotic activity was regarded as a sin, and homosexual inclinations as a lack of manliness and fighting power.

The controversy regarding the extent of homoerotic activity in the eighteenth-century Navy arises from the low number of recorded incidents. While some historians insist that the British sailor's world was indeed as heterosexual as the public wished it to be, others view this as a suspiciously low number. The latter argue that the Navy personnel must have turned a blind eye to homoeroticism, in view of the troublesome court martial and harsh punishment that would have followed. The argument is based on the assumption that in such an isolated, male-only world the men's sexual frustrations should have tempted them more frequently to approach crew members. Furthermore, there is also the thought that homosexual men would have chosen the Navy specifically for the close male-only company, though the work environment hardly tolerated anyone with effeminate character traits. Other possible indicators, such as the sailors' overstated machismo, hedonism or use of homophobic swear words, can equally be taken as supporting evidence for both sides.

When homoeroticism does surface in the Navy sources, it is indeed very often the case of a man having forced sexual contact with a ship's boy. Naturally, cases of sexual contact between two consenting men are less likely to appear, as there needed to be a party with an interest in making it public. In the Seven Years War, during which the Navy employed near one hundred and fifty thousand men and rarely allowed them any shore leave, there were a mere nine courts martial in which people were tried for sodomy. Six out of these involved servants.[52] Some cases relate to one incident only, others to an abuse over a longer period. In 1762, for example, Richard Chilton was hanged for forcing William Hoskins to commit sodomy.[53] William was a fatherless boy from London, who had been brought to the Marine Society three years earlier and had become one of its fife players. For a boy like William it was crucial to prove that he was subjected to threats and did not consent, since both a man raping another and two consenting men having sex were capital offences. Thus Thomas Finley,[54] for example, had embarked a year earlier on what was probably one of the shortest seafaring careers among Jim's comrades. Thomas, the son of a London butcher, had been equipped by the Marine Society on 11 June 1761 and was sent on board the *Ocean*. Only three weeks later he was court-martialled for committing sodomy with a seaman. Strangely, Thomas not only admitted that he had consented, but also that before entering the Navy he was accustomed to 'run about' Birdcage Walk in St James's Park, which was one of the main meeting places for homosexual men in eighteenth-century London. This suggests that he had had regular sexual contacts with men, or possibly had even been involved in prostitution.

Thomas's father did what he could to save his boy. He testified that Tom had always been a good son, that he used to help in the family business, but that he had been inclined to go to sea and one Mr Barratt had enticed him to join the Navy. Yet sadly it was all in vain, and there was no mercy for the fifteen-year-old. Tom was hanged together with the seaman. Young age and naivety did not protect Jim from hanging. Only boys who had not yet reached the age of fourteen could expect leniency. Thomas Finley's unequivocal admission remains puzzling; possibly he was unaware of the consequences. His case also illustrates that Jim's mates did not always have to be forced to tolerate a man's approach. Naivety, susceptibility to bribes, affection and the boy's sexual desire or curiosity could also have played a part, as exemplified by other recorded courts martial, in which seamen lured boys with money and presents, telling them that there was nothing wrong in what they were doing.

While Thomas admitted to consenting, other boys who claimed to have been raped still faced a tough interrogation by the court martial trying to determine if they really did not consent. So, not only had Jim be wary of too much attention from his crew members, if something happened and he wished to complain, he had also to prove convincingly that he was an unwilling victim. Otherwise he would hang next to his molester. Clearly, here lay another reason for Jim to remain silent, and it is conceivable that many culprits used this as a threat to ensure their victims' silence. However, there is one thing that should have worked in Jim's advantage: the lack of privacy on board. Any crew member molesting Jim ran a high risk of being caught, and the culprit had either to be confident that the boy would keep quiet, or that the shipmates would turn a blind eye, or at least that if detected the captain would try to avoid the trouble of a court martial – that is, unless the culprit had no such concerns at all and was just plain desperate or drunk, the latter often being the first line of defence at a court martial.

There were others on board who had a little more privacy and fewer people daring to speak out against them, and they were the officers. If even the captain was involved, then chances were high that nothing would ever make it into our historical documents. In the 1790s, Captain Charles Sawyer's frequent pursuits of the boys on board HMS *Blanche* were apparently well known among his crew.[55] He regularly called the boys into his cabin at night, extinguished the lights and then began touching their private parts. When Sawyer's behaviour became too blatant, his first lieutenant felt that he could no more keep quiet and wrote a letter to the area commodore, Horatio Nelson. It was a difficult decision, because the lieutenant risked both the life of his captain, as well as his own career in the case of the accusations falling through, the boys remaining quiet or being considered untrustworthy at a court martial. To make matters worse, Captain Sawyer was also a well-connected man. Luckily for the first lieutenant, Nelson took the allegations seriously. But rather than order Sawyer's arrest, Nelson instead hoped that Sawyer would do the honourable thing and remove himself from his ship and this world, thus avoiding a scandal. Sawyer did not, and eventually he was dismissed, managing to avoid execution.

The biggest obstacle to a court martial for a rape case was that detailed evidence was needed for a conviction. A witness testifying to penetration and emission was necessary to prove sodomy. Due to their young age, the boys' testimony was often considered unreliable, but who else could testify and take it onto his conscience to have his shipmate hanged? Only two of the nine courts martial during the Seven Years War ended with the accused being hanged, while in three the defendants received between three hundred and a thousand lashes for 'uncleanness or other scandalous actions'. In the remaining four, the accused were acquitted.

The courts martial records trying to establish whether full sodomy was committed exemplify the troublesome and delicate investigation. Their language may disturb the sensitive reader, being the blunt language of sailors, to say the least. However, we should never forget that we are dealing with the alleged rape of minors. In the case against quartermaster James Ball in 1706, for example, we read from the boy's statement in the official court martial records that:

> the said James Ball thrust his finger into his arse which he said hurt him very much but notwithstanding he afterwards forced him and put his cock in his arse. Mr. Rook [the lieutenant present at the surgeon's examination] then asked him what he did further, the boy answered he wriggled about and pissed in his arse.[56]

These were delicate matters expressed in plain sailor terms. James Ball first denied the charge, then claimed the boy was a hermaphrodite, then went for more conventional defence lines by first claiming that he had been drunk and afterwards that the boy only testified against him out of malice. All his defences were in vain, Ball was hanged, and the boy was left unpunished, as the court believed his claim that he had not consented.

Young boys like Jim were certainly easy targets, to be silenced by threats, and with a difficult stand as witnesses at a court martial. On the same day that saw the court martial ordering the hanging of the butcher's son, Thomas Finley, another trial was held in which three boys accused a seaman of the *Crown* of having attempted sodomy with them.[57] Asked why the boys had initially not complained, they stated that they feared that all it would lead to would be a flogging for them. One of the boys was illiterate, and when he responded to the question as to whether he understood the meaning of an oath with the word 'No', the court ruled that he was not able to give evidence. The seaman was finally acquitted, as was, in 1759, William Tremuen of the *Thetis*, who had been accused by the Marine Society boy George Veaux of attempting sodomy with him. In his case the court martial thought George's statement did not appear credible, and none of the other crew members had seen anything.[58]

Apparently, the ships' boys owed their difficult status at courts martial not just to their young age, but also to their reputation for frequently trying to rid themselves of disliked shipmates by wrongly accusing them of attempted buggery.[59] Indeed, buggery allegations often had only other boys as witnesses. Yet one can easily imagine this as resulting from the fact that the boys berthed together, and because they stood by each other against bullying, while the rest of the crew might have been reluctant to send one of their company to the gallows. If the defendant got away alive, then the boy had a problem. Initiating a court martial could not only turn the accused, but the whole crew against the new boy. Thus, even the mischievous boys among Jim's comrades would have been careful about making unfounded accusations. And if it is true that boys often made such claims, then the low number of courts martial only proves that in such cases captains preferred to preserve their ship's reputation.

Punishing the alleged offender with the cat-o'-nine-tails was a less troublesome solution than a court martial.[60] On board Nelson's ship, in 1795, the boy James Martin was punished with thirty-six lashes for committing an 'execrable' act with two seamen – by not specifying his offence any further, Nelson spared his life.[61] Like every captain, Nelson knew that at a time when every seaman was desperately needed, a court martial and a hanging did more damage than good. Ship's boy James Martin was rated as ordinary seaman in the following year. We therefore have to expect that the sexual abuse of boys was probably not as rare as the few recorded cases suggest. The conclusion regarding homoeroticism in the Navy must be that, although this behaviour could be punished with hanging, indicating how subversive it appeared to the authorities, ironically this same severity of punishment ensured that sailors and officers would have been very reluctant to denounce otherwise well-integrated shipmates; the real extent of homoeroticism in the service in the eighteenth century thus remains an unknown quantity.

It was not just floggers and bullies awaiting Jim on board, but also new and deep friendships, entertaining and inspiring characters, and encounters with exciting foreign lands and cultures. Exploration of the fascination eighteenth-century youths had for the sailor lifestyle turns up plenty of examples of the colourful personalities who were now about to make Jim one of them. Sailor John Bechervaise marvelled 'that friendship among seamen (true seamen) is more powerful, more lasting, than among any other class of men'.[62]

Unfortunately, there were also plenty of crew members from whom Jim could pick up some rather bad habits. Many contemporaries on land feared that seamen were not exactly the ideal company for young boys. Samuel Leech, who joined the Navy as a tender twelve-year-old, after a protected upbringing in the country, was shocked.[63] He felt that there were hardly any worse places for the development of the character and morals of a boy than the Navy. For here he was allegedly surrounded by revolting profanity, shameful whoring and many other vices. By the time Leech wrote his memoirs he had become a devout Methodist and lamented: 'How can a boy be expected to escape pollution, surrounded by such works of darkness? Yet, some parents send their children to sea because they are ungovernable ashore! Better send them to the house of correction.'[64] Former cooper's apprentice John Nicol was equally worried:

> I had been much annoyed, and rendered very uncomfortable, until now, from the swearing and loose talking of the men in the Tender. I had all my life been used to the strictest conversation, prayers night and morning; now I was in a situation where family worship was unknown; . . . At first I said my prayers and read my Bible in private; but truth make me confess I gradually became more and more remiss, and, before long, I was a sailor like the rest: but my mind felt very uneasy, and I made many weak attempts to amend.[65]

And satirist Ned Ward had no better words for the Navy and its men:

> It is the sovereign of the aquatic globe, giving despotic laws to all the meaner fry, that live upon that shining empire. It is the New-Bridewell of the nation, where all the incorrigible rascals are sent . . . It is the Christian sanctuary of nonsolvent debtors, and unfortunate whoremasters . . . It is Old Nick's academy, where the seven liberal sciences of swearing, drinking, thieving, whoreing, killing, couzening, and backbiting, are taught to full perfection.[66]

A satirist, a Methodist and a boy brought up by strict religious parents may not be the best judges but, even so, Jim's new comrades were certainly no choirboys. However, the other servants could be a source of help and strength for Jim. Particularly on larger ships, Jim found many boys of his own age, which eased his integration on board. If there was space for leisure and play it would also soften Jim's passage from childhood to adulthood.

Despite being a slave to his officer, Olaudah Equiano, for example, still had fond memories of his time as a ship's boy. He was able to play with a large number of boys on board his ship, which he claimed made his time in the Navy a lot more agreeable and entertaining.[67] It is astonishing how in his autobiography, which was written as a document against slavery, Equiano covers his time as a naval servant in a remarkably positive and non-political tone, compared to the rest of his book. Perhaps in the Navy Equiano felt treated no worse than the ordinary white boys. Many of the boys from non-privileged backgrounds would have not had such close contact with officers as did Equiano. Neither would they have been given such opportunities as being taught arithmetic by the captain's clerk. Here perhaps lay the reason why Equiano felt so attached to his master, Lieutenant Pascal. Though Pascal was his slave master, he also ensured that Equiano received more protection and education than the average Jim Hawkins. Pascal even sent Equiano back to England to attend a school. Whether this was a case of Pascal's paternal feelings, or an attempt to invest in his 'property', is open to debate. The amount of times Equiano uses the word 'we' in the chapters about his service in the Navy certainly suggests that he felt well integrated and had positive memories of being a boy on board a Navy vessel, in spite of all of the hardships and battles.

Some people even feared that the ships' boys were possibly having too good a time. In 1760, a letter writer to the *Grand Magazine* claimed that someone from the Navy had told him that neither the officers nor anyone else on board paid any attention to the youths.[68] Apparently those boys equipped by the Marine Society were known as 'Scape Gallowses', and the first things they learned were blasphemy, chewing tobacco and gaming. And from there they proceeded to drinking and 'talking bawdy', thus becoming within a short period the vilest part of the entire crew. Furthermore, the boys allegedly avoided any work, usually under pretence of having to do some task for their masters. Yet instead they hung around together in the hold, the round tops, or the booms. The anonymous author concluded that the youths would be much better off on board colliers or merchant ships, where smaller crews and a higher workload would guarantee that they were better supervised than in the large warships.

The Marine Society thought such complaints were grossly exaggerated and felt confident enough to include this letter in its publications. The Society argued that misbehaviour, such as blasphemy, was surely more rigorously punished on board than on land, and also that obtaining tobacco and alcohol on board was difficult for the boys. Swearing and drunkenness were indeed punishable offences, though captains were often lenient with regards to the former. The muster lists show that only very few officers allowed their boys to obtain tobacco, and their alcohol rations were usually half of that of the men. Then again, like the sailors, the boys had other ways of getting restricted goods. With regards to the boys' antics, the Society responded in a relaxed manner: 'That lively boys on board ships, should sometimes be saucy, is very easy to be conceived; and it often happens that the same vivacity, under some restrictions, is one reason of their making the best seamen in the world.' One admiral consulted by the Society laughed when he read the complaint that the boys loitered in the round top. He thought that there surely was no better place for them to gather if they wanted to become good seamen. The admiral was right, for nothing could combine both the boys' training and their desire to play better than allowing them to climb freely around in the rigging.

Perhaps the Society had reason enough to be relaxed, for stories of pranks and misbehaviour committed by the boys on board are certainly part of sailors' memoirs of all times. In fact, they are part of almost any published memoirs of a 'working-class' life. Maybe the anonymous letter-writer had assumed that the boys' lives in the limited space of a warship were more strictly controlled, a misapprehension he shared with many magistrates who sent juveniles to the Navy. John Cremer wrote in his memories of being a boy on board a man-of-war that 'It would be teadyous to write of all pranks we naturly took to on board those woodin worlds, for Monkeys cannot be moore mischavos in theair kind.'[69] One sentence delivers enough proof how often the later Captain John Cremer must have played truant when the school-master was teaching the boys how to spell properly. Some of the pranks John recollected are of such a dangerous nature, that, even with the benefit of the advancements in pedagogy of the past two centuries, one would still be tempted to give the rascal a good flogging. John was the lieutenant's son, he kept company with the other officers' sons, and their favourite targets were the poor boys. One of their less brutal pranks was cutting their hammocks at night and letting them fall onto the floor. The adults were not safe from their practical jokes either; those that got them a flogging were likely to have their legs clipped on the way below deck and suffer broken ankles and similar. Once John's gang took the corpse of a sailor and in the darkness threw it at

On the Forecastle (1779), by **W Ward and T Stothard**.

the head of the drunken doctor, who thought that he was being attacked and started wrestling with the dead body.

Sailors lived for months, sometimes for years, without a break in their wooden workshop. It was only natural that seamen recreated on board a little bit of what they missed, and also that they crammed in as much as possible during their brief shore visits. The onboard recreation required some creativity and imagination though, and often only alcohol helped. Captains knew that they had to make sure that time and space was provided for diversions. Captain, later Admiral, Collingwood was rather enthusiastic about the onboard entertainment:

> Every moon-light night the sailors dance . . . and there seems as much mirth and festivity as if we were in Wapping itself. . . . We have an exceedingly good company of comedians, some dancers that might exhibit at an opera, and probably have done at Saddler's Wells, and a band consisting of twelve very fine performers. Every Thursday is a play night, and they act as well as your Newcastle company.[70]

On board Samuel Leech's ship spirits were kept high by an international band: 'the captain procured a fine band, composed of Frenchmen, Italians and Germans, taken by the Portuguese from a French vessel.'[71] The musicians had agreed to serve in the Navy, on condition of being excused from fighting and exempted from being flogged. The *Royal George* had, in 1807, three acting companies performing on alternate nights, nicely graded by social rank.[72] Shipmates with talents in spinning seafaring yarns had cult status. Sam Leech remembered a shipmate called 'Old Dick': 'So bewitching were Dick's stories, that I used to long for the hour when we could lay in our hammocks and listen.'[73] Dick 'was a sort of off-hand novelist; all he cared for was effect, and where truth failed him, fiction generously loaned her services.' Captains who were concerned about the spirit on board can hardly have objected to the occasional street entertainer delivered to them by magistrates under the Vagrancy Act of 1744.

The two greatest temptations awaiting Jim in his new life were alcohol and prostitutes. Both were tolerated to a degree by the officers, knowing that their crews would not function without them. Yet so many misdemeanours, accidents and long-term health damages stemmed from alcohol abuse that one can easily comprehend why alcohol beyond the official rations was banned. Even so, men smuggling alcohol on board, or saving up their rations, still ensured plenty of occurrences of drunkenness. At the same time it is obvious from the way alcohol was distributed, and to a degree also tolerated beyond the official rations, that the Navy knew very well that alcohol was needed to keep the sailors content, as well as fired up when it came to fighting or coping with severe weather conditions. Alcohol was the medication which kept the sailor going, but also frequently the drug that led to his downfall.

Tea, in contrast, took much longer to be accepted in the Navy. Hanway published an essay against the evil habit of drinking tea, the 'Chinese drug' that allegedly caused people to become lazy.[74] Even fifty years later physician Sir Gilbert Blane (1749-1834) still had to convince critics of the positive effects on the sailors' health of drinking more tea and less alcohol, and rebut common fears that the 'relaxing property' of tea would lower the men's fighting spirit.[75] Some of Jim's mates, in receipt of half-rations of alcohol, who had not yet developed a taste for it, sold their rations or swapped them for other goods. Others gave them as presents to their older buddies and protectors among the crew. Grog, wine and tobacco, not money, were the currency in the wooden world.

The temptations were greatest when the ships came into harbour. In wartime the sailors were often not given any shore leave out of fear they would desert – Jim could occasionally be the fortunate exception, though, as officers did take leave and sometimes wanted their servant to accompany them. If Jim was lucky his officer would take him on the odd sightseeing tour around Roman ruins or a shopping trip to a Mediterranean market. Young Edward Barlow was happy to receive some shore leave in Lisbon and marvelled at the local women:

> And also there are in this city many courtesans, many of them both young and handsome, who will call any Englishman or strangers as they walk the streets, and will ask them in as good English as they can speak whether they will come in and drink the wine and take a bit to stay in their longing [sic]; sitting and looking out of their windows upon who passeth by, and they are decked very handsome in apparel and 'gorny' in their hair, finely dressed with ribbons and open sleeves and buttoned jackets, their shifts being as large as half-shirts in England, very neat and handsome.[76]

If the sailors were not allowed to come to the pleasures ashore, then the shore pleasures came to them. As soon as a ship anchored, the 'bum boats' swarmed out and surrounded her. Just as the sailors had boarded their prize ships, now chandlers, dealers, pimps and prostitutes boarded the ship to relieve them of their riches. Women were the most desired 'commodity', which is not unexpected of men who had not had female company for months and whose wives, if they had any at all, were far away. Sometimes hundreds of women entered the ship, and occasionally they even sailed with the ship to the next harbour. According to the Navy Regulations no women were allowed on board apart from those who were the sailors' wives.[77] Now we understand why Charles Dibdin's jolly tar had to sing about a 'wife in every port', and not a girl. The women of course all claimed to be the wives of crew members, and the officers usually did not check for any marriage certificates. Ship's boy Daniel Goodall remembered his first encounter with the bum-boat girls:

> Some of them, it is true, really were the wives of men belonging to the ship, but, if all had been admitted who set up the claim of connubial right, it would have been a clear case of polygamy, for there could not have been less than a proportion of three or four to every man of marriageable age and position on board. As it was, three days sufficed to see fully more than two hundred of the Delilahs of Plymouth settled amongst the crew, not ten per cent. of whom could have made out a feasible claim to marital connection with any of the men.[78]

The wooden world turned into a bawdy-house with raucous partying, drinking, dancing and sex. Amidst all of it was Jim. Whatever his thoughts were, he could not escape this spectacle. It is a scene which has been parodied in numerous jolly caricatures around the turn of the century, depicting the sailor's well-deserved joy after all the hardship, and celebrating those moments in his life which make him even attractive to today's youth. Some of Jim's older mates might have thought this was exactly the reason why they wanted to become sailors. They were about to end their days of virginity. And if homosexuality was indeed that much detested by sailors, then Jim had better prove to his shipmates that he was staunchly heterosexual. We can only speculate about the sex education that Jim might have received from his older shipmates, or the women themselves, but no Navy schoolmaster would have done so, and parents were far away. The lack of wage deductions for medicines to cure venereal diseases in the muster books behind the boys' names could suggest that Jim's comrades might have been a little more careful than their older shipmates. Some boys were perhaps at first as shocked as young Daniel Goodall was about the loose women:

> The brawling and uproar never ceased the whole day long, and sometimes continued through the greater part of the night also. . . . Smoking was quite a prevalent fashion amongst the dear creatures; and, as for swearing they seemed to take quite a peculiar delight in uttering the 'oldest oaths the newest kind of ways', and those ways the most revolting it is possible for even the vilest to imagine. The coarsest seamen on board were far outdone by those damsels.[79]

What Daniel did not consider was that some of the girls might have merely put on a brave face and hidden any vulnerability behind their big mouth, as did some of Jim's shipmates when going into battle. Other boys, whether in retrospect when writing their memoirs or even at the time, were more understanding of the women's plight than Daniel. The humble shoemaker's boy William Robinson observed how the pimps rowing the girls to the boats behaved like slave auctioneers, bluntly telling some of them that they were too old or too ugly to be sold. Despite all the jolly illustrations of the time, it was still prostitution, and William pitied the women and thought the shame rather lay with his shipmates, who had made these women into what they were:

> Of all the human race, these poor young creatures are the most pitiable; the ill-usage and the degradation they are driven to submit to, are indescribable; but from habit they become callous, indifferent as to delicacy of speech and behaviour, and so totally lost to all sense of shame, that they seem to retain no quality which properly belongs to woman, but shape and name. When we reflect that these unfortunately deluded victims to our passions, might at one time have been destined to be the valuable companions and

comforts of man, but now so fallen: in these cooler moments of meditation, what a charge is raised against ourselves; we cannot reproach them for their abject condition, lest this startling question should be asked of us, who made us so?[80]

Captains and officers usually tolerated these offences against the Navy Regulations. It was part of the unwritten laws necessary to keep the sailors happy. If we forget the exploitation of women for a moment, it was indeed the least the officers could do for sexually starved young men in their prime. Most of them were unmarried, and even if they already had girlfriends back home before going to sea, it was virtually impossible to see them and to keep the relationship alive. Daniel Goodall and William Robinson were perhaps not aware that if not for the prostitutes, it might have been their turn to deal with their shipmates' advances.

There was a long list of possible difficulties Jim faced during his integration among sailors, yet after the initial culture shock, the initiation rites, and the finding of friends and protectors among the crew, he was set slowly to become one of them. Even the former cooper's apprentice John Nicol, with his strict religious upbringing, eventually became used to the sailors who had so shocked him at first. And he had kept his juvenile Crusoe-infused enthusiasm for a sea life once his ship was on its way:

> Now I was happy, for I was at sea. To me the order to weigh anchor and sail for the Nore was the sound of joy; my spirits were up at the near prospect of obtaining the pleasures I had sighed for since the first dawn of reason. To others it was the sound of woe, the order that cut off the last faint hope of escape from a fate they had been impressed into much against their inclination and interest. I was surprised to see so few, who, like myself, had chosen it for the love of that line of life. Some had been forced into it by their own irregular conduct, but the greater number were impressed men.[81]

We shall now follow them to sea and try to find out why some of the more experienced sailors did not share new boy John Nicol's enthusiasm.

CHAPTER 7

Jim's Coming of Age at Sea: Masculinity and the Horrors of War

THE moment Jim Hawkins set foot on board he would become acquainted with the common accidents and illnesses that befell the seamen, particularly newcomers. One everyday unpleasantness that Jim was soon to encounter was seasickness. Twelve-year-old Jeffrey Raigersfeld recollected that:

> no sooner were we out of sight of land, than I became so very sea sick as to be unable to assist myself in the least; indeed when crossing the Bay of Biscay, the waves ran so high, and the water out of the soundings caused so bad a smell on board, from the rolling of the ship as it washed from side to side in the between decks, that had any one thrown me overboard as I lay helpless upon the gangway I certainly should not have made the smallest resistance.[1]

Another 'sickness' from which Jim Hawkins was soon likely to suffer was what in those days was frequently called 'nostalgia', that is, homesickness. Naval surgeons even suspected homesickness to be a cause or symptom of scurvy.[2] When the ship departed, and it would dawn on young Jim that the return to his home was in a distant future, if at all, then even the runaways might become pensive. As Mary Lacy remembered:

> After I was got on board, I began to think where I was going; for neither my father or my mother knew where I was all this while, nor what was become of me; therefore my thoughts began to trouble me exceedingly, as I did not know whether I should live to come home again or should ever see my disconsolate father and mother any more. These considerations occasioned me to reflect what sorrow and grief I had brought on my aged parents, who no doubt were very unhappy in having lost me so long.[3]

A remorseful Mary wrote letters to her parents, contemplating why 'children too often grieve and distress their parents by rash and disobedient behaviour', and signing her letters with 'Your undutiful Daughter'.

Other boys struggled with the fact that what had previously been a product of their juvenile imagination was now about to become reality. As most males do at least once in their lives, they would begin to worry if they would be able fulfil the role of the man they aspired to be. The fearlessly masculine sailor was certainly one of the toughest role models to live up to, in a world in which death and danger were often belittled as routine events. Thirteen-year-old James Scott, being trained and armed as a midshipman, pondered this matter:

> I remember well on the following day, when we were receiving our guns, muskets, swords, tomahawks, pikes &c. that my reflections were by no means agreeable. The conviction that they were intended for deadly strife, and that the period might not be far distant when they would be brought into actual use, threw a chill over the enthusiastic ardour that generally governed my feelings respecting the navy. I felt most forcibly that I had not henceforth child's play to encounter, and a feeling allied to fear crept into my mind that I might fail when the moment of trial came.[4]

Other boys kept their enthusiasm and were still eagerly waiting for their first engagement, especially after months of sailing without any incidents. Ship's boy Olaudah Equiano remembered that he was so 'far from being afraid of anything new which I saw, that after I had been some time in this ship, I even began to long for an engagement.'[5]

For some of Jim's mates the initial worries, and the shock of their first taste of naval life, were too great. A few ships' boys were quickly off the ship and back on land; possibly some of them had not been keen on joining the Navy in the first place. During wartime the Navy Regulations forbade any discharges, yet some captains and officers nevertheless just left a servant in the nearest British harbour.[6] They did so occasionally even with men, either letting them go or intentionally giving them opportunities to desert if they felt that the running of the ship would be easier without them. Lack of commitment or fitness, poor health, or a troublesome character led officers simply to give up on a servant. Some of these boys subsequently found themselves in great distress, in an unknown harbour town, with no idea of whom to turn to for help. Others were only too happy to be free again, probably having begged their officer to be discharged, or made it clear in some way that they were not suitable for the job.

Officially, however, in times of war the boy's desire to leave ought to have been ignored. Once Jim enlisted for the Navy he was meant to stick to his commitment, and a change of mind was not allowed. This was something that thirteen-year-old runaway Robert Hay and his caring father had to learn in 1803.[7] On his second day aboard, country boy Robert received a surprise visit from his father, who had found out that his son had volunteered for the Navy, and had thus journeyed all the way from their home village. Robert's father was extremely worried about the bad influence that the seamen might have on his son, and that Robert would take up drinking and swearing. He was determined to take his young runaway home again. Yet Robert's captain made it clear that in the war against France they needed every man, and that even though Robert was still a boy and of not much use at the moment, he would soon become a good sailor. The only possible way off the ship for Robert was if his father would pay a release fee. However, being poor he did not have the required money, and so the concerned father had to give in and leave the ship without his son. Robert's mother was too distressed by the thought of her tender son now being in the company of rough seamen, but his father and sister returned a few days later with new clothes (in blue, so he would fit in better), thread, needles and other necessities. The father also gave Robert a Bible, reminding him to say his prayers daily. Then Robert's ship set sail.

Robert's captain stuck to the rules. He needed the boy as a future sailor in the war against Napoleon. It is, incidentally, interesting to remember that Robert was a runaway: the captain supported the decision of the thirteen-year-old, regardless of his parents' wishes. This stands in contrast to the Marine Society's great efforts fifty years earlier to detect runaways amongst its boys, even if the boy were already on board. Perhaps Robert had also made a good first impression on the captain as somebody worth keeping. Just like any man, Robert had given up his personal liberty until the day the Navy had no more use for him. Any deserters could expect the death penalty. This, however, still did not deter the numerous deserters among seamen – perhaps they knew the Navy hesitated to use the death penalty when sailors were so badly needed. Since the Articles of War of 1749 the death penalty was no longer obligatory. Yet what is remarkable about Jim and his mates is that, based on a statistical sample of careers of ships' boys in the mid-century Navy used for this study, the boys hardly ever deserted, unlike the men.[8] This is surprising if one considers all the troubles the Marine Society had with new boys running away, and also taking account of the young ruffians we have encountered among Jim's comrades.

We could take the absence of desertions among the boys as a strong indication that the vast majority of Jim's mates soon settled successfully into their new life at sea. Maybe it was also unlikely that the boys would run away once their ship had left the home port, considering their young age. Yet unfortunately, we do not know the extent to which captains and officers allowed unhappy boys to depart easily, or whether they were all as strict as Robert Hay's captain. After all, these were inexperienced boys, and their officers were often not in particular need of them, as long as another boy was on hand who could take his position and ensure the officer would get his wage bonus. The ships' muster rolls are a bit vague when it comes to the boys, frequently just noting that a boy had been discharged, but not to which ship.[9]

It is important, though, not to make the mistake of interpreting all these unspecified discharges as discharges from the Navy. It is more probable that the boys were just transferred to another ship. But the limitations of the available historical records remain a problem: the Navy's muster lists were not as concerned with the fate of the unpaid servants as they were with keeping track of the men. When, for example, in the summer of 1758 the gunner of the *Gibraltar*, then anchoring at Cork, was transferred to the *Firedrake* and never appeared on board that ship, this was duly recorded in the *Firedrake*'s muster lists, yet nothing is mentioned about what happened to the two servants he had taken with him from the *Gibraltar*.[10] Notably, towards the end of the eighteenth century when the Navy's muster lists greatly improve in quality, we also notice a few servants being recorded as deserters.

As soon as they were rated as seamen, a number of Jim's mates deserted. At first sight this defies logic, for now the boys actually had something to lose, that is, the wages the Navy owed them. Withholding wages was a handy tool to deter deserters, and it was also a considerable source of interest-free credit for the Navy. Then again, just before the newly-made seamen ran they had often bought clothes and tobacco from the ship's purser in exchange for wage deductions, which would have partly made up for the loss of wages. With this in mind, the Admiralty's strictness when it came to giving out protective clothing beyond the sums the men had already earned appears more understandable. It is hard to say why Jim's mates deserted only after being rated. Maybe they had become disillusioned, realising that their youthful expectations of naval life had nothing to do with its reality. Or perhaps they now felt mature enough to dare to escape. However, they had not only matured, the Navy had also trained them in a skilled occupation that was highly in demand in wartime, and could earn them much higher wages in private shipping. If they themselves did not realise their market value, then a 'crimp' might have let them know.

Crimps operated in harbour towns, luring away sailors of the Royal Navy with promises of high wages in the merchant service. In the summer of 1758, the *Gibraltar*, for example, had many more men go missing than just the above-mentioned gunner and his two boys while anchoring at Cork. Her captain bitterly complained to the Admiralty about his men being tempted onto privateers and merchantmen by local publicans, housekeepers, and crimps, and that even the soldiers at the fort in Cork did not make any effort to stop the deserters.[11] Hence the high number of desertions does not necessarily indicate that Jim and his mates had, once rated, been so unhappy about life in the Navy that even the death penalty did not deter them, as financial reasons might have played a role in their decision to depart.

Many of the deserting former ships' boys ran away when on foreign shores. In the mid century, the North American colonies, and Charleston in particular, were popular places for deserters, since there was always a demand for sailors, and many of the ships were destined to go back to England. The colonies themselves also acted as an escape route for many restless and bold young men, who found life in England too restrictive and planned to start a new life in America. Unfortunately, in the end we can only speculate about the motives of deserters, and it may have been a combination of issues rather than a single reason. The boys Nicholas O'Brien and John Goodman, for example, had together enlisted in the Navy via the Marine Society in 1756 and eventually deserted together in the North American colonies.[12] They had served as captain's servants in the *Union* and the *Neptune* for almost two years, and then as able seamen in the *Zephyr*, which brought them to North Carolina. Nicholas and John might have carried a longer grudge against the Navy, for both of them had already been old enough to serve as paid landsmen when they enlisted, yet they had to remain unpaid servants for nearly two years. The month they ran saw many men deserting the *Zephyr*. The crew had been very sick in the summer with fevers and fluxes, and O'Brien, Goodman and others also had outstanding wage deductions for using medication against venereal diseases. Sick crews made desertions easier, as the ships had to stop more often at harbours to discharge men who were ill. And sick ships also scared away the healthy men and encouraged them to overcome the fear of being punished for desertion – after all, according to the eighteenth-century Navy surgeon James Lind, diseases were by far the deadliest threat the seamen were facing, which takes us straight to the discussion of the next and saddest possible ending of Jim's career as a ship's boy, that is, his early death.

Death was a familiar shipmate of naval sailors in times of war. On most occasions death did not come in the form of a cannonball fired by an enemy ship; death did not storm on board with cutlass and pistol; instead he crawled silently on board in the form of a disease, taking his victims slowly and unspectacularly. Only towards the end of the eighteenth century, with the Enlightenment spurring research into diet and hygiene, could the high rate of death from disease be lowered. Jim's life was indeed in great danger: it is difficult to derive reliable statistics, but based on a sample taken of boys who enlisted during the Seven Years War, each year between fifteen and twenty-five per cent of the ships' boys either died, or were lost out of the historian's sight because they were discharged sick or injured, suffered shipwreck or were captured by the enemy.[13] These are alarmingly high percentages; maybe the sample was an unfortunate one, but without doubt Jim's life was in danger.

Based on the sample, sickness was by far the greatest of Jim's killers, followed by getting shipwrecked and personal accidents, such as falls from great height or drowning. Climbing around in the rigging like circus artists was always dangerous, particularly when done under adverse weather conditions. In addition, the culture of bravado, which was further encouraged by the officers because it strengthened the Navy's fighting power, made the boys prone to disregarding safety precautions. A fall onto the deck meant almost certain death, a fall into the sea yielded better chances of survival. All of these deaths occurred mostly without any direct impact from the enemy, but that is not to say that Jim could completely ignore that threat.

Some boys went straight into battle with minimal time for settling in on board. Fourteen-year-old John Read and thirteen-year-old George Lauder, for example, appeared at the Marine Society in the summer of 1757 to enlist in the Navy.[14] Both youngsters were sent to the brand new frigate *Southampton*, as servants to Captain James Gilchrist. The following month the *Southampton* was plunged straight into action. On her way to Plymouth, she was attacked at midnight by five French privateers, two of them frigates larger than herself. The five were under the command of François Thurot, the most feared French raider of the time. At first, Thurot's frigate engaged in a half-hour long gun battle with John's and George's *Southampton*. When the other four French ships had caught up they tried several times to board the *Southampton*.

The men of the *Southampton* fought off every boarding attempt with much slaughter. Finally, the two French frigates engaged in a ferocious gun battle with the *Southampton*, trying to sink her. This exchange lasted an hour and inflicted heavy damage on the *Southampton*'s masts, sails and hull. It was John's and George's first engagement as powder monkeys, sprinting back and forward between their gun and the magazine below deck, while in the darkness the privateers unleashed their broadsides or tried to force their way on board. Miraculously, the *Southampton* somehow survived the bombardment and all boarding attempts throughout the night. Eventually the privateers gave up, perhaps fearing that British reinforcement was on its way. Maybe George, John and the other Southamptonians afterwards agreed with the famous naval historian William Laird Clowes' later description of François Thurot:[15] that he was not only one of the boldest French corsairs, but also someone who was only bold when attacking helpless merchant ships, but quick on the retreat when met by resistance. Then again, this was a character trait that Thurot shared with many other British and French seafarers.

The Fall of Nelson (*c.*1825), by Denis Dighton.

A powder boy being wounded at the same time as Nelson,
from Denis Dighton, *The Fall of Nelson* (*c.*1825).

147

The *Southampton*, leaking badly, had to turn into Weymouth for repairs. Ten per cent of her crew had been killed or severely wounded. Among those wounded in action was fourteen-year-old John Read. John was left ashore in Weymouth, where he unfortunately disappears from the sources. We do not know if John managed to recover, or died of his wounds, or whether he had become an invalid. With regards to the latter scenario, it is not quite apparent from the records how well public provisions catered for disabled boys. The Navy's sailors had contributions to Greenwich Hospital and the Chatham Chest deducted from their wages, yet seeing that the boys only contributed indirectly (the deductions being taken from their officer's wage bonus) any claims by them might have been difficult. Collections by Marine Society members undertaken in aid of individual boys, and the efforts the Hanway brothers needed to put in to get a blind boy admitted into Greenwich Hospital, suggest that possibly neither of the two funds helped out automatically.[16]

Unlike unlucky John Read, his friend George Lauder survived their first taste of naval warfare unharmed. George did not have much time for reflection, though, for as soon as the *Southampton* was again fit for sea, she was ordered to join Sir Edward Hawke's attack on Rochefort. The *Southampton* got into a fierce battle with a French frigate near Brest. The two ships were very close to each other; the French tried to board, the marines exchanged musket fire, and the sailors began battering each other with their hand-pikes. After half an hour of violent fighting the French surrendered when they became aware that all of their officers had been killed. Another twenty of the *Southampton*'s crew had died in this battle, and at least double the number among the French crew. Our ship's boy George, however, had once again survived. After less than four months in the Navy, the thirteen-year-old boy had now won his first prize money. That was the lottery of the sea. But in spite of his youth George had also already witnessed more slaughter than most humans could stomach in a lifetime. George had survived it all unharmed – at least physically, for we can only speculate about the possible psychological wounds inflicted upon his young mind.

Sailor memoirs often remember the horror of the first encounter with war and death. Thirteen-year-old William Dillon remembered witnessing his first casualty, and learning the lesson that the large wooden splinters which flew across the ship during a gun battle were nearly as deadly as the shot itself: 'I had never seen a man killed before. It was a most trying scene. A splinter struck him in the crown of the head, and when he fell the blood and brains came out, flowing over the deck.'[17] The commonly used term 'splinter' for these deadly wooden fragments is probably another example of the sailors' euphemisms for the most horrific dangers.

In 1794, thirteen-year-old William Parker was about to take part in the century's biggest and bloodiest naval engagement, 'The Glorious First of June'. William had his first taste of death before the battle properly started, as he wrote to his parents: 'We had not fired two broadsides before an unlucky shot cut a poor man's head right in two, and wounded Jno Fane and four other youngsters like him very slightly. The horrid sight of this poor man I must confess did not help to raise my spirits.'[18] Amongst the horrors that young William witnessed was the sinking of the French ship *Vengeur du Peuple*, an event that he also related to his parents:

> The ship that struck to us was so much disabled that she could not live longer upon the water, but gave a dreadful reel and lay down on her broadside. We were afraid to send any boats to help them, because they would have sunk by too many souls getting into her at once. You could plainly perceive the poor wretches climbing over to windward and crying most dreadfully. . . . Oh my dear father! When you consider five or six hundred souls destroyed in that shocking manner, it will make your very heart relent. Our own men even were a great many of them in tears and groaning, they said God bless them.[19]

Evidently, as hardened as seamen were, they were not immune to feelings of compassion towards the sailors fighting against them.

Another 'boy' who at least claims to have fought at the battle of 'The Glorious First of June' was the disguised Mary Anne Talbot. As mentioned earlier, a few question marks crop up throughout Mary Anne Talbot's story, which neither matches with the muster books nor the historical events. Mary Anne writes that she had been a powder monkey on board HMS *Brunswick*, the ship which had engaged in a brutal close-range duel with the *Vengeur du Peuple* and was largely responsible for sending the *Vengeur* and all her men into their watery grave. Mary Anne received a severe wound above her ankle from grapeshot. Grapeshot were usually around eight balls confined to an iron and tied in a cloth, which were then scattered by the explosion of the powder; similarly, canister shot consisted of balls filled into a powder canister, which also scattered by the explosion. Mary Anne remembered that, after being hit by grapeshot:

> I attempted to rise three times, but without effect, and in the last effort part of the bone projected through the skin, in such a manner as wholly to prevent my standing, if I had been able to rise. To complete my misfortune, I received another wound by a musket-ball, that went completely through my thigh, a little above the knee of the same leg, and lay in this crippled state till the engagement was over.[20]

She was now in great danger of receiving a deadly infection, of bleeding to death or requiring an amputation. Mary Anne mentions nothing. She must have stopped the bleeding somehow, although it is also possible that the musket ball went, for example, straight through the muscles, or at least hit no major blood vessel. She could have done what Scottish boy Daniel Goodall did when he was hit in the leg: Daniel took the silk neckerchief he was wearing and bound it around his thigh as tightly as he could, in order to avoid bleeding to death.[21] The sailors' accessories were evidently not merely items of fashion.

Like so many boys, thirteen-year-old David Farragut, training to become an officer, also vividly remembered the first casualty he witnessed:

> I shall never forget the horrid impression made upon me at the sight of the first man I had ever seen killed. He was a boatswain's mate, and was fearfully mutilated. It staggered and sickened at first; but they soon began to fall around me so fast that it all appeared like a dream, and produced no effect on my nerves. I can remember well, while I was standing near the Captain, just abaft the mainmast, a shot came through the waterways and glanced upwards, killing four men who were standing by the gun, taking the last in the head and scattering his brains over us. But this awful sight did not affect me half as much as the death of the first poor fellow. I neither thought of nor noticed anything but the working of the guns.[22]

David suggests that the young boys were eventually numbed towards the slaughter around them. They simply carried on with their duties ignoring the horrors. Ship's boy Olaudah Equiano casually noted 'remarkable' incidents during their attack on Louisbourg in 1758, such as the lieutenant being shot through the mouth while giving orders, or Olaudah marvelling at the scalp of an Indian chief that had been taken off by a Highlander.[23] Robert Hay saw one of his messmates dashed into pieces by a cannon shot: 'His flesh, as I collected the scattered fragments of it, creeped to my hand as if unwilling to part.'[24]

Evidently, the Navy needed to recruit their men at a very young age not just for the sake of getting them used to the natural hardships of a life at sea, but also so that they became accustomed to the horrors of war. In the words of naval surgeon Thomas Trotter: 'The mind, by custom and example, is thus trained to brave the fury of the elements, in their different forms, with a degree of contempt, at danger and death, that is to be met with no where else, and which has become proverbial.'[25] Thirteen-year-old William Dillon, later Vice Admiral of the Blue, remembered of his first battle: 'Never having been before present in an action of the kind, my curiosity and anxiety were beyond all bounds. The danger to which I exposed myself had not the slightest influence over me.'[26]

Facing dangers without fear, even with intentionally displayed unaffectedness, was the culture the Navy fostered, both among the men and the officers. It was probably the only defence mechanism to cope with what was the most dangerous profession of the time. However, we also have to remember that once again we are reliant on the available sources. Someone like William Dillon knew that even his private letters could be read by others, who would judge his suitability for a career in the Navy. Neither on board, nor in letters or memoirs, was there any space for admitting feelings that people might perceive as a weakness. William was thirteen years old, he had experienced an abrupt change in his living circumstances, and was now suddenly trapped in a dangerous adult world far away from the safety of his home and family – nobody would have been surprised, if, in a moment of privacy and reflection, a few tears rolled down his young face. But he mentions nothing. Especially since the execution of Admiral John Byng in 1759, for failing to do his utmost to recapture Minorca, the upper classes at sea were as much afraid of showing anything that could be viewed as cowardice or lack of masculinity as the lower classes.

Fourteen-year-old ship's boy Samuel Leech from the lower deck delivered a slightly more thoughtful analysis of his first engagement than William Dillon: he admits that even in old age remembering the events from his childhood was very painful.[27] This is what he recollected from his battle experience against an American ship in 1812:

> Our men kept cheering with all their might. I cheered with them, though I confess I scarcely knew for what. Certainly there was nothing very inspiriting in the aspect of things where I was stationed. So terrible had been the work of destruction round us, it was termed the slaughter-house. Not only had we had several boys and men killed or wounded, but several of the guns were disabled.[28]

From his shipmates Sam copied the ways to cope with the situation; carrying on with the fight appeared the only option:

> Our men fought like tigers. Some pulled off their jackets, others their jackets and vests; while some, still more determined, had taken off their shirts, and, with nothing but a handkerchief tied round the waistbands of their trowsers, fought like heroes. . . . I also observed a boy, named Cooper, stationed at a gun some distance from the magazine. He came to and fro on the full run, and appeared to be as 'merry as a cricket.' The third lieutenant cheered him along, occasionally, by saying, 'Well done, my boy, you are worth your weight in gold.'[29]

Everyone had to put on a brave face; anything else would have been dangerous. Some just functioned, others swallowed their anxieties, as Sam did:

> I have often been asked what were my feelings during this fight. I felt pretty much as I suppose every one does at such a time. That men are without thought when they stand amid the dying and the dead, is too absurd an idea to be entertained a moment. We all appeared cheerful, but I know that many a serious thought ran through my mind: still, what could we do but keep up a semblance, at least, of animation? To run from our quarters would have been certain death from the hands of our own officers; to give way

to gloom, or to show fear, would do no good, and might brand us with the name of cowards, and ensure certain defeat. Our only true philosophy, therefore, was to make the best of our situation, by fighting bravely and cheerfully.[30]

Charles Pemberton, though a pacifist, claimed that he just fought himself into frenzy and did not have any of the serious considerations Leech mentions:

> I had no time to be frightened during all this, for I was not in my right mind – I was in a whirl: the bustle, hallooing, hurraing, crashing, cracking, rattling, thundering, whizzing, and whistling, made me drunk and delirious; like a fellow in a tavern, who, when he is in the third heaven of jollity, smashes tables and chairs, dishes and glasses – dashes his fist through the door-panels and the windows, all senseless of the scarifying and bruises he inflicts upon himself in the indulgence of this fun: mine was an excitement even to frenzy, from the strangeness, and wondrous novelty of my position; and I dare say, if any one had set me the example, I should have ran away and hid myself if I could; only, it happens, that there are no back doors to escape by in these affairs.[31]

Charles had experienced the classic fight-or-flight mode, the rush of adrenalin, the additional blood streaming into his brain, a state in which physical pain is hardly recognised.

While fear might not be tolerated in this macho culture, irony was the accepted alternative. The sailors' outspoken trivialisation of death and injuries was one of the aspects that had initially impressed Jim Hawkins. Now it was harsh reality. The Navy needed the devil-may-care sort of seaman, and Jim had to adopt that attitude if he wanted to survive mentally unharmed. Sailor William Robinson described a fierce naval battle he was involved in as 'a grand display of fireworks, at the expense of John Bull; no gala night at Ranelagh or Vauxhall, could be compared to it.'[32] During the battle, one of William's shipmates had the calves of both of his legs shot away. His legs needed to be amputated immediately. Though no anaesthetics were used, William proudly pointed out that throughout the operation his mate did not utter a single syllable. Only at the end of it he exclaimed: 'Now to the devil with all the shoe-makers, I have done with them!'[33]

For those who survived there was the bonus of having tales to tell of fearless action in battle to make other sailors and people on land envious of not having lived through such character-forming events, rather than thanking the Lord that they had been spared from such slaughter. It is impossible to say how many boys and men fought themselves into a frenzy like Charles Pemberton, and how many quietly harboured such deeper concerns as ship's boy Sam Leech, who later in life became a devout Methodist:

> I thought a great deal, however, of the other world; every groan, every falling man, told me that the next instant I might be before the Judge of all the earth. For this, I felt unprepared; but being without any particular knowledge of religious truth, I satisfied

myself by repeating again and again the Lord's prayer, and promising that if spared I would be more attentive to religious duties than ever before. This promise I had no doubt, at the time, of keeping; but have learned since that it is easier to make promises amidst the roar of the battle's thunder, or in the horrors of shipwreck, than to keep them when danger is absent, and safety smiles upon our path.[34]

Sam was nevertheless amazed by the display of courage by his shipmates. On one occasion, when some of his crew got ready to board a small vessel, Sam observed how they got into their barge 'in as fine spirits as if they had been going on shore for a drunken spree. Such is the contempt of danger that prevails among sailors.'[35] There are stories of men sneaking into the small boats sent out to cut loose enemy ships, eager not to miss out on the action. The image of Hanway's bold youths 'whose Heads are turned to War' comes back to mind, and the young men's search for fight and thrills, glory and gain. Then again, cutting loose or plundering harmless merchant vessels promised a different kind of adventure from engaging in a close-range battle with an enemy warship. Enemy broadsides were not impressed by courage and manliness: their death came in the form of a lottery.

Sam Leech writing his memoirs of his wartime boyhood at sea is a notable exception, for which we must be thankful, amongst the thousands of ordinary

British Sailors Boarding a Man of War (1815), by J A Atkinson: the recapture of HMS *Hermione*, which had been handed over to the Spanish by ship's boy James Allen and his fellow mutineers.

ships' boys. Leech had a purpose: having become a Methodist, he wished to expose the brutality of naval war. The vast majority of stories of boys on the lower deck, however, remain left to our imagination when interpreting the Navy's official documents. The foregoing story of the two Marine Society boys George Lauder and John Read of the *Southampton* was chosen at random and was traced with the help of the Navy's muster rolls and battle reports. We could have chosen countless other ships' boys who had similar wartime experiences. Their dramatic fights and fates remain hidden behind sober entries in the Navy's records, in which captains describe battles like games of chess, leaving little space for individual heroics and suffering. Sam Leech gives us some insights into the nature of battle for a powder monkey, who had to sprint through a hailstorm of musket fire, cannon balls, wooden splinters, canister and grapeshot:

> My station was at the fifth gun on the main deck. It was my duty to supply my gun with powder, a boy being appointed to each gun in the ship on the side we engaged, for this purpose. A woollen screen was placed before the entrance to the magazine, with a hole in it, through which the cartridges were passed to the boys; we received them there, and covering them with our jackets, hurried to our respective guns. These precautions are observed to prevent the powder taking fire before it reaches the gun. . . . The roaring of cannon could now be heard from all parts of our trembling ship, and, mingling as it did with that of our foes, it made the most hideous noise. By-and-by I heard the shot strike the sides of our ship; the whole scene grew indescribably confused and horrible; it was like some awfully tremendous thunder-storm, whose deafening roar is attended by incessant streaks of lighting, carrying death in every flash, and strewing the ground with the victims of its wrath: only, in our case, the scene was rendered more horrible than that, by the presence of torrents of blood which dyed our decks. . . . The cries of the wounded now rang through all parts of the ship. These were carried to the cockpit as fast as they fell, while those more fortunate men, who were killed outright, were immediately thrown overboard.[36]

Beginning with having to supply his cannon, Sam soon had to provide for not one but three to four guns, as the boys next to him were wounded. Sam saw two of them fall in almost the same instant: one boy was hit in the leg by a large shot, the other had grape or canister shot crushing through his ankle. A stout Yorkshireman lifted the boy in his arms and quickly carried him into the cockpit, to the operating theatre. Here the two wounded boys would have been greeted by a fearsome sight: the surgeon and his mate smeared with blood from head to foot, looking more like butchers than doctors. Amidst the ongoing roar of battle the surgeon would hastily go to work. The two boys knew what to expect next; fear of infection determined the drastic step. For the first boy it was the entire leg, for the second boy 'just' the foot. The operation was done without any anaesthetics and in a hurry, for if it took too long the boy could die of shock or bleeding to death, or the wounds could become infected. Antiseptic practice was unknown.

First the surgeon took a knife to cut through the boy's skin, tissues and muscles right down to the bone, then he pulled back the flesh, so that he could take his saw and cut the bone a little higher up the leg.[37] Even for the hardened seamen, who assisted the surgeon by holding down the patients, amputations were the worst sight of them all. Sam Leech witnessed how the surgeon was 'using his knife and saw on human flesh and bones, as freely as the butcher at the shambles does on the carcass of the beast!'[38] The two boys on Sam's ship survived their operation, but they were now invalids for the rest of their lives. It was a rude awakening for Sam that this had little to do with his childhood fantasies. The enemy's guns were fired indiscriminately, and the young boys were as much a target as any grown man. Two other boys on board Sam's ship were killed in the same battle. A seaman witnessing their death told Sam that one of them had the powder that he carried catch fire, which almost burned the flesh off his face. The boy was in great agony, the seaman explained to young Sam, but 'luckily' he was soon relieved from his pain by a passing shot which cut him in half.

In 1794, thirteen-year-old future admiral William Dillon had among his gun crew a man called John Polly, who was very short in stature and joked to William that there was nothing to worry, because with such a small stature any shot would always pass over you. 'The words had not been long out his mouth when a shot cut his head right in two, leaving the tip of each ear remaining on the lower part of the cheek,' William still remembered graphically fifty years later. This was Dillon's first taste of battle. Any movies displaying such scenes of violence today would be deemed unsuitable for thirteen-year-olds. Yet Dillon claimed that even at his young age this did not shake his sense of duty: 'There was no withdrawing from our situation, and the only alternative was to face the danger with becoming firmness. The head of this unfortunate seaman was cut so horizontally that anyone looking at it would have supposed it had been done by the blow of an axe. His body was committed to the deep.'[39] The sailor's funeral was a quick affair; Jim Hawkins, regardless of his heroics, had no Nelsonian funeral to expect. There may have been a plinth waiting for fallen admirals, but Jim was often straight away tossed overboard to make space.

The agony did not stop with the battle: some of the wounded still struggled with death for days – fourteen-year-old Sam Leech tried to help as much as he could:

> One poor fellow who lay with a broken thigh, begged me to give him water. I gave him
> some. He looked unutterable gratitude, drank, and died. It was with exceeding difficulty

Learning the alphabet in an early nineteenth-century children's book: 'Z for Zeal'.

I moved through the steerage, it was so covered with mangled men, and so slippery with streams of blood. . . . I remember passing round the ship the day after the battle. Coming to a hammock, I found some one in it apparently asleep. I spoke: he made no answer. I looked into the hammock; he was dead. My messmates coming up, we threw the corpse overboard; that was no time for useless ceremony. The man had probably crawled to his hammock the day before, and, not being perceived in the general distress, bled to death! O War! who reveal thy miseries.[40]

Others had to come to terms with the loss of their friends – as Sam observed, with different reactions:

There was a poor boy there crying as if his heart would break. He had been servant to the bold boatswain, whose head was dashed to pieces. Poor boy! he felt that he had lost a friend. I tried to comfort him by reminding him that he ought to be thankful for having escaped death himself. . . . Some who had lost their messmates appeared to care nothing about it, while others were grieving with all the tenderness of women.[41]

Learning maths in an early nineteenth-century children's book:
'Nautical Arithmetic – Subtraction'.

These were all deaths related to fierce naval battles, but we should perhaps remember the statistics which tell us that in the mid century in most cases Jim's death would not happen in battle. One just has to follow, for example, the numerous unfortunate Marine Society boys who in 1757 joined the *Ramillies*,[42] Sir Edward Hawke's flagship in the abandoned attack on Rochefort, in which George Lauder took part in the *Southampton*. On board the *Ramillies* were three fatherless boys from Cambridgeshire, fourteen-year-olds William Finch and John Woolett, and sixteen-year-old James Gray. The three were transferred from the *Ramillies* to the *Prince George*, where in April 1758 a fire broke out which killed half of the crew. Terror and chaos reigned on board, as the *Prince George*'s chaplain Sharp remembered: 'I must be deficient even to attempt a description of the melancholy scene that was now before me; shrieking, cries, lamentations, bemoanings, raving, despair, and even madness itself, presented them-selves.'[43] Fires were a constant danger – a careless cook or smoker, or a candle – and with all the wood, the tar and the powder, a small fire would quickly develop into a major disaster. On the *Prince George* more lives could have been saved, complained the chaplain, had the merchant ships in the vicinity not kept a safe distance and been more concerned with fishing up geese, fowls, tables, chairs and other goods from the burning ship than with picking up her crew.

Meanwhile, those Marine Society boys who had stayed on the *Ramillies* did not fare any better than the three Cambridgeshire lads. Having been checked and considered healthy at the start of their career by the Society's surgeon, two thirds of them became ill on board the *Ramillies*. Five died in consequence at the hospital, and a further two were discharged sick and never returned. The rest had recovered their health, and seventeen Marine Society boys were still serving on board the *Ramillies*, when one evening in February 1760 disaster struck, one which was to live on in the local memory for decades to come. On her way from Plymouth to join Admiral Boscawen's Channel fleet, the *Ramillies* was caught by a violent gale, and while the crew struggled with a badly leaking hull, the wind pushed her further eastwards than anyone noticed. Land came in sight, land which to the master looked like Rame Head, the entrance to the Plymouth Sound. He concluded that returning into the safety of the Plymouth Sound was the best way out of danger.

There must have a been a look of horror on the faces of the master and the captain when they realised that what they considered to be Plymouth Sound was in fact the treacherous Bigbury Bay, and they were steering straight into it. Their desperate attempts to turn the ship around only led to the sails being torn apart and the masts being broken. The only option left was to drop the anchors and get rid of what was left of the masts, to stop the ship being pressed into the bay. For a moment it even appeared as if this final measure might get the situation under control. Big warships like the *Ramillies* carried several large anchors, yet however heavy these anchors were, the weak link remained the cables connecting them to the ship, and the *Ramillies'* cables snapped. At this point she was a hopeless case, and there was nothing her men could do to prevent her from ramming straight into the Bolt Head cliffs. The sailors were crushed on the rocks or drowned as the ship broke apart.

Many eighteenth-century sailors were bad swimmers; the Navy preferred to keep it that way, to curb desertions. There are plenty of stories of sailors who, when their ship's final hour had struck, would rather head for the stock of rum than for the water. And even the good swimmers on board the *Ramillies* that evening had few chances of survival, what with the rocks, the storm, the currents and the breaking ship. More than seven hundred drowned with the *Ramillies*, and only twenty-seven men survived, none of the Marine Society boys being amongst them. Over the following days, the corpses were washed onto the Devon shore, where surely local wreckers already waited like vultures to pick them over, together with anything else of value which might present itself – not a glorious end for Jim Hawkins, to be torn apart by the very people for whom he was sent to fight. But perhaps both Jim and the wreckers just did what they were obliged to in order to survive. Nowadays there is a car park on the site where most of the sailors from the *Ramillies* were thrown into a mass grave. 'Come, all you pretty fair maids, weep with me, who lost your loves on the *Ramillies*,' the sailors sang in the decades to come. The careers of the ships' boys on board the *Ramillies* were short ones and unhappy ones, and they ended with not a Frenchman in sight. The sea demanded its toll of lives, careless of how young those lives were.

In some cases, Jim's career was cut short by being captured by the enemy. Unfortunately, at this point it becomes almost impossible for the historian to continue tracing the boy's story. Experiences in captivity varied; most likely Jim's captors were French. Apparently the treatment of prisoners of war was comparatively humane throughout the century, unlike in more recent years. Nevertheless, imprisonment, regardless of where, was always highly dangerous in the eighteenth century, because of the likelihood of the prisoners falling victim to disease. With regards to our 'sample boys' in the Seven Years War, there are allegations that one in eight prisoners died,[44] although prisoners with fatal battle injuries distort the statistics. In 1811, physician Gilbert Blane rebutted claims that French prisoners were maltreated in Britain by stating that only one in fifty-five died.[45] Luckily for Jim, prisoners were usually only held until an exchange was arranged. It was even more gentlemanly for the officers, who were allowed to walk free under the promise that they would not serve in the Navy until they had been officially exchanged with a prisoner.

To us today all this sounds an unbelievably honourable sport, but perhaps nationalism has indeed removed Europeans very far from this world over the past two centuries. Napoleon worsened relations by rarely allowing any prisoner exchanges; he claimed that many English seamen simply did not want to be returned to their 'floating prisons', that is, the Royal Navy. Napoleon may have been right that many did not want to re-enter the Royal Navy, but they certainly also did not fancy staying in a French prison where they had their possessions taken away and endured pitiable food rations, as well as dangerously unhygienic conditions.

We find a few colourful stories of captured boys in the published memoirs, although it is hard to say how representative their adventures were. Fifteen-year-old George Mackay was one of those boys from better-off families aiming at an officer's career. He was taken in August 1794 by two French frigates off Algeria.[46] George was angry that his crew seemed more concerned about hiding their prize money than putting up a fight against the French, 'with the exception of a few who, like true British tars, finding they were in the hands of the enemy, broke open the spirit-room and in a few minutes totally forgot the situation.' After a few days sailing, George and the other prisoners reached Toulon. They then had to endure a hundred-mile march northwards to their prison in Gap – an unpleasant ordeal for sea legs. Once they reached their inland destination, George was allowed a remarkable freedom of movement, presumably because of his family background. He even had money sent to him from the prize agent from Livorno. Fortunately for George he also spoke a little French.

However, despite such advantages George had had enough after one year of being a prisoner and tried to escape. Even so, he was caught on both attempts. Another year passed, and there was still no prisoner exchange in view. George made a third attempt, managing to get as far as Paris, where he was once again apprehended and returned to Gap. This time they put him in a prison for thirty days as a punishment. But that was not the worst: George also heard that during his absence his ship's crew had been exchanged with French prisoners. Remarkably, George was then allowed to make his own way to Toulon, to arrange his exchange, but that did not work either. Instead he fell in love with a fourteen-year-old French girl, but sadly she soon died of the smallpox, leaving George depressed and ill in hospital until 1798. Frustrated about now spending his fourth year in captivity, George embarked on another escape attempt. Finally he was successful, running away via Switzerland and Germany. Happy about being free again, in Cuxhaven, Northern Germany, George boarded the packet boat to Yarmouth, which delivered him back to England – and straight into the arms of the press gang. George was immediately back in the wooden world and on his way to the West Indies before there was any chance of paying a visit to his home.

The most cheerful boyhood prisoner-of-war story is to be found in Sam Leech's memoirs. Having been captured by an American ship in 1812, fourteen-year-old Sam already felt perfectly at home among the American sailors as he was brought to New York as prisoner. He even messed with them: 'All idea that we had been trying to shoot out each other's brains so shortly before, seemed forgotten. We ate together, drank together, joked, sung, laughed, told yarns; in short, a perfect union of ideas, feelings, and purposes, seemed to exist among all hands.'[47] When they arrived, Sam, his crew and his ship were proudly presented to the New Yorkers. As Sam's ship lay in the harbour, her crew waiting for an exchange, the clever youngster found a profitable activity: he started tour-guiding curious New Yorkers around the ship, colourfully describing to them all the battle action, and pointing out places were particular individuals had died. His American visitors took their young English guide to their hearts. The word spread in New York about the courteous English boy who would take visitors on a tour of the ship and relive the battle in which this ship of the mighty Royal Navy had been captured by American sailors. All the while, Sam not only saved up money for his plan to escape, but also developed a liking for the Americans which made him think that the New World could be a better future home for him than old England.

The happiest end to Jim Hawkins' career as a Navy servant was being rated as a paid seaman. According to the Navy Regulations, rating was to be based strictly on seafaring experience. An able seaman had to have served at least three years, whilst an ordinary seaman was commonly assumed to have at least one year's experience. However, following the careers of a sample of boys in the mid century shows that in practice length of service was often irrelevant when it came to rating the boys.[48] Some of Jim's mates were rated as able seamen within two years or even less, whilst others remained servants for many more years. Age appears to have been the more decisive factor. In the mid century, Jim's comrades were rated as ordinary seamen mainly between the age of seventeen to nineteen, and as able seamen between eighteen and twenty-one, seemingly independent of their actual number of years at sea. There was also no step-by-step career ladder, and captains took some liberties when rating. Some lads progressed straight from servant to able seaman, others were first made ordinary seaman and then later able seaman. There was no examination or formal procedure in the rating of the boys; it was merely a matter of the captain having the letters 'ab' or 'ordy', rather than servant, scribbled behind Jim's name in the muster book's column for quality. Most servants were allowed to skip the quality of a 'landman', the lowest 'rank' on board.

Admittedly, the Navy's muster lists contain some curious examples of boys being rated, so caution must be exercised when drawing conclusions from the entries. Those servants from better-off families, for example, who were destined for an officer's career, could go on a rollercoaster of ratings in the muster book. They often progressed rapidly to midshipmen, despite the Navy Regulations forbidding the rating of anyone above his ability and experience, and specifically stating that a midshipman had to have served four years at sea and had to be 'in all Respects qualified for it'.[49] The memories of William Robinson's tyrannical twelve-year-old midshipman spring into mind.[50]

Boys aiming at an officer's career were sometimes mustered with no apparent logic, going from servant to midshipman, to able seaman and back to servant, or whatever appeared convenient, while in practice they were steadily educated to become officers. And then there were even those among them whose names were listed in the muster books, when in reality they were nowhere to be seen on board. Instead they were clocking in their years of seafaring experience safely on land, whilst being taught the art of navigation in schools – and also no doubt, indirectly, the art of creative muster-book keeping. Novelist Patrick O'Brian, in his *Master and Commander* (1970), has the lieutenant of Jack Aubrey's ship explain to the newly arrived 'landsman' and surgeon Stephen Maturin:

> Never let a mere word grieve your heart. We have nominal captain's servants who are, in fact, midshipmen; we have nominal able seamen on our books who are scarcely breeched – they are a thousand miles away and still at school; we swear we have not shifted any backstays, when we shift them continually; and we take many oaths that nobody believes.[51]

Although the pedantic historian feels the urge to point out that the quality of a captain's servant had already been abolished at the time in which O'Brian placed his novel, we should take the warning words of his lieutenant seriously.

Yet all the oddities in the rating apart, it appears that for humble future seamen such as Jim, the Navy had an age concept according to which servants were commonly rated as ordinary seaman around the age of eighteen, and/or as able seaman around nineteen to twenty, regardless of how many years they had been collecting seafaring experience. Rating all boys at ages from eighteen to twenty-one was in any way only fair, as others at the same age and with no seafaring experience could enter the Navy as paid landsmen. Although the boys were indeed already taking part in the sailing of the ship before being rated, turning seventeen to twenty-one-year-olds into wage-earning adults still differed very positively from the long unpaid servitude some boys faced in apprenticeships on land. With regards to becoming a fully-paid adult speedily, the Navy outdid other career options open to poor boys, and the hope for prize money promised even more.

Further advancement within the Navy was difficult for Jim because of his humble origins, but not impossible. Petty officer rank was something Jim could set his eyes upon, yet *From Powder Monkey to Admiral* (1870), W H G

Kingston's boys' fiction set in Nelson's Navy, was just that, a fiction. It is no wonder that Kingston's novel was criticised for giving ordinary boys an impossible ambition, though admittedly by his time class barriers had hardened. Yet also in the eighteenth century, the lonely inn at the coastal road to Bristol, in which Jim Hawkins had grown up, yielded a rather unrealistic promise for the lively youth: the inn was named the Admiral Benbow after Admiral John Benbow (1653-1702), whom people said had risen from humble origins to admiral. Benbow was an exception, if not partly a myth. Class mattered when it came to the highest ranks, although education, connections and merit could get those from the lower middle class a long way up the ranks in the eighteenth-century Navy.

Among the poorest, however, even an ambitious and bright ship's boy like Robert Hay ran against the class boundary: Robert had bought himself an old map, and practised with his master's mathematical instruments in his cabin, but could not surmount the barrier arising from his social background which did not allow him to check the sun on deck with those instruments:

> To get any opportunity of taking the meridian altitude of the sun, and thereby ascertaining the latitude by observation, was of course wholly out of the question. But circumstances occurred which enabled me to get the ship's place at noon, almost every day, and of course to trace on the chart with a pencil her daily course and progress.
> It was a rule aboard that every midshipman should send in daily to the Captain on a slip of paper a statement of the course and distance made good since the noon of the day before, the ship's present latitude and longitude, both by observation and dead reckoning, together with the bearings and distance of the point of land we intended first to make. These slips, quaintly called day's works, were generally handed to the ward-room sentinel, who sent them into the Captain by one of the boys. I took care to throw myself pretty frequently in the way of these little errands, and had thus the means of seeing almost every day the ship's place at noon, as stated in the accounts of several different observers.[52]

But in the end Robert demonstrated how class barriers could be overcome and progress be made outside the Navy. Back on land, he was able to enrol for a course in navigation and eventually became a captain of a trading boat on the canal. Wise career moves between Royal Navy and merchant shipping, and gaining access to education, could allow the successful rise of less-privileged boys. The prime example is the failed grocery-shop boy and collier apprentice Captain James Cook. Young James Cook was fortunate enough to have his first school education paid for by his father's employer.

In the Navy, it was crucial for Jim to have a good relationship with his master or another officer. The Navy was an organisation arranged into many separate divisions, its ships. Whoever wanted to make a career in this organisation had to stick close to those at the top of these divisions, choose a patron, and follow him through the ranks of the organisation. Next to Benbow, there were a few other personalities who made it from relatively humble beginnings to the highest ranks. Rear Admiral John Pasco (1771/4- 1853), famous for rephrasing Nelson's signal that 'England expects that every man will do his duty' at Trafalgar, was the son of a caulker from the Plymouth dockyard. John Smith, Post Captain, was allegedly the only Marine Society boy ever to reach such a high rank.[53] Smith's mother died when he was very young, and his father became insane, lost all his money and died in a lunatic asylum, leaving nothing for his children. Smith was apprenticed to a cooper, but broke off his apprenticeship aged sixteen and applied to the Marine Society in 1797.

However, John Smith had also attended a boarding school before his father died, and his relatives included Rear Admiral Isaac Smith and the wife of Captain James Cook. So, although poor, he had family connections and education, which aided his rise. On board the Marine Society's training ship, young John was already described as jolly, fresh-faced, and a very good boy and reader,[54] and Smith was clever enough to make use of the Marine Society's influence.[55] Promoted to lieutenant in 1805, he first asked the Society to put its weight behind his promotion to commander in 1809, which the Society did by writing to the Admiralty. The Admiralty appeared slightly offended, telling the Society that there were plenty of equally qualified candidates in the Navy. But three years later his attempt was successful. This time the Society put its full weight behind Smith, arguing that Smith's promotion would also be a recognition of its work over the past fifty years and an encouragement to all their boys. Smith was promoted to commander in July 1812 and to captain in 1822. The Society thought that Smith's rise was proof of the refreshing meritocracy that the Navy allowed. Yet his case also exemplifies that he was the only one of the twenty-five thousand Marine Society boys who ever made it this far, and that possibly without Smith getting the Society to act as his patron over years, and turning the matter of his promotion into an acknowledgement of the Society's value in general, he might not have progressed.

On the Isle of Wight, people still tell the story of Admiral John Hopson, who had apparently been an orphan and parish apprentice to a tailor before he ran away to sea. And then there was Rear Admiral Thomas Troubridge (c.1756-1807), the son of a pastry-cook with a shop in the Strand.[56] Troubridge was even created a baronet in 1799. Ironically it was Troubridge who, when asked how he defined mutinous behaviour among his sailors, allegedly came up with the most sarcastic and arrogant expression of class barriers: 'whenever I see a Fellow look, as if he was thinking, I say that's mutiny.'[57] Troubridge considered sailors who had learned to read and write to be a potential nuisance. Charles Pemberton's comments come back to mind, that those men who had been promoted from the ranks, or from the mast, were often the harshest disciplinarians.[58] Possibly there is an element of truth in this assertion, be it because 'it is their turn now', as Pemberton suggested, or because such men felt that they had to draw a clear line in order to be accepted in their new class.

Naval historian Nicholas Rodger has suggested that until the 1790s the Navy had been comparatively open to individuals rising on merit, although perhaps not to those from the poorest, but at least from the lower middle classes. The sons of warrant officers, for example, had good chances of progress, and even a few commissioned officers had come from before the mast. The upper classes on land occasionally voiced their irritation about the rough characters from lower birth who had climbed the social ladder through naval service. To Rodger, the introduction of the three-class system for boys in 1794 signified the putting up of more solid barriers to upward mobility.[59] From then on it was predetermined who could become an officer even before the youths were at sea and could prove their suitability. However, according to historian Samantha Cavell's recent research, even in the early years of the tripartite class system boys from less privileged families were still able to progress.[60] Indeed, the muster books still show movements of boys from second- to first-class boys. Only once Napoleon was defeated and demobilisation began did the Navy's class barriers become more rigid. At that point, the Navy had increased its popularity hugely with its celebrated victories, yet the posts available were greatly reduced. Thus, while the French navy had moved in the spirit of the revolution from promoting sailors according to merit rather than birth, the British Navy was about to move in the opposite direction.

However, even in the days of Jim Hawkins, when the boys were still all labelled as servants, in practice the division of who was meant to become an officer or not was already there. It manifested itself, for example, when the boys were taught separately by the schoolmaster on board, or when the privileged servants received personal training from their officers. Furthermore, those with career ambitions usually acquired their navigation skills in schools on land, which poor boys could not afford. It needed an exceptionally self-motivated boy, together with a patron, to rise through the ranks. But let us not be too self-righteous, and forget that even in many large organisations today – whether Navy, business or politics – patronage, loyalty, connections and education are still factors which can facilitate progress.

165

Jim Hawkins clearly faced great dangers when he set foot on board, dangers of which his teenage mind had probably not been aware. But if he managed to stay alive, it was guaranteed that worries like poverty or the servitude of an apprentice, which once drove many of Jim's mates into the Navy, would be consigned to the past. Yet was all this a permanent improvement, or only temporary? We shall see next what happened when the war which had dragged so many of Jim's comrades to sea suddenly came to an end.

CHAPTER 8

Jim's Return from the Sea

SIX years after thirteen-year-old Robert Hay had sneaked out of his family home in Paisley one morning and run away to the Navy, and five years after he had last seen the home shore, Robert's ship finally returned to Britain:

> Early in July 1809 we struck soundings in the British Channel. It would be difficult to describe the sensations which pervaded our minds when soundings were first announced. The sound operated like a charm. All the endearing recollections of wives, children, parents, brothers, sisters and friends rushed with intense pleasure of the mind. Even those who had not relatives to excite such pleasure, cast their thoughts back to the days of youth and rejoiced over the endearing scenes of nativity.[1]

Years had sometimes passed when Jim Hawkins finally returned home. Most of the boys were recruited into the Navy in times of war, and they had to serve at least until peace arrived. Visiting home in between was hardly possible; only letters could have kept Jim in touch with his family or friends. Those who, like Robert Hay, had living parents to whom to return, were not just full of joy, but also a little anxious when they knocked at the door of their family homes, worrying if their parents were still in good health. A feeling of guilt about not having been there as a support might have crept into the minds of former runaways who had matured at sea. Jim might knock, the door open, joy and celebrations erupt – but not always, though. Sometimes there would be a look of confusion, for Jim would have grown up at sea, so much so that some parents struggled to recognise their sons. Robert Hay, and also Sam Leech's cousin, who had been at sea for eleven years, played a heart-warming trick on their mothers when they returned: the mothers not recognising their sons, they introduced themselves as good friends of their sons, told them about all the adventures they had been through together, and only at the very end of their stories did they reveal their true identity. Only sailors had a knack for spinning such a good yarn.

Spinning a dramatic yarn, or singing the same, was one of the skills Jim might acquire during his years at sea. A few made good use of this by publishing their memoirs. The Marine Society boy Thomas Potter Cooke (1786-1864) even did one better and became a famous actor and stage

Turner, *A Sailor Relating his Adventures* (1803).

manager in London, specialising in playing sailors. Cooke, the son of a surgeon, had run away and enlisted via the Marine Society as a tender ten-year-old, pretending to be thirteen.[2] He served until the Peace of Amiens in 1802. Two years later he started his career as an actor. Audiences loved Cooke for giving the sailors he played not just a romantic touch, but that of 'thoughtfulness and mystery, deep-toned passion and pathos'[3] – adjectives which were rarely applied to Jack Tar at the beginning of the eighteenth century. Charles Pemberton, a runaway from very poor parents who had been pressed into the Navy, also tried his hand at acting and theatre managing after his time at sea, although with less success than Cooke.[4] Pemberton was a sailor of great intellect, but perhaps this had also made him an outsider on board; he was often appalled by the behaviour of his shipmates. Pemberton eventually found his calling not as a religious preacher, as did other former sailors who were shocked by their shipmates' behaviour, but by becoming a lecturer for the Mechanics' Institutes, which offered educational opportunities for the working poor. Sailors turned actors like Cooke and Pemberton were rare exceptions, though. For others their storytelling and singing talents earned them a few drinks or some free nights at an inn, but this was nothing to make a living from. Jim had to make a decision about his future, whether there was a place for him to settle down, or whether he would continue to sail across the oceans and follow the sailor's maxim 'a Rowling Stone never gathers Moss'. Yet was this decision entirely up to him?

T P Cooke as Ben Backstay.

T P Cooke as Long Tom Coffin.

If Jim wanted to stay at sea he had to face the peacetime labour market. Most boys had been drawn into the Navy by war, but what happened when peace returned? The Navy's demand for manpower during peacetime amounted to only about an eighth of the number of men required during wartime. Hence only an eighth of Jim's comrades could remain in the Royal Navy. Even those who stayed were not guaranteed permanent employment, for until 1853 there was no such thing as continuous service; instead sailors were hired whenever needed. Jim had been trained as a sailor, he had fought for King, country and commerce, but when peace came his seafaring future was suddenly uncertain. The question is whether the peacetime economy offered

T P Cooke as a tipsy sailor (1828).

sufficient employment opportunities. It was a question which worried not only Jim, but also the people back home on land. They feared the release of thousands of men, 'all accustomed to the use of arms, and many of them to rapine and plunder', as the eighteenth-century economist Adam Smith wrote.[5]

Demobilisation was often marred by a notable rise in crime back home, and on the seas, too. Privateers sometimes just continued what they had been doing all the time, the difference being that their raids were no longer sanctioned by the British government. Their labels in British eyes changed from privateer to pirate, but their actions remained almost the same, depending upon how much they were driven by plunder or by nationalism and anti-Catholicism. Worried about unemployed sailors, some concerned thinkers suggested at the end of the Seven Years War that seamen should be given land for free along the southern coastline of England and in the western isles of Scotland.[6] Others proposed to settle them in the new territories just won in Canada. And Jonas Hanway, always a man for practical solutions, thought of combining his two favourite charities, the Marine Society and the Magdalen Hospital, by safely marrying off the returning sailors to repenting prostitutes. It is possible that some of Jim Hawkins' mates indeed joined the likes of Long John Silver to make a living. Some historians argue that the difficult labour market in effect often forced Jim into a life of violent crime and piracy,[7] where he also hoped that prizes and ranks would be more fairly distributed than in the Navy.

But the life of an outlaw was not the only option. Things did not look that bleak, as Jim could hope to take over the jobs of deceased seamen in the Royal and merchant navies. Many experienced old salts never returned to the labour market, having become casualties of war. Even the usually upbeat Marine Society, which proudly advertised that the majority of the ten thousand men and boys it had clothed during the Seven Years War had found employment soon after the war, had to add that it only referred to those who had survived.[8] The supply of sailors was furthermore reduced by seamen who had already retired from seafaring, or were about to, and who had only been called back into it by war. And finally, the number of available seamen was lowered further, as most of the foreigners who had filled the gaps in British crews were forced to leave. Extraordinary allowances for foreigners on board British ships went back to the limitations directed by the Navigation Acts. Although these foreigners had done their duty as England expected, the larger part of them now had to vacate their jobs in favour of British sailors – bad news for them, good news for Jim.

Commercial interests had been the driving force behind eighteenth-century wars, and as long as these wars went in Britain's favour an increase in commerce, and hence more jobs for Jim, could be expected. Wars were often global conflicts, and the desire to open up and dominate trading opportunities with the aid of Britain's protectionist Navigation Acts stood at their heart. However, Jim did not always reap all the commercial benefits for which he fought: the increase in British maritime trade was met by an increase of the ships' ton-per-sailor ratios, which means that Jim's employment chances did not expand quite as rapidly as British trade.[9] There was no marked increase in wages for sailors throughout the eighteenth century, suggesting that there was at least no shortage of seamen – with the exception of wartime. There would have been good times and bad times for Jim if he chose to stick to seafaring. Yet it is perhaps impossible to give a definitive answer on his future prospects at sea, as being a sailor was never a permanent employment, being always influenced by seasons, trade volumes, politics and hostilities, and also dependent upon Jim's personal health, luck and ability to lay by money for hard times.

On the other hand, if Jim ended his seafaring career, and abandoned his youthful dreams of fortune and self-fulfilment, then he would receive, just like any sailor and soldier, an important reward designed to help him settle down on land: the liberty to take up any trade he desired in any town he wanted.[10] This was a useful perk at a time when changing one's place of abode or trade was heavily restricted by settlement and apprenticeship laws, and by the privileges of corporations. Jim was given a flexibility which others seeking employment did not have, or only achieved by moving illegally and having to live in fear of being deported or prosecuted. Unfortunately, in most cases our Jim had gone to sea at an early age and had not learned fully any trade. Some servants to warrant officers might have picked up a bit of their master's trade while at sea. Much depended on Jim's eagerness to make productive use of the idle time on board, as well as having the fortune to encounter shipmates willing to share the secrets of a trade or give him unselfish career advice.

An ambitious boy like Robert Hay, brought up by poor but caring parents, managed to get a taste of various arts while at sea. He learned how to make and sell straw hats, how to shape and sew his clothes, and how to turn wood, as well as some arithmetic, French, and how to play the German flute. Then one day the ship's carpenter approached the then sixteen-year-old Robert and joked that a boy of his age should not still be a 'shoe-boy' to an officer, and told him it was much better to learn the shipwright's business. Robert understood that here was a unique opportunity. He moved from being a servant to being rated as one of the carpenter's crew on board, and learned a skill to build upon in his later life on land. On land, shipwrights and caulkers were quite distinct, but at sea Robert learned some of everything, thus keeping his future options open. Furthermore, now aged sixteen and thus earlier than many apprentices on land, Robert was paid for his work and even made something extra whenever his crew helped with the repairs of merchant vessels. And by necessity and wisdom Robert invested this money in some tools of the trade.

A further aid in settling down on land was that Jim would receive a substantial amount of money when he was paid off in the form of his wages and prize money; he was forced to save up his money by the Navy withholding his pay, and by not having many opportunities to spend money. The only question was whether to use this lump sum as an aid to settling down, or whether to act according to maritime custom and spend it all at once as if there were no tomorrow. As long as the sea was his only home, the latter option appeared the 'safer' action, for his time on land was brief, places to invest money were hard to find, and money taken on board could be lost. Evidently, much of Jim's success in settling down depended on his ability to

A Rich Privateer Brought Safe into Port,
by Two First-Rates (1782), by **Carington Bowles**.

change the attitudes he had acquired among seafarers. Sometimes loyalty to old shipmates who had settled down would help Jim with reintegration into life on land. Reunions with former shipmates could be moving scenes: 'Observe the grasp of each other's hand; the delight that glows on their countenances as each looks at the other, and marks the change made by the encroachments of time, which warns him that in his face too are the marks of increasing years',[11] wrote sailor John Bechervaise about two old shipmates meeting each other – such a heart-warming description, it might fuel the case for the study of homoeroticism in the Navy. Yet it can also be interpreted in the context of Bechervaise's speculations about what both men might have been through together, how close they may have been for years, and for how long they might have been out of contact with each other. The rich one always gives to the poorer one, Bechervaise enthused, and in the sailor tradition: 'A public-house almost invariably follows the meeting, which most probably is prolonged till one or both are intoxicated'.

Love, or the longing for it, should nevertheless not be underestimated as an incentive for Jim to settle down. Ever since he had reached puberty, the women to whom Jim had been close had usually been those who were paid for their attentions. If Jim had a childhood sweetheart at home, it was possible that during his long absence she had found a new partner. 'A wife in every port' sounded appealing, but there were times when the sailor worried if his favourite wife back home was any more capable of controlling her urges than he was. Hudson's hornpipe ditty 'Jack Robinson' spelled out the sailor's worst fears:

> The perils and dangers of the voyage were past,
> And the ship at Portsmouth arrived at last,
> The sails all furled, and the anchor cast,
> The happiest of the crew was Jack Robinson.
> Says the lady, says she, 'I've changed my state,'
> 'Why, you don't mean,' says Jack, 'that you've got a mate;
> You know you promised me.' Says she, 'I couldn't wait,
> For no tidings could I gain of you, Jack Robinson.'[12]

If there were any among Jim's mates that turned into Jack Robinson, then that was clearly an incentive not to settle down. As Jack sang:

> 'But to fret and to stew about it's all in vain,
> I'll get a ship and go to Holland, France or Spain,
> No matter where; to Portsmouth I'll ne'er come again,'
> And he was off afore you could say Jack Robinson.

All those whose sweethearts were still available were at least warned by 'Jack Robinson'. Jealousy could overcome Jim's desire to rove about the oceans, as much as a feeling of responsibility about remaining close to his ageing parents, and if Jim longed for a steady relationship, then he needed to stay nearer to home. Jim would often make various attempts to settle down, repeatedly being called back to seafaring by the need for money or a longing for the excitement of the sea. Remarkably, many of Jim's mates were still put off by the more confined workplaces on land, even though after their first voyages they should have learned that ships, too, were very confined workplaces.

For some of Jim's fellow ships' boys the end of hostilities came too early, that is, before they had been rated as seamen. These boys faced the most difficult future. The reduced number of servant positions in the peacetime Navy were mainly reserved for the sons of wealthier families, and the labour market was flooded with sailors who were better qualified than they were. The plight of these lads was also of great concern to the Marine Society, which feared in the 1760s that a lot of them would be left stranded at the end of the Seven Years War. For a charity which wished to encourage more youngsters to go to sea, and thought that sending them to sea would also eradicate the problem of teenage delinquency, a failure to reintegrate on the part of these returnees would have put the entire undertaking into question. The last thing the Society wanted was to see their boys back on the streets, hardened by the slaughter at sea, and with no prospect of future employment.

When complaints about discharged boys 'lurking about' the streets of harbour towns reached the Society,[13] it sprang into action. The logical idea was to place these boys as apprentices in the merchant navy or in waterborne trades, so that the youths could build on their seafaring experience, and also so that they would be readily available if war broke out again, and this was a direction which some servants would have taken even without the Society's assistance. One of those servants yet to be rated, paid off by the Navy at the end of the Seven Years War, was Mary Lacy. Her master, the carpenter, had always promised that he would apprentice her to his trade after the war. The boatswain on board her ship, however, had warned Mary not to rely too much on the carpenter's promises,[14] but the former nevertheless advised Mary still to embark on an apprenticeship as a shipwright, and not to be put off by the further seven years of training. Learning a proper trade, the boatswain explained to Mary, was much safer than merely remaining a sailor, at a time when so many sailors were being paid off.

Other boys might have been a lot less keen on entering an apprenticeship, for it entailed the long servitude that they had tried to avoid by enlisting in the Royal Navy. The particular nature of young Jim's new apprenticeship certainly mattered. The Marine Society hoped to be able to get the masters to bind the discharged servants for only three to five years, depending on how long the youngsters had already served at sea, so that the boys would be out of their apprenticeships at around the age of nineteen. But the Society also knew very well that while the supply of boys exceeded the demand, the masters had the stronger bargaining position, and would try to bind the boys for as long as possible as apprentices, to make the most out of their cheap labour. Even worse, at the bottom end of maritime apprenticeships there was not even a guarantee for continuous employment, as some apprenticeship indentures contained clauses which ruled out any work being provided during the winter months, and this would also mean no food and accommodation. Other apprenticeships were at least promising some unspecified alternative employment on land for the winter, whatever that might turn out to be.

The Marine Society inserted advertisements in newspapers and put up posters in public places, inviting all boys who had been discharged from the Navy to apply to the Society. Captains of paid-off ships were asked to send all boys younger than seventeen, who had no means to support themselves, nor any larger sums of money due to them, and who were also unlikely to be rated soon. The boys were kept in ships for up to three months, or until the Society found an apprenticeship for them. In Chatham, Portsmouth, and Plymouth the Society had old naval vessels at its disposal – the Lords of the Admiralty had requested them from the King, in acknowledgement of the many good young seamen provided by the Society and also of the importance of preventing them from becoming vagabonds or thieves.[15] Lists were prepared of all the boys, recording how long and in what quality they had served, whether their parents were alive and, if so, whether they were able to care for their son. The lists were sent to the secretary of the Society in London, and the Society then invited owners and masters of ships and water-related businesses, or any other interested masters, to inspect the boys as potential apprentices.

Finding placements for the boys was no mean task. The Society even asked for masters from the colonies, if the boys were willing to bid farewell to Britain.[16] Ideally, all boys would have received apprenticeships at sea. However, the Society was disappointed by the response of maritime masters. By December 1763, out of 295 former Navy servants the Society had placed only twenty-nine in merchant shipping, fifteen with fishermen, and nine with watermen and lightermen. Instead of staying connected to water, seventy-one had been placed in a 'mechanic trade', seventeen with manufacturers, six in public houses, one in agriculture, and sixty-seven had been given some pocket money so that they could return home and find themselves some work.[17] It seems that for many of Jim's younger comrades the sea remained only a temporary episode in their lives. The uplifting aspect for the Marine Society was that in the case of eighty boys the naval officers agreed to keep them for three more years as servants in peacetime.

As masters were difficult to find there was the danger that some youngsters would end up in apprenticeships where they would be misused as cheap labour. The Society's dream of binding the boys only till the age of nineteen remained a dream for many of the ex-Navy servants. Instead they were bound until their early twenties. According to John Fielding, the difficulty in finding a decent master on land was due to the fact that boys were often rejected merely because they had been at sea.[18] The Royal Navy, the very institution to which the 'Idle Apprentice' had been sent so that he would be taught proper discipline, now apparently served as a badge of dishonour. To be fair to the Navy though, it never intended to be a re-educational institution for society's misfits. Furthermore, one very important aspect that Fielding failed to mention was that the bad reputation of these boys did not just come from having served in the Navy, but rather more from the fact that Fielding and the Marine Society had praised their schemes as police measures. It was no wonder that the public now feared that a boy coming from the Marine Society could be a troublesome youth.

In the Society's records, we only discover a few cases of masters who actually found their new apprentices too ill-disciplined. One waterman complained that his apprentice John Rustoll, a sixteen-year-old son of a soldier, behaved 'most dangerously bad'.[19] The Society could only advise him to seek the help of a magistrate. Another master returned his boy, complaining of his very evil conduct in drinking, swearing and such like.[20] The Society cancelled the indentures, lodged the boy in the Hoxton workhouse, and started to look for a master at sea – once again the only solution for a misbehaving boy appeared to be a maritime apprenticeship. Use of 'naval language' had also put an end to the short interlude as an apprentice on land of John Cremer: 'I being bred on board a man-of-War,' John writes, he used to address his master's maid as 'bitch'.[21] This delighted his fellow apprentices, but not his master, who terminated John's apprenticeship, leading John's family to the realisation that the only solution for the boy was to send him off to sea again.

The master of the Hoxton workhouse, where the Marine Society temporarily lodged some of the boys returned from the Navy, visited the Society one day in 1763 to complain that the behaviour of the lads was outrageously bad. His complaint was supported by the Society's apothecary

Henry Haskey, who, when visiting the accommodation, found that the youths were 'very insolent' towards him.[22] The workhouse master pleaded with the Society not to send any more older lads, as they appeared uncontrollable. The father of Thomas Stillwell visited the Society and begged them to send his son to sea again, 'on account of the temptations Youth are exposed to when unemployed.'[23] John Fielding, however, proudly noted that remarkably few of his boys had reappeared at his court for criminal offences,[24] although it probably comes down to how we want to read such a statement, and furthermore, once again the death toll, and also the fact that the boys had matured at sea, should be taken into account.

Behind those sometimes 'jolly' stories of young sailors failing to re-integrate into society on land lay more serious issues: in all those years Jim's mates had not only been detached from their homes, so that some felt nowhere really at home, they had also spent their formative years in the Navy. They were used to being shouted or even beaten out of bed by the boatswain and having their lives regulated like clockwork. So far, being on land had meant living as if there were no tomorrow, spending their money knowing that the time for shore leave was limited. And that is exactly how many of Jim's mates behaved when they were fully discharged and paid off. They entered the harbour towns with pockets full of cash, spent it all, lived like a bird freed from its cage, and when the money ran out, they did not know where to find their next berth. It did not help that they were paid in lump sums. Sailors often struggled to arrange their life on land now that it was in their own hands, sometimes (intentionally or not) they did not even speak the same language any more, and many are said to have been naive and easy prey for dubious traders. Ransome, the cabin boy in Stevenson's novel *Kidnapped* (1886), had been frightened by the sailors' stories of what life on land was like: 'In a town, he thought every second person a decoy, and every third house a place in which seamen would be drugged and murdered.'[25]

At the end of the eighteenth century, naval physician Thomas Trotter summarised the problems the returned Jim Hawkins faced:

> Excluded, by the employment which they have chosen, from all society, but people of similar dispositions, the deficiencies of education are not felt, and information on general affairs is seldom courted. Their pride consists in being reputed a thorough bred seaman; and they look upon all landmen, as beings of inferior order. This is marked, in a singular manner, by applying the language of seamanship to every transaction of life, and sometimes with a pedantic ostentation. Having little intercourse with the world, they are easily defrauded, and dupes to the deceitful, wherever they go: their money is lavished with the most thoughtless profusion; fine clothes for this girl, a silver watch, and silver buckles for himself, are often the sole returns for years of labour and hardship.[26]

Satirist Ned Ward left a less compassionate description of the seaman back ashore at the beginning of the eighteenth century, though in between the lines Ward, too, delivered the reasons why life in the Navy had transformed Jim: the suppressed frustrations, the denial of women, the brutal discipline – some of Jim's mates could not handle living without restrictions.

> Sometimes we met in the street with a boat's crew, just come on shore in search of those land debaucheries which the sea denies 'em; looking like such wild, staring, gamesome, uncouth animals, that a litter of squab rhinoceroses, dressed up in human apparel, could not have made, to me, a more ungainly appearance. They were so mercurial in their actions, and rude in their behaviour, that a woman could not pass by 'em but they fell to sucking her lips, like so many horseleeches. They were ready to ride her in the open street, as if they were absolute strangers to Christian civility, and could have committed a rape in public, without a sense of shame, or fear of danger. . . . Every post they came near was in danger of having its head broke, for every one, as he passed by, would give the senseless block a bang with his cudgel, as if he wished every post he met to be either the purser or the boatswain.[27]

Quite a few of Jim's mates returned home with injuries which possibly hindered their settling down; the wooden legs were an obvious reminder of their naval service. A pay-out from the Greenwich Hospital fund could soften the resocialisation. The noise of war, the thundering cannons that always appear in sailors' memoirs, was also still echoing: many sailors had their hearing damaged. But some scars went deeper – wounds that were less obvious, scars that also shine through in Ned Ward's description above of the sailor ashore. Dependency on alcohol, the medication that had helped many to cope with the cold and cruelty of a life at sea, was one of the long-term hurts. Yet more generally, now that he was back on land and alone, it would become obvious whether the sailor's bravado, the defiance of death and mutilation celebrated in Charles Dibdin's songs, had been genuine or just a show.

The boys had left home and been exposed to slaughter and battle stress at a very young age – had they really ever assimilated this, or had they just locked it away in a sea chest deep down in their memory, hoping that it would never be opened? Today we immediately think of post-combat or post-traumatic stress disorders. The eighteenth century was only beginning to grasp such problems. Occasionally 'nostalgia', sleeplessness, anxiety, emotional outbursts and melancholy were observed. People noticed unusually high numbers of cases of madness among sailors. According to physician Sir Gilbert Blane, insanity was seven times more common in the Royal Navy than among the general population.[28] He reckoned that lunacy appeared in about one in a thousand sailors. But these were only the sailors who had become unfit during their service, were properly diagnosed and lodged in the Navy hospitals. Most sailors, however, were just paid off, without anyone inspecting their mental health.

Blane blamed the fact that sailors frequently accidentally hit their heads against the ships' wooden beams for the high number of lunatics. And as these injuries were in Blane's view often sustained when intoxicated, he thought that the alcohol had increased the effect of the blows to their brains. Again alcoholism was regarded as a cause rather than a consequence. Of course, banging one's head on board an eighteenth-century man-of-war was easily done; some tourist visitors to HMS *Victory* in Portsmouth have painfully figured that one out. But next to the high alcohol consumption itself there were plenty of other physical and psychological impacts that could have had a negative effect on Jim's mental health. It was not just battle stress. There was, for example, Jim's abrupt and early separation from family and home, the sudden loss of attachment figures – for the orphans among Jim's comrades these factors had already had an impact even before they went to sea. Furthermore, sexually transmitted diseases and malnourishment could also have affected the sailors' mental health.

The Navy contracted private asylums such as Hoxton House, to care for those who had undoubtedly lost their sanity at sea. The majority of the patients in Hoxton could not be cured, however, and were transferred to Bethlem Hospital (Bedlam), London's infamous madhouse.[29] As Bethlem entered the eighteenth century, sailors became its main patients.[30] Two thirds never made it out of the hospital. Here the most unfortunate of Jim's mates ended as a cheap spectacle for curious Londoners: for one penny, visitors gained entry to the hospital and laughed at the 'freak show'. Some of the visitors brought long sticks, so that they could poke and provoke the patients. They were laughing at Jim, whom they had sent to sea to fight for Britain's empire and whose emotional wounds they did not understand. They had not seen the carnage his young eyes had had to witness. They did not know how an abrupt separation from parents and home can trigger negative emotional reactions. They did not know how it felt to spend every day in the wooden world, at the mercy of the elements and of the officers. When describing the sailors' culture of dealing with the dangers at sea, historian Isaac Land reckoned that they 'cultivated fatalism until it was almost an art form', and that: 'Rather than seeking solutions, sailors learned to feel pride in their ability to "take it", whether the "it" in question was flogging, privation, or danger.'[31] Although Land does not draw any conclusion from this, his words lead one to think of what psychologists call 'learned helplessness', that is subordination to seemingly unavoidable events, which would have made it hard for Jim to muster the spirit for taking life on land into his own hands.[32] An uncomfortable anxiety about the challenges he faced on land could have crept into his mind.

Jim was now without his shipmates, the family who had surrounded him every day during the years in which his brain and ways of thinking matured. Jim had spent his puberty in the wooden world; unlike others of his own age, he had not yet learned how to relate to people outside his core family. He only knew friend or foe, shipmate or Frenchman; all was black and white with no shades of grey. That is why sailor crews were such an exclusive gang. Jim was likely either to consider everyone on land an enemy, as Stevenson's boy Ransome did, or as a trustworthy mate and thus become one of the many 'dupes to the deceitful' that Thomas Trotter saw among the sailors. Even relations with his own family could be difficult. Some sons of sailors struggled to establish any emotional bond with their returned seafaring fathers. When eleven-year-old Christopher Thomson's father came back from the Napoleonic War, Christopher found his father 'a strange austere being; his manners were at first terrifying to me'.[33] Christopher thought that his father had been demoralised by his wartime experiences, that his 'isolation of all society except those hardened, and framed to legal murder, and to laugh at danger' had turned him into a harsh being for whom he felt no affection. John James Bezer, whose father returned one-eyed and an alcoholic from the sea, feared that he must have been 'unmanned' by the floggings he had received in Nelson's Navy, and that: 'Brutally used, he became a brute – an almost natural consequence.' Frank Gifford, whose father went to sea in the mid-eighteenth century, blamed his father's long absences for never being able to establish a relationship: 'I had not grown up with him and he was too prone to repulse my little advances to familiarity with coldness or anger.'

Hence perhaps the bigger obstacles to Jim's settling down were not in the labour market, but inside his own head. Jim had lost his roots early on in life – the idea of now permanently settling down in one place, and entering lifelong commitments, might have scared him. Jim did not see that in the eyes of others he was equally trapped in his wooden world. Finding a purpose and meaning in life could help Jim overcome his new challenges, and it is perhaps no coincidence that a few of the memoir-writing ships' boys, whom we shall revisit for one last time, found in religion the strength to carry on with their post-sea life.

Some exceptional ships' boys who published their memoirs have accompanied us throughout the book. Now, at the end, it is time to pick up their stories for one more time, and see what they had to say about their lives after coming of age at sea. Though exceptional, their stories illustrate some of the common opportunities and difficulties Jim Hawkins faced when trying to settle down back on land. One of our most frequent companions was Sam Leech, the naive twelve-year-old who enlisted in the Royal Navy in 1810. We last encountered him during the Anglo-American War as a prisoner of war in 1812, where he was making some pocket money by showing curious New Yorkers around on board his ship and retelling the story of how she was taken by the Americans. While his shipmates patiently waited for a prisoner exchange, Sam was making plans for his escape. Sam did not just want to escape from prison, he had also had enough of the 'obnoxious discipline' of the Royal Navy and, despite his young age, intended to settle in the United States. North America remained an escape for young men who found life in Britain too restricted by rigid class barriers. Sam's American visitors encouraged him in his design, some offering a free dinner or even an apprenticeship if he made it. Sam convinced another boy, twelve-year-old James Day, to join him, and the two eventually dared to escape.

New York was still ten miles away, which was quite a distance for boys with sea-legs. The two were exhausted two or three miles before New York and had to call at a tavern on the road to spend the night there. Those drinking in the tavern were quite excited when they heard where the boys were from, and all night long the two had to entertain them with retelling the stories of the battle and singing sea songs. It was a very merry night, Sam recalled. The landlord refused to charge them for his hospitality. The first night in a proper bed after years of hammocks felt a bit strange, yet what to the boys was the greatest pleasure of all was waking up the next morning at their own leisure, without being driven out of bed by a swearing boatswain.

Sam and James eventually enlisted for the US Navy. Knowing full well that if captured by the British they would be hanged for deserting to the enemy, both assumed wrong names and claimed to be from Philadelphia. However, once the boys realised that the US Navy was already full of fake Philadelphians who could not name a single street in Philadelphia, nor speak with a proper American accent, they became sure that if ever captured by the British they would never pass as Americans. Hence both preferred to retreat onto land and return to New York. Here Sam began to learn the trade of a shoemaker with a deserted British army soldier. For a while it looked as if Sam would settle in New York as a shoemaker, until the day the youth had a surprise encounter which caused a relapse into his old addiction, the sailor's life: Sam ran into his older cousin, one of the young men who had once enticed him to go to sea.

Sam's cousin had by now become an American and happened to be in port on an excessive celebration of his prize money. Sam enlisted once again for the US Navy. It was of course foolish, for the United States were still at war with his native country, and Sam's ship was promptly captured. Sam ended up in a British prison in Cape Town. He remained there for eight months, luckily undetected. Yet when the US and Britain ended their hostilities, Sam realised with horror that the prisoners of war were to be taken first to England and then released. Sam already saw himself hanging from the yardarm. The war might have been over, but the British were still determined to set examples to deter the frequent desertions to America among its sailors. As England came in sight, Sam did his best to appear as ignorant as possible of it, deliberately asking a great many questions about the country. What made Sam panic even more was the story they told of another youth among the Americans brought to England, who swore that he was American until the point when his unsuspecting mother arrived at the port to bring her son a fresh shirt. Allegedly, the British lieutenant had politely asked her to come on board with her fresh shirt and find her son, which she did. Then he had the boy hanged in his new shirt.

Luckily for Sam his mother was not waiting with a fresh shirt for him, and he was eventually shipped back to the United States. Sam bade farewell to England with mixed feelings and thoughts about his future. He was no more the naive young boy who longed for adventures at sea. Now Sam and the other released veterans idealised a much quieter way of living, at least for the moment:

> I was happy, and yet sad. Happy because I was now safe; sad, because I was again leaving the soil which held my mother and my friends. On the whole, my joyous feelings prevailed. . . . During the voyage, a great deal was said about quitting the seas and settling down in quietness ashore. One of our shipmates, named William Carpenter, who belonged to Rhode Island, had a particular enthusiasm in favor of farming. He promised to take me with him, where I could learn the art of cultivating the soil. Many of us made strong resolutions to embark in some such enterprise. The pleasures of agriculture were sung and praised among us in so ardent a manner, that he must have been incredulous indeed, who could have doubted, for a moment, the certainty of quite a number of our hands becoming farmers, whenever we should gain the land. . . .
>
> Said one, 'If I ever get home, you won't catch me on board of a ship again.' 'Yes,' said another; 'farmers live well, at any rate. They are not put on allowance, but have enough to eat: if they work hard all day, they can turn in at night; and if it blows hard, the house won't rock much, and there's no sails to reef.'[34]

All those grave resolutions were, of course, forgotten once they arrived in New York and received their lump-sum pay. Sam, though still just a boy, was paid one hundred dollars, and what followed was according to Sam a life of dissipation and folly: 'Drinking, swearing, gambling, going to the theatre, and other kindred vices, took up all our time as long as our money lasted. We felt as if New York belonged to us, and that we were really the happiest, jolliest fellows in the world.'[35] In sober moments, Sam tried to leave this life and try one more time to settle down as a shoemaker. But he pictured the life around the shoe-bench as a worse confinement than prison and hence kept on roving around town with his shipmates. One after the other, all of them had to go back to sea. Sam became philosophical: 'Their dreams of ploughing the land evaporated, leaving them what they were before, and what most of them remained until death, the ploughmen of the ocean.'[36] Sam too went back to sea, he joined an American man-o'-war, which, thanks to a flogging captain, this time turned out to be as brutal as the worst Royal Navy ships. Eventually Sam deserted again, ending up impoverished on the freezing winter streets in America, begging from door to door and singing and telling sea stories for alms. Sam had hit the low point of his life. But maybe that was what he needed. Sam was now reaching the end of his teenage years, and it was time to abandon the life of the sailor before it was too late.

Remembering the praises he had sung of the quiet farmer's life, Sam indeed began a new life in agriculture and, equally importantly for him, he finally followed the promises he had made whenever death was near, and became a devout Methodist. He found a 'meaning' which spurred him on. He also wrote to his mother back in England, both knowing that it was still impossible for him to return home. Sam then became a store owner, founded a family, and moved around in the United States, enjoying the quiet life. When his mother wrote to him that it was finally safe to return, he treated his entire family with a vacation to England. The year was 1841, and Sam was finally back home, thirty years after he had left as a young ship's boy.

Another boy we have frequently encountered is Daniel Goodall, the Scottish runaway who enlisted in the Navy in 1801. Daniel had at first been terrified by his rough new company, then found some great protectors and friends among the crew, only to discover that they were the ringleaders of a failed mutiny on board HMS *Téméraire*. Twenty months in the Navy were enough for Daniel to start longing for a quieter life on land. However, after only two and a half years on land, and hostilities between Britain and France being renewed, Daniel had become bored and went back to sea. Once again the sea exerted a strange fascination or addiction; despite all the dangers and hardships they had encountered, the boys still struggled to settle down in a quiet life and felt that irresistible 'longing for the Blue Water', as Daniel put it.[37]

The slight change that Daniel made was that this time he went on board as a 'lobster': he joined the marines. He does not reveal why he changed, but perhaps he was hoping for an easier time on board, or it had something to do with the *Téméraire* mutiny. Daniel served on 'happy ships' and encountered an abundance of gentlemanly and brotherly characters among officers and men. The numerous pursuits and captures of relatively defenceless merchant-men, and all the prize money gained, played a great part in Daniel's high spirits at sea. Daniel's career ended abruptly in 1813, when he lost a leg in battle. Even though the fevers which befell him after the amputation almost

Greenwich Pensioners Playing 'Sling the Monkey' (*c.*1835),
George Cruikshank. While the others try to harass the 'monkey'
with knotted handkerchiefs, he tries to mark one of them with a piece
of chalk and this person will become the next 'monkey'.

killed him, Daniel never lost his positive attitude and survived against all odds in the Navy's famous Haslar Hospital at Portsmouth. He was full of praise for the dedication of its staff, as well as for the compassion of his old captain and crew.

After he was released from Haslar, Daniel collected his pay and his pension from Greenwich and then returned to his native Scotland and his old friends. He even started to work again at his old master's business, and he remained there until the end. Unlike Sam Leech, Daniel kept fond memories of the Navy. Although he had seen horrible violence, he had encountered incredible companionship in the face of death and also profited a fair bit from the war. In fact he was even proud of his wooden leg and very flattered when he realised that forty years later, in the mid-nineteenth century, the young men around him were more excited than ever about hearing his old sailor yarns of the golden age of sail that was now over – so much so that one of them, who was connected to the press, encouraged Daniel to write his memoirs. Robert Louis Stevenson probably also knew such young men who surrounded an old 'sea dog' like Daniel in a tavern, and he just transferred them one hundred years into the past, into Jim Hawkins' Admiral Benbow inn, where they admired the old 'sea dog', Captain Billy Bones, and his terrifying stories.

Another Scottish boy, the bright and ambitious runaway Robert Hay, had already shown during his time on board that he was willing to make use of any learning opportunity on offer. We would expect Robert to have done well in whatever future career he chose, and so he did. When Robert finally returned to his home in Paisley after eight years at sea, his mother did not even recognise her son. Still hungry to learn, and keen to avoid the monotonous and sedentary work behind the loom from which he had once run away, Robert enrolled in a school to learn the art of navigation. His mother feared that this could only mean that her beloved son would once again leave her for years, and so she convinced him to learn the art of bookkeeping as well. Robert then became a captain of a trading boat on the canal. In 1813, when Robert was in his mid-twenties, it was time to leave the waters and settle down. He became a clerk and storekeeper, and later in life even a newspaper editor.

The disguised ship's boy, Mary Lacy, the lively girl who had been left lovesick by a dance-floor Casanova and had run away to sea in 1759, also thought that it was wiser to learn a trade on land. Although her carpenter's promises about arranging an apprenticeship remained drunken empty phrases, she eventually gained an apprenticeship as a shipwright in Portsmouth dockyard in 1763. Seven years later she received her shipwright's certificate. Yet she could not work long in her trade, and rheumatism forced her to resign only a year later. Rheumatism was one of the long-term damages of living at sea; in the long run, the warming effects of alcohol were no substitute for being properly dressed. However, Mary successfully applied for a yearly pension of £22 from the Admiralty, which she received, despite her true sex being revealed. Mary Lacy had sexual affairs with both men and women, yet she had no desire to meet her old love again, although he had repeatedly enquired about her at her parents' house. Historian Suzanne Stark speculates that the young man anyway merely served in her autobiography as a romantic and more conventional reason for Mary going to sea, while in reality her true motivation had been the desire to break out from the restrictions placed on females and to take on a male identity instead.[38] Thirty-three-year-old pensioner Mary wrote her autobiography, after which we lose track of her.

The greatest fame among our collection of ships' boys, however, would fall on Olaudah Equiano, the enslaved African child. Equiano had bravely fought with his master, Lieutenant Pascal, during the Seven Years War, yet when returning to England, Pascal sold him on to a merchant from Virginia. Equiano protested in vain that Pascal had no right to do this. Even worse, Pascal also pocketed all of Equiano's prize money. However, Equiano was then able to work his way up in his new master's trading enterprise. He received further education, and eventually, aged in his early twenties, the new master allowed him to buy his own freedom. Years of trading and travelling followed, until Equiano finally settled in London and became a prominent campaigner in the anti-slavery movement. His autobiography was a great asset in the campaign. Olaudah Equiano died in 1797, ten years before his anti-slavery campaign saw the success of the Act for the Abolition of the Slave Trade in 1807. It was history's gain that this ship's boy, whose heroics as a powder boy opened this book, had managed to dodge all the French broadsides.

Epilogue

FINALLY, we return to Jim Hawkins' description of his terrifying lodger Billy Bones:

> His stories were what frightened people worst of all. Dreadful stories they were; about hanging, and walking the plank, and storms at sea, and the Dry Tortugas, and wild deeds and places on the Spanish Main. By his own account he must have lived his life among some of the wickedest men that God ever allowed upon the sea; and the language in which he told these stories shocked our plain country people almost as much as the crimes that he described. My father was always saying the inn would be ruined, for people would soon cease coming there to be tyrannised over and put down, and sent shivering to their beds; but I really believe his presence did us good. People were frightened at the time, but on looking back they rather liked it; it was a fine excitement in a quiet country life; and there was even a party of the younger men who pretended to admire him, calling him a 'true sea dog,' and a 'real old salt,' and such like names, and saying there was the sort of man that made England terrible at sea.[1]

As Stevenson penned this colourful description of the storytelling old sea dog, and equally in the century in which Stevenson had placed his story, it was such mythologised images of deep-sea sailors that often led boys to ignore or even celebrate the dangers awaiting them at sea. The Royal Navy needed to get the likes of Jim Hawkins at a young age, not only so that they became used to the roughness of the elements early on, but also so that they were numbed to the horrors of naval warfare. Mature landsmen were not just lacking the robustness, they also lacked the necessary naivety and adventurousness to throw themselves into what was the most dangerous profession of the time. By viewing the sailors' culture through the prism of youth culture this book has tried to explain why many boys would not have been deterred by the threats to their lives awaiting them at sea, as glorification or trivialisation of dangers are an ingredient of many youth cultures, and were certainly present among sailors.

Although life at sea propelled the real Jim Hawkins into a coming of age and a meeting of the demands of manhood, it also preserved his youthful attitudes and unsettledness.[2] The study of sailors' culture in the light of youth behaviour opens up many other interesting avenues which go beyond the scope of this book. For example, if the sea service was an escape route for unsettled and impoverished youths, one may argue that it had a stabilising effect on British society at home, similar to the role played by the American colonies. It absorbed great numbers of potentially subversive young men, and thus made a political revolution back home in Britain less likely.

A further interesting question is that if deep-sea sailing was indeed something many men turned to only in their teens and twenties, and if seafaring was often only a casual employment, then a far greater share of the British population than hitherto thought had at one point been at sea – perhaps a share big enough to talk of a 'maritimisation' of British society and culture. One contemporary observer, in 1772, reckoned that one in seventy was a seaman.[3] Yet with war drawing so many men temporarily to sea at some stage in their lives, the ratio of people with maritime experiences would have been much higher.

Over the course of a conflict such as the Seven Years War, for example, the Royal Navy alone employed roughly five per cent of the male population. Many of the older and younger males of that population would have gathered maritime experiences in previous or later conflicts. And to that number we must add all those employed in private shipping and in trades related to seafaring. Thus the sailors' culture exerted a strong influence on general culture in Britain. This may have had effects on a variety of aspects of British life, from its notions of masculinity to the incredible wealth of popular music and storytelling this country has produced over the past two centuries.

Beyond the study of eighteenth-century sailors, an approach akin to this study could also usefully be applied to other trades, cultures and times; for example, comparison with a study of the romance and reality, and the later romanticisation and iconisation in youth culture, of nineteenth-century North American cowboys could provide an interesting analogy. There are also potential contemporary comparisons and resonances when one considers the struggles to settle down, reluctance to relinquish youthful behaviour and insecure working conditions characterised by short contracts and flexible workplaces common today in creative industries such as music, film and television. In such professions, the difference between romance and reality, and the difficulty of integrating work into a family life, often lead to a career change in the late twenties.

Also noticeable with regards to the general history of youth is that the history of ships' boys contains a very strong element of what the Germans call *wanderlust*, the desire to roam. In social and economic history the term usually refers to travelling apprentices offering their services wherever they found a demand, and hence it also includes an element of 'wandering' being forced upon youths by economic circumstances. This *wanderlust* and also *fernweh*, an aching to see distant places, appear to be a constant feature in the history of European youth. The story of Jim Hawkins and his real-life counterparts is perhaps one of the most wonderful expressions of this phenomenon. Whether this *wanderlust* of the youth is innate or has an external impetus, resulting from social and economic circumstances, is open to debate. A simple explanation for the *wanderlust* of youth could be that it is the only stage in life in which an individual can follow such urges; she or he has reached a certain physical fitness and maturity, but is not yet bound to commitments such as a family or the possession of means of production, making youthful dreams of a different life elsewhere appear realisable.

Just as the term *wanderlust* includes an element of economic necessity, it was not just the desire to see the world that led the real Jim Hawkins into the arms of the Royal Navy, but also dire financial pressures and family tradition. We have seen that often unemployment and the loss of one or both parents caused Jim to fall on hard times, and the sea appeared as an ideal solution to his problems. Some of Jim's mates were even pushed towards the sea by other people, not by the Navy's press gang, but by authorities on land. Parish overseers, magistrates, churchwardens, dissatisfied apprenticeship masters and struggling parents all tried to place boys in the Navy, in line with the common stereotype illustrated by Hogarth's *Idle Apprentice*, that for boys who had failed to settle in any trade the last resort must be the sea. Furthermore, eighteenth-century poor laws, apprenticeship laws, and laws against vagabonds and rogues, all ignored the personal liberty of the children of the poor and gave local authorities the power to force them into the sea service. However, the impression gained in this study is that all this was only successful in cases where the boy and the Navy were willing to co-operate.

Using the Navy or the Army to get rid of troublesome youths had a wide public backing at all times and in all countries, regardless of the fact that no navy was ever enthusiastic about such recruits. Although by taking such youths on board the Navy may have acquired the Billy Bones types who made England so 'terrible at sea', it also gave the Navy a difficult task in supervising these crews, and it made society dread what would happen once these hardened old sea dogs were released back onto land. Some readers may have been surprised and disappointed that those numerous mischievous boys from neglectful parents are such a far cry from the well-behaved Jim Hawkins and his caring mother. Yet such readers should consider the following: the fact that Jim and his friends pocketed the old pirate Captain Flint's treasure at the end of *Treasure Island*, without considering that they had even less of a moral right to the riches than did Long John Silver and his gang (who had murdered and plundered to accumulate the treasure), is a clear indication of an opportunism and cheekiness in Jim Hawkins' character which we would have found equally among many real-life ships' boys.

We might criticise the imperfection of the attempts of organisations like the Marine Society to use the Navy as a surrogate family and disciplinarian for troubled boys, but today, despite much greater wealth and knowledge, we are not much closer to solving the problems of neglected youths. Even now, proper affectionate parenting is hard to replace; crime rates among children in institutional care are still depressingly high. The Navy was perhaps never the ideal solution. Yet, even two and a half centuries later, the Marine Society's basic idea, of somehow taking the children away from the inner-city and its negative peer pressures, and ensure closer adult supervision, possibly in the form of exciting, team-building sailing trips, appears worth considering.

In addition, the other concern of the Marine Society, to 'breed up' more sailors for Britain's emerging empire, and thus avoid the dangerous manning shortages the Navy experienced at the outbreak of hostilities, was not one to be solved quickly. In the eighteenth century, it was simply impossible to expect private shipping to train as many sailors as were needed during wartime. There was no need for such a large pool of sailors in times of peace, and many of those drawn to sea at war would have found themselves unemployed, or employed in other trades on land, for long periods in their working lives. There was no alternative to dragging landsmen to sea in times of war, thus it was the recurrence of war itself which provided Britain's much needed 'nursery' of seamen,[4] as it increased the Navy's demand for boys. Furthermore, it led landsmen and former or occasional sailors into the Navy, where they learned or brushed up their seamanship.

It is remarkable that, with its officer-servant model, the eighteenth-century Navy held at least officially onto the system of paternal guidance, a system which also governed the lives of eighteenth-century youths on land in the form of the master-apprentice relationship. The reality on board, however, looked very different: it resembled more the dawning world of the (manu)factories, where one master supervised a large workforce, with the youths being trained among the workers and in an increasingly regulated manner. The retention of the old paternal concept seems even more remarkable when considering that the Navy was thus prevented from creating a larger 'nursery' of seamen, since the number of trainees was always limited to the number of servants allowed to each captain and officer. One would think that it might have been more sensible to enlist more boys and train them, rather than having to reject so many because there were not enough servant placements.

Yet perhaps such thoughts ran contrary to the Navy's general philosophy that it consisted of individual ships, all with a fixed complement, with fixed positions and an exact idea of how wide the hierarchical pyramid on board could spread at the bottom in relation to the top.[5] In a way, the Marine Society's training ship acted as a temporary holding ship, but it could only take around one hundred boys. In 1810, the Society received a rather angry letter from Admiral Sir Roger Curtis, demanding that the Society send all its boys to the *Royal William*, where they would be held and then distributed.[6] Yet, surprisingly, the Society bluntly told him that it would never do so, arguing that this would lessen 'the confidence which the lower Class of People place in the Society; as the Friends of the Boys expect to be informed when they take leave of them, what Ships they are to serve in.' Fifty years of recruiting boys had perhaps led the Society to the conclusion that it could take better care of the future ships' boys than could the Navy.

That the real Jim Hawkins was likely to encounter a bit of 'Rum, Sodomy and the Lash' in the Navy might not be surprising, yet what is shocking is the high casualty rate. The boys would have been at risk from diseases, etc., in other walks of life, too, but nowhere near as much. Even in unhealthy London, children who reached their teens had passed the greatest dangers and actually had the lowest death rate of all age groups.[7] The statistics of this study may be blurred by the insufficiencies of the source material, but they remain disturbing. With diseases and shipwrecks as the major threats, being a boy did not mean that Jim was more protected than the men, since the whole crew – men and boys – literally sat in the same boat. Neither did the enemy's broadsides and boarding attempts take any consideration of minors on board. Thus there is one aspect which the ships' boys definitely shared with their fictional equivalent Jim Hawkins: they were placed in situations which forced them to stop being a boy and to take on adult responsibilities. To master these situations is a theme of many boys' daydreams, a theme so effectively used by Stevenson in *Treasure Island*. Yet for these real-life ships' boys it was also the harsh daily reality.

However, the wisdom of hindsight in view of more recent extremes of behaviour from World War II, when Japanese teenagers 'volunteered' (under heavy peer-pressure) as Kamikaze pilots, and German teenagers were propelled into the final battle for Berlin, encourages us to be a little more critical towards the adults responsible for making use of these boys' disregard for dangers and their easily ignited patriotic or religious spirits, and for sacrificing them in a conflict for which they were too young to judge the necessity. As sailor Charles Pemberton, who was pressed into the Navy as a seventeen-year-old in 1807, sarcastically warned: 'But what would become of the navy, if its seamen were instructed to think, or allowed to reason? Their daring intrepidity would dwindle in calculations, their reckless bravery would evaporate in foresight and caution . . . men won't fight, if ever they acquire the knack of asking for whom or for what.'[8] Rear Admiral Thomas Troubridge must secretly have agreed, with his comment that to him any sailor who looked as if he was thinking was a mutineer.

The issue goes a little beyond the scope of this book, as it leads us not only to having to judge the necessity of each of the eighteenth-century wars in which Britain was involved, but ultimately also to debate the legitimacy of the social order of eighteenth-century Britain and its distribution of wealth. The official reasons for going to war were commonly no different from any other century or any other country: war was always presented as a defensive act, a response to an enemy plotting an apparently unprovoked attack/invasion or exploiting other lands preferably under British control. The Marine Society thought that, for example, in case of the Seven Years War, it had 'pleased divine Providence to involve this Nation in a further War'.[9] Hanway declared: 'It is beyond dispute, that they [the French] ever behold with envious eyes the bounties which heaven bestows on this nation, and are watchful of opportunities to ravish them from us.'[10] Yet there were a few others like Admiral Nelson's cousin Horatio (Horace) Walpole (1717-1797), who wrote that he was anxious to have peace and did not care a farthing for the interests of the merchants.[11] To Walpole, the ordinary sailors killed and injured were 'as valuable, as a lazy luxurious set of men, who hire others to acquire riches for them'. Pacifists often suffer the wrath of nationalists, and Walpole bitterly concluded: 'I am a bad Englishman, because I think the advantages of commerce are dearly bought for some, by the lives of many more.'

As the justification for war is often in dispute, it may be fair to give teenage minds a little more time to develop before allowing them to follow their juvenile thirst for joining the action, so that they are mature enough to have come to the realisation that going to war is not like going to a football match; it is about killing people and being killed. Even today, the Royal Navy and British Army still take their recruits at a young age. At the start of the twenty-first century, the UK's minimum recruitment age at 16 is the joint-lowest in Europe, and the UK is the only European country to send minors (under-eighteens) frequently into battle. Two hundred years earlier, ship's boy Sam Leech was a mere fourteen years old when he had his first taste of naval battle. Seeing the surgeon in the ward-room cut like a butcher into his friend's leg, first with a knife, then with a saw, while the battle was still in full rage, was a scene that remained with Sam for the rest of his life: 'Such scenes of suffering as I saw in that ward-room, I hope never to witness again. Could the civilized world behold them as they were, and as they often are, infinitely worse than on that occasion, it seems to me they would forever put down the barbarous practices of war, by universal consent.'[12]

Notes on Sources and Literature

Tracing Jim's Career in the Royal Navy

The main aids to keeping track of Jim's mates, and anyone else who served on the lower deck in the eighteenth century, are the Royal Navy's muster lists and pay lists held at The National Archives (TNA) in Kew, London. Recorded by captain and purser, with the assistance of the master and the boatswain, these lists have survived in an impressive quantity. They are easily available to any interested reader. The books are big and bulky, and anyone browsing through a few musters in the reading room of The National Archives is soon covered in a mixture of dust, dirt and historic scraps. The main purpose of the lists was to determine every man's wage. The thoroughness with which they were kept is nowhere better illustrated than by the muster book with The National Archives reference number *ADM 36/10744* (and pay book *ADM 35/216*) from the year 1790: like all musters it lists each individual recruit, the price of anything he had obtained on board from the purser and that had later to be deducted from his wage (beds, clothes, tobacco, medicines against venereal infections), as well as any occurrences of discharges, deaths and desertions with the exact date. What makes *ADM 36/10744* so special is that it was kept by William Bligh and his ship was the infamous *Bounty*. Even after a year-long odyssey of over three and a half thousand nautical miles across the Pacific and Indian Oceans in the small launch in which the mutineers had left Lieutenant Bligh and those loyal to him, Bligh had held on to the books. Once in England, Bligh, the master John Fryer and the boatswain William Cole completed their duty to sign the final muster books, listing every man's wage deductions for what they had obtained on board, and recording every mutineer as a deserter together with the exact date they had 'run' – all for a ship which had actually never returned to England but had remained with the deserters at the other end of the globe. Evidently, another raison d'être of the muster lists was to keep track of deserters and mutineers.

Unfortunately, when it comes to boys the muster and pay-book keepers were a lot less diligent. Possibly because a servant was not paid directly by the

Navy, and he was only of importance in determining the wage of the officer he was officially serving, the entries for the boys are sometimes inaccurate. Anyone researching the career of an ordinary boy in the eighteenth-century Navy should therefore be aware that it may be a painstaking search, for once the boy is discharged from his ship the books often fail to record to which ship he had been transferred. The best guess is usually the ship his master went to, or any other ship anchoring in the vicinity. Such unspecified discharges of boys should, however, never be taken as a definite and final discharge from the Navy, a mistake frequently made by historians. To genealogists these unspecified discharges are a great nuisance and possibly the end of their research, but they should take consolation in the fact that to the historian wishing to compile statistics on the careers of the average Jim Hawkins the problem multiplies into an utter nightmare. Representative statistics are difficult to derive with such a high likelihood of losing boys out of sight. Only once the boys are rated as men their careers are easy to trace.

For this book a sample of 262 boys was followed into the Navy in the mid-eighteenth century. The sampling techniques, research problems and individual careers were presented in Roland Pietsch, 'Ships' Boys and Charity in the Mid-Eighteenth Century' (unpublished PhD thesis, University of London, 2003, pp.201-211, 299-357). N A M Rodger's *Naval Records for Genealogists* (1984, 1998), as well as Randolph Cock and N A M Rodger's *Guide to the Naval Records in the National Archives of the UK* (2006, 2008), give a general introduction into the muster lists and other naval records.

Only at the end of the eighteenth century, when the officer-servant model was abolished and the boys were paid directly, and when perhaps the spirit of the Enlightenment improved the Royal Navy's attitude towards record-keeping in general, do these insufficiencies in the muster books disappear. The careers of boys are from then on easy to follow. The lists in general are still an underused historical resource and beg for more statistical analysis of seafaring careers. Any sailor careers thus followed can be complemented by further Navy records, such as the captains' logs and letters, the Admiralty's correspondence, courts martial records, the Navy Regulations and other material listed in the bibliography.

The Marine Society Boys

The Marine Society's records are an exceptional resource for finding out more about the background of the real-life Jim Hawkins. Held at the National Maritime Museum (NMM) in Greenwich, London, they include registers of its boys, as well as minutes of the Society's meetings and correspondence. While this book has made extensive use of the Society's records of the early years in the mid-eighteenth century, the correspondence and minutes of later years, particularly during the wars with Revolutionary France, are still crying out for more detailed research. Yet perhaps even more promising for further research would be an analysis of the Society's boys sent to the merchant navy, as this book focuses solely on Royal Navy servants. For those interested in tracing ancestors in the Marine Society's records, my article on 'A Boyhood at Sea' (*Genealogists' Magazine*, 2001) gives some guidance. The Society's boy registers can be analysed speedily thanks to computer technology. For this book, my own database, as well as that of Dianne Payne and the work of Roderick Floud's research group (all listed in the bibliography under databases), allowed quick surveys covering both the eighteenth and the nineteenth centuries. Overly enthusiastic users of computerised historical registers have to be slightly careful, though, with drawing conclusions from blanks in columns: blanks can mean anything from the information not being recorded, not being known, or whatever is asked for in the column headline not being the case. One also has to watch out for inconsistencies in the recorded information over the decades. Both problems tend to be hidden in computerised sources and only become apparent when looking at the originals.

The seemingly endless number of publications by Jonas Hanway (the bibliography only contains works relevant to the Marine Society), as well as the writings of John Fielding about his work, give a more lively insight into the history of the Marine Society. Their pamphlets can be read among the rare books at the British Library and other large libraries. The most modern biography of Jonas Hanway was produced by James S Taylor (1985), while John Fielding needs a new biographer, the works about his life being slightly outdated. Fielding's consolation may be that he is the star of Bruce Alexander's recent historical crime novels.

Literature

This book is a first, as so far no book has been written on the ordinary ships' boys, the Navy's servants, in the eighteenth century. More work has been done on boys from better-off families destined to become officers and on midshipmen, most recently in D A B Ronald's *Young Nelsons* (2009), as well as in the many general books on the eighteenth-century Navy and in biographies of naval heroes such as Horatio Nelson. Nelson and Napoleon still draw the biggest audiences, and hence a lot has been written on the Navy at the turn of the century but comparatively little about the mid century, where Stevenson had placed Jim Hawkins' quest for *Treasure Island*. N A M Rodger's *The Wooden World* (1986) is still the standard for the Navy in the mid century. Anyone interested in particular aspects of the history of ships' boys can take as guidance the literature references provided in the chapters and in the bibliography. Most exciting may be reading the stories of the sailors themselves; that is, memoirs such as those of Samuel Leech and Robert Hay, which have been reprinted and are therefore easily available.

A matter close to the heart of this book is to try to make a small contribution to drawing naval history out of its isolation and embedding it in the general social, youth and cultural history of the eighteenth century. Some cultural historians, like Isaac Land with his fascinating study of *War, Nationalism and the British Sailor* (2009), have developed a taste for naval history. Yet cultural and naval historians still sometimes seem to lead an almost parallel existence. Perhaps there is a cultural barrier between both, due to the fact that the plain-talking naval historians are scared off by the vast repertoire of theories, enthusiasm for new models and long-winded language common in cultural history; while the cultural historians in turn are daunted by the nautical jargon, in-depth factual knowledge and conservatism of the naval historians. As a doctoral student, I often found myself in the middle, feeling equally intimidated by the literature and language of both camps. It needs a bit of the naive courage of a Jim Hawkins to enter enthusiastically a new world with all its strange and colourful characters and language.

Notes to the Text

Preface: 'To the Hesitating Purchaser'
1. Title of poem by R L Stevenson opening *Treasure Island*.
2. R L Stevenson, *Treasure Island* (London 1883, 1927), pp.1-2.
3. A slight alteration of Ian Dury's song of 1977.
4. R L Stevenson, *Treasure Island* (London 1883, 1927), pp.4-5.

Chapter 1 Seafaring Boys in the Eighteenth Century: Fiction and Reality
1. Olaudah Equiano, *The Interesting Narrative of the Life of Olaudah Equiano* (Boston 1791, 1995, Bedford edition), pp.76-77.
2. For an overview of the sea novels which influenced Stevenson see Harold Watson, *Coasts of Treasure Island* (San Antonio 1969). For representations of eighteenth-century sailors and officers in fiction, poetry and art see Charles Robinson, *The British Tar in Fact and Fiction* (London & New York 1909) – slightly dated, but written with the loving touch of a collector.
3. The most curious edition that I own of *Mr Midshipman Easy* is one published in the Soviet Union (Progress Publishers: Moscow 1982), with an introduction in Russian and the text in English for English language students – another proof that British stories of seafaring boys even crossed the twentieth century's ideological borders of popular culture, despite the rather elitist moral of *Midshipman Easy*'s story.
4. Like *Treasure Island* in 1966, *Jack Holborn*, too, was adapted by West German television in the form of a (Christmas) mini-series in 1982, and thus had an impact on the childhood of this book's author and probably on his later research interests. Also adapted for a West German Christmas mini-series were Stevenson's David Balfour adventures, *Kidnapped* and *Catriona*, in 1978. Incidentally, the 1966 adaptation of *Treasure Island* was directed by Wolfgang Liebeneiner, the man in charge of Joseph Goebbel's last and never-finished Nazi propaganda movie *Das Leben geht weiter* (Life goes on) – the film is still lost and should really start a treasure hunt no less exciting than that of Jim Hawkins.
5. The most recent work is D A B Ronald's *Young Nelsons* (Oxford 2009). Biographies of famous captains, and general books on the eighteenth-century Navy, also usually cover the training and roles of these boys, particularly once they were rated as midshipmen.
6. Hanway, *Reasons for an Augmentation of at least Twelve Thousand Mariners* (London 1759), p.92.
7. TNA, ADM 2/81, 30/08/1758, pp.62-63.
8. George Samuel Parsons, *I sailed with Nelson* (London 1973), p.247 (my thanks go to Professor Roger Knight for finding the quotation).
9. It is conceivable that in times of war these apprentices were declared as servants by their

masters, to cash in the wage bonus. Apprentices had a proper indenture with their master, intending to learn their master's specialist trade. In terms of social status they may have been somewhere in the middle between the servants of upper-class and lower-class backgrounds. On a few occasions commissioned officers, even admirals, also brought apprentices with them. The nature of their apprenticeship is not entirely clear. Presumably they were bound by an indenture to their master, who with the help of his connections would have the lad employed or trained in any maritime business, with the master receiving whatever wages the boy was earning in exchange for providing living expenses, pocket money, etc.

10. Anecdote in Glyn Williams, *The Prize of all the Oceans* (London 1999), p.168.

11. See *Regulations of the Marine Society: Historical Account* (London 1772), p.10.

12. Hanway, *A Letter from a Member of the Marine Society* (London 1757, 3rd ed.), p.10, and NMM, MSY/A/1, 22/03/1759.

13. See for example the French prisoners of *Royal George* at the battle of Quiberon Bay in 1759, also TNA, ADM 36/6702, pp.19-20; ADM 36/6127, p.187 (no.1017), p.195 (no.105).

14. See J C Beaglehole, *The Life of Captain James Cook* (London 1974), p.141.

15. N A M Rodger, *The Wooden World* (London 1986, 1988), p.320. See also Edward Barlow's memoirs as an apprentice in the seventeenth-century Navy, when his master and the captain ask him to pretend to be another servant to collect the boy's wages – in *Edward Barlow's Journal of his Life at Sea*, vol.1 (London 1934), pp.47-48.

16. *Regulations of the Marine Society: Historical Account* (London 1772), p.10 (fn.), (in 2nd ed., 1775, pp.9-10). Officially, the act 22 George II, c.33, s.II, par.33 (1749), threatened any officer signing a false muster with dismissal from the Navy.

17. TNA, ADM 1/5179, 16/04/1794.

18. Peter Earle, *Sailors* (London 1998), pp.17-26, gives a concise overview on boys in merchant shipping.

19. See TNA, ADM 7/393-397, and Peter Earle, *Sailors* (London 1998), pp.200-1.

20. Estimating the numbers of seamen outside the Navy is difficult, especially since many were only seasonally or temporarily employed. See for example David J Starkey, 'War and the Market for Seafarers in Britain, 1736-1792', in Lewis R Fisher & Helge W Nordvik (eds.), *Shipping and Trade* (Pontefract 1990), pp.28-29, 40-41; or Ralph Davis, *The Rise of the English Shipping Industry* (Newton Abbot 1962, 1972), p.323; as well as N A M Rodger, *The Wooden World* (London 1986, 1988), p.149.

21. William Robinson, *Jack Nastyface* (London 1836, 1973), p.66.

22. Britain was not the only country who failed in this respect. The only successful example was perhaps seventeenth-century France, where Jean-Baptiste Colbert (1619-1683) introduced the *Inscription Maritime* and *Classes Maritime*, a rotational service combined with a registry for seamen.

23. TNA, ADM 2/1056, 28/11/1760, p.330 (also pp.337, 341, 356-357, 366). See also TNA, ADM 2/1056, 20/11/1759, p.192 (mob in Stockton freeing pressed sailor), TNA, ADM 2/1057, 08/03/1762, pp.1-2 (rioters destroying the house where Captain Fortescue kept his rendezvous), or the massive opposition William Spavens recalls when his gang tried to press men during the Seven Years War in Spavens, *The Narrative of William Spavens* (Louth 1796; London 1998), pp.21-22.

24. In the summer of 1762, for example, magistrates in Suffolk committed several officers of the press gang to prison – see TNA, ADM 2/1057, 20/07/1762, p.59. For civilian collaboration

see also J S Bromley, 'The British Navy and its Seamen after 1688: Notes for an Unwritten History', in S Palmer & G Williams (eds.), *Charted and Uncharted Waters* (London 1981), pp.151-152.

25. Acts 2 & 3 Anne, c.6 (1703); and 4 & 5 Anne, c.6, 19 (1705). Building on older laws: 27 Henry VIII, c.12 (1530/1); 1 Edward VI, c.3 (1547); 3 & 4 Edward VI, c.16 (1549-50); 5 Elizabeth I, c.4 (1562); 39 Elizabeth I, c.3 (1597-8); 43 Elizabeth I, c.2, s.v (1601); 21 James I, c.28, s.I, par.33 (1623); 3 Charles I, c.4, s.22 (1627); and for a fine to force masters to accept parish apprentices: 8 & 9 William III, c.30, s.v (1697).

26. In fact, such apprentices were even forbidden to volunteer (or to be pressed) for the Royal Navy until the age of eighteen (2 & 3 Anne, c.6, s.iv [1703]).

27. Peter Earle, *Sailors* (London 1998), pp.22-23.

28. See Hanway, *Reasons for an Augmentation of at least Twelve Thousand Mariners* (London 1759), pp.94-96, and John Fielding, *An Account of the Receipts and Disbursements Relating to Sir John Fielding's Plan* (London 1769), pp.7-9.

29. *An Account of the Hospital* (London 1749), p.xvii.

30. See Ruth K McClure, *Coram's Children* (New Haven 1981), pp.126, 150.

31. Charles Dickens, *Oliver Twist* (London 1838, 1992), p.24.

32. See 2 & 3 Anne, c. 6, s.xvi (1703) (building on 39 Elizabeth, c. 4 [1597-8]; and 11 & 12 William III, c.18 [1700]). Vagabonds were specified in the Vagrancy Act 17 George II, c.5 (1744). For the Seven Years War period see public notices for hot press allowing the impressment of any idle and disorderly landsman, in *London Magazine*, March 1756, p.145 & August 1761, p.446. In the Admiralty's correspondence see, for example, letter to regulating captains in TNA, ADM 2/718, 18/08/1761; or letter to magistrate James Forster in TNA, ADM 2/716, 17/09/1760, pp.189-190; also Admiralty Board minutes in TNA, ADM 3/65, 21/12/1756.

33. See Stephen Gradish, *The Manning of the British Navy During the Seven Years War* (London, 1980), p.84; and N A M Rodger, *The Wooden World* (London, 1986, 1988), p.170; and as an example TNA, ADM 2/525, 30/03/1759, p.81. See also Hanway on rejection of magistrate men in his *Letter from a Member of the Marine Society* (London, 1757, 3rd ed.), pp.22-23.

34. See for example TNA, ADM 2/1056, 04 & 05/01/1760, pp.207-208.

35. See for example the cases of Muller and Dring in TNA, ADM 2/1056, 21/12/1759, pp.202-203 & 02/04/1760, p.244.

36. Samuel Leech, *A Voice from the Main Deck* (London 1857, 1999), p.22.

Chapter 2 Jim's Troublesome Youth on Land: 'The Idle Apprentice Sent to Sea'

1. Edward Coxere, *Adventures by Sea of Edward Coxere* (Oxford 1945), p.4.

2. Acts 2 & 3 Anne, c.6 (1703); and 4 & 5 Anne, c.6, 19 (1705). See also chapter 1.

3. Sometimes there was an additional bonus for the parish overseer: each parish was responsible for looking after its poor, being funded by a poor-rate tax from local property owners, yet sending a poor boy to another parish near the water for an apprenticeship relieved the overseer of the responsibility to care for the youth in future. The boy would be able to claim his settlement (commonly after forty days of residence) in the new parish, depending where his ship was registered. The settlement was a much desired certificate which confirmed entitlement to poor relief in a parish. It was issued by parish overseers or churchwardens and signed by two Justices of the Peace, and was commonly gained by either being born or being

apprenticed in a parish.

4. *Regulations of the Marine Society: Historical Account* (London 1772), p.41.

5. John Fielding, *An Account of the Origin and Effects of a Police Set on Foot by His Grace the Duke of Newcastle in the year 1753* (London 1758), pp.17-19.

6. Henry Fielding, *The History of Tom Jones, a Foundling* (London 1749, 1997), pp.33, 37, 66-67.

7. John Fielding, *An Account of the Receipts and Disbursements Relating to Sir John Fielding's Plan, for the Preserving of Distressed Boys, by Sending them to Sea* (London 1769), pp.2-5.

8. Claim made by Hanway, *The Defects of Police* (London 1775), p.31. Recent historical research suggests that the share of hanged teenagers was not quite as high – see for example Peter King, *Crime and Law in England, 1750-1840* (Cambridge 2006).

9. See acts 27 Henry VIII, c.12 (1530/1); 1 Edward VI, c.3 (1547); 3 & 4 Edward VI, c.16 (1549-50); 5 Elizabeth I, c.4 (1562); 39 Elizabeth I, c.3 (1597-8); 43 Elizabeth I, c.2, s.v (1601); 21 James I, c.28, s.I, par.33 (1623); 3 Charles I, c.4, s.22 (1627); and for a fine to force masters to accept parish apprentices see 8 & 9 William III, c.30, s.v (1697).

10. Workhouses, intended to house the poor and sick, had been growing in numbers since the seventeenth century, as such 'indoor relief' promised to make it easier to care for and check on poor-relief claimants. A badge sewn to the clothes commonly identified inhabitants of a parish workhouse.

11. Edward Ward, *The London Spy*, edited by Paul Hyland (London 1709, East Lansing, 1993), p.245.

12. In this respect, Queen Anne's laws promoting maritime apprenticeships for the children of the poor were already progressive, as they bound the boys only until the age of twenty-one.

13. Act 7 George III, c.39, s.xiv (1767).

14. Reading a collection of apprenticeship court cases one realises that it is no wonder that when the slavery of Africans on the colonial plantations was abolished in the early nineteenth century, it was often continued under the guise of apprenticeships, so bad were the indentures in some apprenticeships. In eighteenth-century Britain there were cases of destitute boys who had been tricked into signing apprenticeship indentures that virtually enslaved them – see for example the case of thirteen boys who ended up in the care of the Marine Society in 1760: a ship's carpenter and an old sergeant of the Marines had made them sign indentures which literally enslaved them for work in the American plantations (NMM, MSY/A/1, 28/02/1760, 20/03/1760).

15. Trying to amend this and to make an appeal easier, an act was passed in 1747 (20 George II, c.19, s.3), ruling that any parish apprentice, and those whose fee had been below five pounds, could appeal to any two justices and achieve a discharge without having to pay a fee.

16. See for example Robert B Shoemaker, *The London Mob* (London 2004), p.17.

17. See *Edward Barlow's Journal of his Life at Sea*, vol.1 (London 1934), pp.16-20.

18. Mary Lacy, *The History of the Female Shipwright* (London 1773), reprinted in *The Lady Tars* (Tucson 2008), pp.61-65.

19. Advertisement for *The Apprentice* in the *London Magazine*, January 1756, pp.3-5.

20. See for example Philippe Ariès, *Centuries of Childhood* (Paris 1960; London 1996); John R Gillis, *Youth and History* (London 1974, 1981); or Ilana Krausman Ben-Amos, *Adolescence and Youth in Early Modern England* (New Haven & London 1994), pp.183-205.

21. Admittedly many boys in pre-industrial Europe left home at least temporarily at a much earlier age.

22. John Fielding, *Newgate Magazine*, vol.II (London 1766), p.783.

23. Hanway, *Observations on the Causes of the Dissoluteness which Reigns Among the Lower Classes of the People* (London 1772), p.15.

24. Welch, *Observations on the Office of Constable* (London 1754), pp.26-28.

25. See Paulson, *Popular and Polite Art in the Age of Hogarth and Fielding* (Notre Dame/London 1979), pp.16-17, 22-23; and *Emblem and Expression* (London 1975), pp.72-73.

26. The usual fifteen holidays per year would have been a meagre consolation – for holidays see Tim Hitchcock, *Down and Out in Eighteenth-Century London* (New York 2004), p.183.

27. See Hanway, *Observations on the Causes of the Dissoluteness which Reigns Among the Lower Classes of the People* (London 1772), p.23. London's Bridewell, having been among the first of its kind, turned the name Bridewell into a generic term for all similar houses of correction. Hanway found during a visit to the Bridewell that the discipline there was in his eyes very lax – see Hanway, *The Defects of Police* (London 1775), p.35.

28. Leech, *A Voice from the Main Deck* (London 1857, 1999), p.11.

29. R L Stevenson, *Kidnapped* (London, 1886, 1895), pp.42-43, 63. Stevenson had placed the adventures of David Balfour in the 1750s, just like those of Jim Hawkins.

30. In M D George, *London Life in the Eighteenth Century* (London 1925, 1992), p.226, n.37.

31. Hanway, *The Defects of Police* (London 1775), pp.33-35, 79-80. The most infamous example of such a failed apprentice turned criminal was Jack Sheppard from Spitalfields, London's most celebrated burglar and partly the real-life model for Macheath, John Gay's central figure in the *Beggars' Opera* (1727). Jack left his apprenticeship because he had become 'weary of the yoke of servitude', as novelist Daniel Defoe writes, and because he was more attracted by London's nightlife, ignoring the curfews that had been imposed on him by the master's wife – see Lucy Moore, *The Thieves' Opera* (London 1997), p.192.

Chapter 3 Poor Jim: Charity and the Marine Society

1. *Edward Barlow's Journal of his Life at Sea*, vol.1 (London 1934), p.31.

2. Hanway, *A Letter from a Member of the Marine Society* (London 1757, 3rd ed.), pp.16-17.

3. For the beginning of Fielding's initiative see John Fielding, *An Account of the Origin and Effects of a Police* (London 1758), p.20-21; *Public Advertiser*, 29/03/1756, 10/04/1756, 27-28/04/1756, 03/05/1756, 16/06/1756, & 09-11/07/1756; TNA, ADM 2/704, 20/04/1756, p.227; also TNA, ADM 1/922, Henry Osborne, 09/05/1756; and *The Origin, Progress, and Present State of the Marine Society* (London 1770), pp.2-3, 6; *Regulations of the Marine Society: Historical Account* (London 1772), pp.1-2; also John Pugh, *Remarkable Occurrences in the Life of Jonas Hanway* (London 1787, 1788), pp.139-140. Powlett is also spelled Henry Pawlett.

4. John Fielding, *An Account of the Origin and Effects of a Police* (London 1758), p.22.

5. TNA, ADM 2/704, 28/04/1756, p.274 (to Hanway); Hanway, *Three Letters on the Subject of the Marine Society: Letter III* (London 1758), p.5.

6. NMM, MSY/A/1, 29/07/1756; John Fielding, *An Account of the Origin and Effects of a Police* (London 1758), pp.22-23; *Public Advertiser*, 30/07/1756-04/08/1756; Fielding, *An Account of the Receipts and Disbursements Relating to Sir John Fielding's Plan* (London 1769), p.14.

7. NMM, MSY/A/1, 27/04/1759.

8. NMM, MSY/A/1, 08/12/1757.

9. *Regulations of the Marine Society: Dedication* (London 1772, 1775), p.xv; also p.xix of Introduction.

10. See Ruth McClure, *Coram's Children* (New Haven 1981), pp.47-48; and Donna Andrew, *Philanthropy and Police* (Princeton 1989), p.63.

11. *Instructions to Apprentices placed out by the Stepney-Society* (London 1759), pp.3-4.

12. *Instructions to Apprentices placed out by the Stepney-Society* (London 1759), pp.3-4.

13. Paul Langford identifies him as Benjamin Disraeli's father, not grandfather, in Langford, *A Polite and Commercial People* (Oxford 1989, 1998), p.489.

14. See *Public Advertiser*, 10-13/05/1757; *London Magazine*, May 1757, p.257; also performance of *Acis and Galatea* in *Gentleman's Magazine*, June 1757, p.285.

15. TNA, ADM 1/922, Henry Osborne, 26/05/1756; ADM 2/704, 27/05/1756, p.449. A year later an act (31 George II [1757], c.10, s.xvi) was introduced which aimed to insure naval officers against such dangers, by ruling that they could keep the boy's pay if they had been unaware that their servant was an apprentice.

16. *Public Advertiser*, 15/03/1756.

17. Hanway, *Reasons for an Augmentation of at least Twelve Thousand Mariners* (London 1759), p.104.

18. See NMM, MSY/A/2, 17/01/1765, 31/01/1765, 29/08/1765, 10/10/1765, 21/11/1765.

19. NMM, MSY/A/2, 06/04/1769; MSY/A/4, 25/06/1772.

20. NMM, MSY/G/2, p.115, 19/09/1818.

21. *Regulations of the Marine Society: Historical Account* (London 1772), pp.42-45 (also following quotations).

22. Figures (until Dec. 1905) according to report to Board of Trade in 1906 (NMM, MSY/J/3, Appendix A, p.3). The 4,787 boys equipped for the Royal Navy during the Seven Years War have been added to the total. Some, though very few, double-counted boys may be included in the totals. The 387 boys aided after returning from the Seven Years War are not included in the total. A lesser-known aspect of the Society's work is that it also supported girls. William Hickes had ordered that part of his bequest was to be used for arranging apprenticeships for girls (not in seafaring though). From 1771 to 1978, the Society sponsored nearly two thousand apprenticeships and scholarships for girls.

23. TNA, ADM 1/923, Osborne, 20/11/1756.

24. *Public Advertiser*, 03/11/1756.

25. NMM, MSY/A/1, 19/04/1759. A 'fife' is a boy who has been trained to play the fife.

26. NMM, MSY/K/1.

27. HM Sloop *Thorn* (1799), HM Frigate *Solebay* (1814), HM Frigate *Iphigenia* (1833), HM Frigate *Venus* (1848), HM Frigate *Warspite* (1862), and the new *Warspite* (formerly *Conqueror/Waterloo*) (1877).

28. NMM, MSY/A/1, 12/05/1757, 19/05/1757, and 15/09/1757; Hanway, *Three Letters on the Subject of the Marine Society: Letter I* (London 1758), p.21, and *Letter III*, p.46; and Hanway, *Account of the Marine Society* (London 1759, 6th ed.), p.57. There were also plans to teach boys to play the drum.

29. NMM, MSY/O/11, no.711, and Don Kingston, great-great-grandson of William Stevens, in correspondence with the author (13/04/2001).

30. The main author of these instructions was Hanway (see NMM, MSY/A/1, 26/05/1757). For the complete instructions see the Society's rules in Hanway, *Three Letters on the Subject of the Marine Society: Letter III* (London 1758), pp.56-60.

31. See dedication to public in *Regulations of the Marine Society* (London 1772, 1775), p.vii.

32. Josiah Woodward, *The Seaman's Monitor* (London 1705, 1767), pp.iii, 5-6, 23-26, 32-34. Woodward wrote at the turn of the century, but his works were still being published in the middle of the eighteenth century.

33. In case of the landsmen the Society promised right from the start a set of clothing to anyone who could produce a certificate from a regulating captain, testifying that he had enlisted. Captains knew of the Society and would have certainly sent all of their new recruits to the office. And at times, the Society clothed not just landsmen volunteers but also men forced into the Navy by civil magistrates, men rated as ordinary seamen, as well as distressed seamen who returned from prisons in France – see NMM, MSY/A/1, 26/05/1757; Hanway, *Three Letters on the Subject of the Marine Society: Letter II* (London 1758), pp.10-11, and *Letter III* (London 1758), pp.16-17, and *An Account of the Marine Society* (London 1759, 6th ed.), p.52. Once the Admiralty decided that all men from London, volunteers and pressed, were first kept on board a tender, and the Society began to give out its clothing on board, the identification of those who could count as original Marine Society recruits became impossible – see NMM, MSY/A/1, 22/12/1757; Hanway, *Three Letters on the Subject of the Marine Society: Letter III* (London 1758), pp.25-26; NMM, MSY/F/1, p.95 (payment to captain's clerk on board for helping with the distribution of the equipment).

34. See for example NMM, MSY/A/1, 26/05/1757, 14/05/1761, 29/07/1762, 04/11/1762; also NMM, MSY/H/2, no.4158.

35. James Lind, *An Essay on the Most Effectual Means of Preserving Seamen in the Royal Navy* (London 1757, 1762), p.xvii.

36. James Lind, *An Essay on the Most Effectual Means of Preserving Seamen in the Royal Navy* (London 1757), pp.3-4.

37. M D Hay (ed.), *Landsman Hay* (London 1953), p.221.

38. *Gentleman's Magazine*, April 1757, p.150.

39. See Greg Dening, *Mr Bligh's Bad Language* (Cambridge 1992), pp.133-140.

40. See Hanway, *A Letter from a Member of the Marine Society* (London 1757, 3rd ed.), p.22.

41. Hanway, *A Letter from a Member of the Marine Society* (London 1757, 3rd ed.), pp.32-33.

42. See Gilbert Blane, 'Statements of the Comparative Health of the British Navy, from the year 1779 to the year 1814, with Proposals for its Farther Improvement', in *Medico-Chirurgical Transactions*, vol. 6 (1815), p. 542.

43. Clean clothing was especially important when considering that washing the body was difficult during the voyage, as fresh water was too dear, and soap was expensive and less effective in salt water – see N A M Rodger, *The Wooden World* (London 1986, 1988), p.107.

44. For quotations see Lind, *An Essay on the Most Effectual Means of Preserving Seamen in Royal Navy* (London 1757), pp.1-4.

45. Lind, *Two Papers on Fevers and Infection* (London 1761, 1763), p.31.

46. Lind, *An Essay on the Most Effectual Means of Preserving Seamen in the Royal Navy* (London 1757, 1762), pp.2, 4.

47. One consequence of this increasing recognition was the emergence of the Divisional System in the 1770s, whereby the men were divided into small groups and supervised by a midshipman – the system was not only to ensure discipline on board, but also so that someone would keep a close eye on each man's cleanliness and clothes. The Marine Society had already advocated a similar system to inspect the sailors and their clothes back in 1758, so that it would not just be their boys who were properly dressed – see Hanway, *Two Letters: Letter IV* (London 1758),

p.3. In 1759, Captain Richard Howe (later Admiral Lord Howe), in the oldest ship order book we know of, made his midshipmen responsible for checking the men's clothes, cleanliness and whether they had sold or lost any of the clothes supplied to them – see Brian Lavery (ed.), *Shipboard Life and Organisation* (NRS 1998), pp.74-75, 82-91.

Chapter 4 The Typical Jim Hawkins

1. Founder Jonas Hanway is pictured addressing the committee; Lord Romney sits in the chair (a reminder that this is an official engraving, as in reality Romney rarely found the time to act in his role as chairman), while treasurer John Thornton is counting the finances.
2. The statistical analysis of the boys was made possible by three databases. First of all, I am indebted to Dianne Payne, who allowed me to use her database on the Marine Society's boys in the 1770s. Another big help was the group project by Roderick Floud, *Long-Term Changes in Nutrition, Welfare and Productivity in Britain*. And finally I made use of my own database of the Society's recruits, attached on a CD in Pietsch, 'Ships' Boys and Charity in the Mid-Eighteenth Century' (unpublished PhD thesis, University of London 2003).
3. NMM, MSY/H/2, no.4404.
4. NMM, MSY/H/2, no.2602 (Dowsett); MSY/H/1, no.1915 (Woodward). Also MSY/H/2, no.4210 (Richard Phillips).
5. Acts 2 & 3 Anne, c.6, s.I (1703).
6. NMM, MSY/H/2, no.3763.
7. NMM, MSY/H/2, no.2972, also no.3118.
8. NMM, MSY/H/2, no.3008.
9. *Regulations of the Marine Society: Historical Account* (London 1772), p.10.
10. NMM, MSY/H/1, no.1252.
11. Inoculation was replaced at the beginning of the nineteenth century by vaccination, and thanks to worldwide vaccination campaigns smallpox was finally eradicated in the late twentieth century. For more on smallpox see the works by Peter Razzell, *The Conquest of Smallpox* (Sussex 1977), and *Population and Disease* (Sussex 2007); also Ruth McClure, *Coram's Children* (New Haven 1981), p.207. There are allegations against British troops apparently using biological warfare in the Seven Years War and in the American War of Independence, by trying to spread the smallpox among Indian tribes and US troops with infected cloths.
12. NMM, MSY/H/1, no.2264.
13. NMM, MSY/A/1, 26/06/1760; *General Evening Post*, 17/01/1758; *Public Advertiser*, 07&09/04/1758.
14. *Regulations of the Marine Society* (London 1772), p.11.
15. Hanway, *A Letter from a Member of the Marine Society* (London 1757, 4th ed.), p.17.
16. A remark taken from Roderick Floud, Kenneth Wachter, Annabel Gregory, *Height, Health and History* (Cambridge 1990), p.166.
17. Comparison made in Roderick Floud, Kenneth Wachter, Annabel Gregory, *Height, Health and History* (Cambridge 1990), pp.166, 176, 197.
18. NMM, MSY/H/2, no.2925.
19. Taken from Peter Earle, *Sailors* (London 1998), p.18.
20. NMM, MSY/A/1, 27/04/1758. NMM, MSY/H/2, nos.4027, 4200; TNA, ADM 36/5515, p.8, no.5; ADM 36/6776, p.237, no.376; ADM 36/6777, p.257, no.376; ADM 36/6778, p.106, no.376.

21. *The Female Cabin Boy*, a folk song from *c*.1730, reprinted in Terry Castle (ed.), *The Literature of Lesbianism* (New York 2003), pp.248-249.

22. The memoirs of both women are reprinted in *The Lady Tars* (Tucson 2008).

23. See Suzanne Stark, *Female Tars* (London 1996, 1998), pp.107-110.

24. NMM, MSY/A/1, 08/11/1759; and MSY/H/2, no.3511.

25. NMM, MSY/H/2, no.3631.

26. NMM, MSY/A/1, 08/01/1762.

27. NMM, MSY/H/2, no.3442.

28. NMM, MSY/H/2, nos.2414, 2415.

29. Michael Lewis, *A Social History of the Navy* (London 1960), p.58.

30. Based on estimates given in John Landers, *Death and the Metropolis* (Cambridge 1993), p.180.

31. See Dianne Payne, 'Children of the Poor in London' (unpublished PhD thesis, University of Hertfordshire 2008), p.159.

32. See for example Hanway, *Observations on the Causes of the Dissoluteness which Reigns Among the Lower Classes of the People* (London 1772), pp.5-6; *Defects of Police* (London 1775), p.31; and *Regulations of the Marine Society* (London 1772), pp.12-13.

33. *Public Advertiser*, 29/01/1757.

34. Hanway worried as much about the increased business competition from Jewish merchants as about the religious impact their naturalisation might have on Christianity in Britain. Nevertheless, the Society had an active Jewish committee member in the person of Michael Adolphus.

35. Solomons is mentioned in Todd Endelman, *The Jews of Georgian England* (1979, Michigan 1999), p.116.

36. NMM, MSY/O/2, 1777, no.1061.

37. NMM, MSY/O/2, 1778, no.458.

38. NMM, MSY/A/2, 12/04/1764.

39. Olaudah Equiano, *The Interesting Narrative of the Life of Olaudah Equiano* (Boston 1791, 1995). For the controversy regarding Equiano's birthplace, see Vincent Carretta, *Equiano, the African: Biography of a Self Made Man* (Athens, Georgia 2005).

Chapter 5 Jim's Motives: Sailors and Youth Culture

1. *Public Advertiser*, 16/12/1754.

2. For statistics on delinquency see NMM, MSY/O/1-4, analysed with the help of Dianne Payne's computerised database.

3. Hanway, *Three Letters on the Subject of the Marine Society: Letter II* (London 1758), p.7.

4. Hanway, *A Letter from a Member of the Marine Society* (London 1757, 3rd. ed.), p.8.

5. *Regulations of the Marine Society* (London 1772), pp.12-14.

6. William Robinson, *Jack Nastyface* (London 1836, 1973), pp.25-26.

7. Hanway, *Three Letters on the Subject of the Marine Society: Letter I* (London 1758), p.6. See also Butler Swift's poem *Tyburn to the Marine Society* (1759), in which the Tyburn gibbet curses the Society for robbing him of those who were normally raised to feed him.

8. Hanway, *Two Letters: Letter IV* (London 1758), p.34.

9. NMM, MSY/A/1, 13/09/1759; MSY/H/2, no.3525; MSY/U/21; MSY/F/1, 20/09/1759, p.184.

10. *Old Bailey Proceedings Online* (www.oldbaileyonline.org, accessed 07/04/2009), April 1804,

trial of William Barrett (t18040411-81).

11. *Old Bailey Proceedings Online* (www.oldbaileyonline.org, accessed 07/04/2009), September 1793, trial of George Mackay (t17930911-14).

12. *Old Bailey Proceedings Online* (www.oldbaileyonline.org, accessed 07/04/2009), July 1798, trial of George Renny (t17980704-21).

13. *Old Bailey Proceedings Online* (www.oldbaileyonline.org, accessed 07/04/2009), February 1814, trial of Richard Mills (t18140216-79).

14. See Pietsch, 'Ships' Boys and Charity in the Mid-Eighteenth Century' (unpublished PhD thesis, University of London 2003), pp.134-135.

15. Daniel Defoe, *Robinson Crusoe* (London 1719, 1975), p.7.

16. Gordon Grant, *The Life and Adventures of John Nicol* (London 1822, 1937), pp.36-38.

17. M D Hay, *Landsman Hay* (London 1953), pp.27-31.

18. William Robinson, *Jack Nastyface* (London 1836, 1973), p.19.

19. *Edward Barlow's Journal of his Life at Sea*, Basil Lubbock (ed.), vol.1 (London 1934), pp.19-28.

20. Mary Lacy, *The History of the Female Shipwright* (London 1773), in *The Lady Tars* (Tucson 2008), p.65.

21. *Gentleman's Magazine*, March 1759, p.125.

22. *Edward Barlow's Journal of his Life at Sea*, Basil Lubbock (ed.), vol.1 (London 1934), pp.41, 60.

23. See appendix of M D George, *London Life in the Eighteenth Century* (London 1925, 1965), pp.420-421.

24. Tobias Smollett, *The Adventures of Roderick Random* (London 1748; Oxford 1999), p.30. Smollett had himself at one point in his life been a surgeon's mate in the Navy.

25. Adam Smith, *An Inquiry into the Nature and Causes of the Wealth of Nations* (London 1776; Indiana 1994), p.126.

26. Since 1653 Royal Navy wages stood at 24s per month for able seamen, 19s for ordinary seamen, and 18s for landsmen. Sixpence towards the Greenwich Hospital, and 1s for the Chatham Chest, were subtracted from the pay. The Navy's wages remained unchanged until 1797, the year of the naval mutinies coinciding with a big jump in inflation and the suspension of the Pound's gold convertibility through the Bank Restriction Act (37 George III, c.45). In merchant shipping in comparison, where peacetime wages also remained remarkably steady around 25s, the extra demand for sailors in wartime put seamen in a better bargaining position, and wages could rise up to 60s or even 70s per month.

27. See E G Thomas, 'The Old Poor Law and Maritime Apprenticeship', *Mariner's Mirror*, vol.63 (1977), pp.154; and Ralph Davis, *The Rise of the English Shipping Industry* (Newton Abbot 1962, 1972), p.119.

28. Samuel Richardson (presumably), *Apprentice's Vade Mecum*, ed. by Augustan Reprint Society, nos.169-170 (London 1734; Los Angeles 1975), pp.51-52.

29. See NMM, MSY/A/1, 08/01/1762; *Regulations of the Marine Society* (London 1772), p.41; and Hanway, *A Letter from a Member of the Marine Society* (London 1757, 1st ed.), p.29.

30. James Boswell, *The Life of Samuel Johnson* (London 1791), quoted in Christopher Lloyd, *The British Seaman* (London 1968, 1970), p.209.

31. *Edward Barlow's Journal of his Life at Sea*, vol.1 (London 1934), p.61.

32. *Edward Barlow's Journal of his Life at Sea*, vol.1 (London 1934), p.28.

33. William Robinson, *Jack Nastyface* (London 1836, 1973), p.135.

34. Thomas Trotter, *Medicina Nautica* (London 1797), pp.35-36.

35. W H G Kingston, *From Powder Monkey to Admiral* (London 1870, 1910), pp.7-8.

36. Thomas Trotter, *Medicina Nautica* (London 1797), pp.35-36.

37. Charles Dibdin, *The Sea-Songs of Charles Dibdin* (London 1852?), p.20.

38. William Spavens, *The Narrative of William Spavens* (Louth 1796; London 1998), p.1.

39. John Nicol, *The Life and Adventures of John Nicol* (London 1822, 1937), p.37.

40. Adam Smith, *An Inquiry into the Nature and Causes of the Wealth of Nations* (London 1776; Indiana 1994), p.127.

41. Excerpt of a ballad reprinted in Charles Robinson, *The British Tar in Fact and Fiction* (London & New York 1909), p.369.

42. Leech, *A Voice from the Main Deck* (London 1857, 1999), p.62.

43. Smith, *An Inquiry into the Nature and Causes of the Wealth of Nations* (London 1776; Indiana 1994), p.127.

44. Leech, *A Voice from the Main Deck* (London 1857, 1999), pp.10, 12.

45. Leech, *A Voice from the Main Deck* (London 1857, 1999), p.14.

46. Leech, *A Voice from the Main Deck* (London 1857, 1999), pp.41-42.

47. Charles Dibdin, *The Sea-Songs of Charles Dibdin* (London 1852?), p.96.

48. Reprinted in Charles Robinson, *The British Tar in Fact and Fiction* (London & New York 1909), p.421.

49. *Edward Barlow's Journal of his Life at Sea*, vol.1 (London 1934), p.28.

50. Cindy McCreery, 'True Blue and Black, Brown and Fair: Prints of British Sailors and their Women During the Revolutionary and Napoleonic Wars', *British Journal for Eighteenth-Century Studies*, vol.23 (2000), p.146.

51. Defoe cited in Peter Earle, *Sailors* (London 1998), p.31.

52. Edward Ward, *The Wooden World dissected* (Edinburgh 1707, 1779), p.75.

53. Edward Ward, *The Wooden World dissected* (Edinburgh 1707, 1779), p.75.

54. John Fielding, *A Brief Description of the Cities of London and Westminster* (London 1776), p.xv.

55. See, for example, Captain Graham's defence for pressing a man in TNA, ADM 1/3681, 05/01/1779, p.135; also in Nicholas Rogers, *Crowds, Culture and Politics in Georgian Britain* (Oxford 1998), p.110.

56. Isaac Land, *War, Nationalism, and the British Sailor* (New York 2009), pp.39, 43-44.

57. Thomas Trotter, *Medicina Nautica* (London 1797), p.35.

58. *A Letter to a Naval Officer from a Friend* (London 1797), p.11, by an unknown author, cited in Isaac Land, *War, Nationalism, and the British Sailor* (New York 2009), p.39.

59. Peter Burke, *Popular Culture in Early Modern Europe* (Aldershot 1978, 1994), pp.43-46.

60. Isaac Land, *Domesticating the Maritime* (unpublished PhD thesis, University of Michigan 1999), pp.225-248; and Land, 'The Many-Tongued Hydra: Sea Talk, Maritime Culture, and Atlantic Identities, 1700-1850,' *Journal of American and Comparative Cultures*, vol.25, nos.3-4 (December 2002), p.416. Land argues that there were various maritime subcultures (linked to circumstances, trades, localities and nationalities), instead of just one homogenous, nationwide or even transnational maritime culture, as suggested by Rediker and Linebaugh in *The Many-Headed Hydra* (London 2000).

61. Charles Dibdin, *The Sea-Songs of Charles Dibdin* (London 1852?), p.11.

62. *The Letters of Private Wheeler, 1809-1828*, edited by B H Liddell Hart (Adlestrop,

Gloucestershire 1951), p.47; see also p.46.

63. See Peter Linebaugh & Marcus Rediker, *The Many-Headed Hydra* (London 2000); and Marcus Rediker, *Between the Devil and the Deep Blue Sea* (Cambridge 1987, 1998).

64. M D Hay, *Landsman Hay* (London 1953), pp.44, 72, 94, 108-109, 201.

65. See Isaac Land, 'The Humours of Sailortown: Atlantic History Meets Subculture Theory', in Clark, Owens & Smith (eds.), *City Limits* (Montreal 2010), pp.329-331.

66. M D Hay, *Landsman Hay* (London 1953), p.190.

67. Charles McPherson, *Life on Board a Man-of-War* (Glasgow 1829), p.1, also in Isaac Land, *War, Nationalism, and the British Sailor* (New York 2009), p.41. For the uniform look of contemporary youth cultures see for example the photo collection by Mollison & Morris, *The Disciples* (London 2008).

68. John Cremer, *Ramblin' Jack* (London 1936), pp.39, 194.

69. Remarkably, the first ship's boy with a tattoo I ever came across pre-dated Cook's explorations. In 1763, fourteen-year-old Marine Society boy Henry Rowning (NMM, MSY/H/3, no.43) had upon his return from sea service his name written on his right arm. If this was some sort of tattoo, then it is noteworthy, as the question of how far tattooing had disappeared in European culture after the Middle Ages, and only re-emerged in the late eighteenth century with Cook's explorations of the Pacific (together with the Polynesian loan word 'tattoo'), is still debated in academia – see Jane Caplan (ed.), *Written on the Body* (London 2000), pp.xv-xx; and Nicholas Thomas in discussion with the author (02/2003).

70. Charles Dibdin, *The Sea-Songs of Charles Dibdin* (London 1852?), p.96.

Chapter 6 Jim's Life on Board

1. *Edward Barlow's Journal of his Life at Sea*, vol.1 (London 1934), p.33.

2. Mary Lacy, *The History of the Female Shipwright* (London 1773), reprinted in *The Lady Tars* (Tucson 2008), p.67.

3. *Historical Account* in *Regulations of the Marine Society* (London 1772), pp.14-15.

4. Hanway, *A Letter from a Member of the Marine Society* (London 1757, 1st ed.), p.10, and NMM, MSY/A/1, 14/04/1757.

5. Hanway, *A Letter from a Member of the Marine Society* (London 1757, 4th ed.), p.10.

6. John Fielding, *An Account of the Origin and Effects of a Police Set on Foot by His Grace the Duke of Newcastle in the year 1753* (London 1758), p.24.

7. See the letter to *Grand Magazine* in June 1760, reprinted in the British Library's 1760 edition of Hanway, *An Account of the Marine Society* (London 1759, 6th ed.), pp.152-153.

8. Hanway, *Two Letters: Letter IV* (London 1758), p.29.

9. John Fielding, *An Account of the Receipts and Disbursements Relating to Sir John Fielding's Plan* (London 1769), pp.9-10.

10. Hanway, *A Letter from a Member of the Marine Society* (London 1757, 4th ed.), pp.10-11. See also Hanway, *An Account of the Marine Society* (London 1759, 6th ed.), pp.54-55.

11. See Ruth K McClure, *Coram's Children* (New Haven 1981), pp.219-20, and Victor Neuberg, *Popular Education in Eighteenth Century England* (London 1971).

12. See the 'Additional Regulations' (1756), in *Regulations and Instructions Relating to His Majesty's Service at Sea* (1757, 9th ed.), pp.191-232; and TNA, ADM 2/81, 30/08/1758, pp.62-63.

13. Olaudah Equiano, *The Interesting Narrative of the Life of Olaudah Equiano* (Boston 1791, 1995, Bedford edition), p.65.

14. Mary Lacy, *The History of the Female Shipwright* (London 1773), reprinted in *The Lady Tars* (Tucson 2008), pp.66-67.

15. Mary Lacy, *The History of the Female Shipwright* (London 1773), reprinted in *The Lady Tars* (Tucson 2008), p.66.

16. See for example Hanway, *A Letter from a Member of the Marine Society* (London 1757, 3rd ed.), pp.10-11, 13; and *Christian Knowledge made easy* (London 1763), pp.4, 69 (letter to commanders).

17. Mary Lacy, *The History of the Female Shipwright* (London 1773), reprinted in *The Lady Tars* (Tucson 2008), pp.81, 88.

18. Pietsch, 'Ships' Boys and Charity in the Mid-Eighteenth Century' (unpublished PhD thesis, University of London 2003), p.324.

19. NMM, MSY/A/2, 04/11/1762.

20. Equiano, *The Interesting Narrative of the Life of Olaudah Equiano* (Boston 1791, 1995, Bedford edition), p.83.

21. Mathew Barker, *Greenwich Hospital* (London, 1826), cited and interpreted in Isaac Land, *War, Nationalism, and the British Sailor* (New York 2009), p.35.

22. Daniel Goodall, *Salt Water Sketches* (Inverness 1860), p.21.

23. Mary Anne Talbot, *Life and Surprising Adventures of Mary Anne Talbot* (London 1809), reprinted in *The Lady Tars* (Tucson 2008), p.157.

24. Mary Lacy, *The History of the Female Shipwright* (London 1773), reprinted in *The Lady Tars* (Tucson 2008), pp.75-76.

25. Taken from Roy & Lesley Adkins, *Jack Tar* (London 2008), p.3.

26. Daniel Goodall, *Salt Water Sketches* (Inverness 1860), pp.4-5.

27. M D Hay (ed), *Landsman Hay* (London 1953), pp.43-44.

28. Leech, *A Voice from the Main Deck* (London 1857, 1999), pp.20-21.

29. Leech, *A Voice from the Main Deck* (London 1857, 1999), pp.28-29, 40.

30. Sir William Henry Dillon, *A Narrative of my Professional Adventures*, vol.1 (NRS 1953), p.23.

31. Walter's story is taken from John Sugden, *Nelson* (London 2004, 2005), p.611.

32. Taken from B R Burg, *Boys at Sea* (Houndmills & New York 2007), p.111.

33. Taken from Roy & Lesley Adkins, *Jack Tar* (London 2008), p.10; see also Aaron Thomas, *The Caribbean Journal of a Royal Navy Seaman, 1798-1799* (http://scholar.library.miami.edu/thomas, accessed 22/11/2009). However, it appears that Joseph was one of the 'Jolly Boat Boys' and possibly already twenty years old (according to TNA, ADM 36/13726, p.14, no.309).

34. Charles Robinson, *The British Tar in Fact and Fiction* (London & New York 1909), p.91.

35. Mary Lacy, *The History of the Female Shipwright* (London 1773), reprinted in *The Lady Tars* (Tucson 2008), pp.73, 79.

36. NMM, MSY/G/1, p.110.

37. Edward Coxere, *Adventures by Sea* (Oxford 1945), p.7. Edward served on board a merchantman.

38. Goodall, *Salt Water Sketches* (Inverness 1860), p.126.

39. William Robinson, *Jack Nastyface* (London 1836, 1973), p.55. See also the eighteenth-century ballad *The Jolly Sailor's True Description of a Man-of-War* mentioning random beatings by ten-year-old midshipmen, in Charles Robinson, *The British Tar in Fact and Fiction* (London & New York 1909), p.409.

40. Charles Pemberton, *The Autobiography of Pel. Verjuice* (London 1929), p.148.

41. For the *Hermione* mutiny see Dudley Pope, *The Black Ship* (London 1963).

42. See *The Trial of the Mutineers, late of his Majesty's Ship Téméraire, held on board the Gladiator, in Portsmouth Harbour, January 6, 1802* (London 1802), and Goodall, *Salt Water Sketches* (Inverness 1860), pp.37-46.

43. See John Cremer, *Ramblin' Jack* (London 1936), p.44.

44. Cited in Peter Earle, *Sailors* (London 1998), p.97.

45. See also D A B Ronald, *Young Nelsons* (Oxford 2009), p.87.

46. Mary Lacy, *The History of the Female Shipwright* (London 1773), reprinted in *The Lady Tars* (Tucson 2008), pp.71-72; and NMM, MSY/H/2, nos.3319-3327.

47. Equiano, *The Interesting Narrative of the Life of Olaudah Equiano* (Boston 1791, 1995, Bedford edition), pp.65-66.

48. NMM, MSY/A/1, 27/10/1757.

49. TNA, ADM 2/1056, 24/10/1760.

50. NMM, MSY/A/1, 16/03/1758; and MSY/H/2, no. 2226 (Arpin); TNA, ADM 51/3748; ADM 1/1893, Richard Hughes (no mention of the affair).

51. Phrase in 22 George II, c.33, s.II, par.29 (1749).

52. TNA, ADM 12/26; ADM 1/5295-5302.

53. TNA, ADM 12/26, pp. 33-35; NMM, MSY/H/2, no.4153 (also Hodgkins).

54. NMM, MSY/H/2, no.4334 (also Findall); TNA, ADM 1/5300, 02/07/1761 (Newton/Finlay).

55. See B R Burg, *Boys at Sea* (Houndmills & New York 2007), pp.92-94.

56. TNA, ADM 1/5266, 09/10/1706, taken from B R Burg, *Boys at Sea* (Houndmills & New York 2007), pp.34-35.

57. TNA, ADM 1/5300, 02/07/1761 (Berry); NMM, MSY/H/2, no.3742.

58. TNA, ADM 12/26, pp.16-21; MSY/H/1, no.1183.

59. Arthur N Gilbert, 'Buggery and the British Navy, 1700-1861', *Journal of Social History*, vol.10 (1976), pp.72-98.

60. In support see Markus Eder, *Crime and Punishment in the Royal Navy of the Seven Years War* (Aldershot 2004), p.76.

61. In Richard Woodman, . . .*of Daring Temper* (London 2006), p.42.

62. John Bechervaise, *A Farewell to my Old Shipmates and Messmates* (Portsea 1847), p.17-18 (also 5-6, 11-17, 20, 40); also in Isaac Land, *War, Nationalism, and the British Sailor* (New York 2009), p.38.

63. Leech, *A Voice from the Main Deck* (London 1857, 1999), p.63.

64. Leech, *A Voice from the Main Deck* (London 1857, 1999), p.64.

65. Gordon Grant, *The Life and Adventures of John Nicol* (London 1822, 1937), p.41.

66. Edward Ward, *The Wooden World dissected* (Edinburgh 1707, 1779), p.2.

67. Equiano, *The Interesting Narrative of the Life of Olaudah Equiano* (Boston 1791, 1995, Bedford edition), p.65. See also Shaun Regan, 'Slavery, Service, and the Sea: Olaudah Equiano and the Seven Years' War', in Frans De Bruyn & Shaun Regan (eds.), *The Culture of the Seven Years' War: Empire, Identity, and the Arts* (forthcoming publication).

68. See British Library's edition of Hanway, *An Account of the Marine Society* (London 1759), p.145.

69. John Cremer, *Ramblin' Jack* (London 1936), pp.46-62.

70. Citation taken from N A M Rodger, *The Command of the Ocean* (London 2004), pp.504-505.

71. Leech, *A Voice from the Main Deck* (London 1857, 1999), p.51.

72. See Rodger, *The Command of the Ocean* (London 2004), p.504.

73. Leech, *A Voice from the Main Deck* (London 1857, 1999), p.146.

74. Hanway, *A Journal of Eight Days' Journey from Portsmouth to Kingston upon Thames . . . an Essay on Tea* (London 1756).

75. Gilbert Blane, 'Statements of the Comparative Health of the British Navy, from the Year 1779 to the Year 1814, with Proposals for its Farther Improvement', in *Medico-Chirurgical Transactions*, vol.6 (1815), p.525.

76. *Edward Barlow's Journal of his Life at Sea*, vol.1 (London 1934), p.63.

77. See 'Additional Regulations' in *Regulations and Instructions Relating to His Majesty's Service at Sea* (1787, 12th ed.), p.200.

78. Goodall, *Salt Water Sketches* (Inverness 1860), pp.25-26.

79. Goodall, *Salt Water Sketches* (Inverness 1860), p.26.

80. Robinson, *Jack Nastyface* (London 1836, 1973), pp.88-91.

81. Grant, *The Life and Adventures of John Nicol* (London 1822, 1937), pp.38-39.

Chapter 7 Jim's Coming of Age at Sea: Masculinity and the Horrors of War

1. Cited in D A B Ronald, *Young Nelsons* (Oxford 2009), p.86.

2. See Jonathan Lamb, *Preserving the Self in the South Seas* (Chicago & London 2001), pp.120-121.

3. Mary Lacy, *The History of the Female Shipwright* (London 1773), reprinted in *The Lady Tars* (Tucson 2008), pp.70, 73.

4. Cited in Roy & Lesley Adkins, *Jack Tar* (London 2008), p.23.

5. Equiano, *The Interesting Narrative of the Life of Olaudah Equiano* (Boston 1791, 1995, Bedford edition), p.65.

6. See for example complaint by Captain O'Hara, in NMM, MSY/A/1, 27/04/1758.

7. M D Hay, *Landsman Hay* (London 1953), pp.34-38.

8. For deserting ships' boys in the mid century see Roland Pietsch, 'Ships' Boys and Charity in the Mid-Eighteenth Century' (unpublished PhD thesis, University of London 2003), pp.230-235.

9. See the notes on the Navy sources at the end of this book, and also Pietsch, 'Ships' Boys and Charity in the Mid-Eighteenth Century' (unpublished PhD thesis, University of London 2003), pp.201-204.

10. TNA, ADM 36/5667, pp.126-127 (nos.129 & 148), p.134 (no.221), p.221 (nos.31 & 46); ADM 36/5669, p.112, no.31; ADM 36/5595, p.147 (no.5).

11. TNA, ADM 1/2210, William McCleverty, 11/07/1758.

12. Also Nicholas Brian. NMM, MSY/H/1 (nos.182 & 213). TNA, ADM 36/6943, pp.3-4, 58-59 (nos.48 & 75); ADM 36/6944, pp.213-214 (nos.12 & 28); ADM 36/6200, pp.19-20 (no nos); ADM 36/6218, p.100 (nos.728 & 742); ADM 36/7099, pp.10, 30 (nos.40 & 41).

13. Pietsch, 'Ships' Boys and Charity in the Mid-Eighteenth Century' (unpublished PhD thesis, University of London 2003), pp.236-240.

14. NMM, MSY/H/1 (nos.1167 & 1169); TNA, ADM 36/6683, pp.3, 50, 146 (nos.39 & 40).

15. William Laird Clowes, *The Royal Navy*, vol.3 (London 1898), p.296.

16. In the Hospital's *Digest of Minutes* (TNA, ADM 67/266) the policy towards servants seems

nowhere discussed. More research is needed. A famous example from a later period, according to Pieter van der Merwe of the National Maritime Museum in Greenwich, was Tom Allen, who in old age was admitted into the Hospital on the basis of having once been Nelson's servant. For the Marine Society's collections see for example NMM, MSY/A/1, 27/10/1757, and for the blind boy: NMM, MSY/A/2, 28/02/1765, 07/03/1765, 14/03/1765, 25/04/1765, 01/08/1765.

17. Sir William Henry Dillon, *A Narrative of my Professional Adventures*, vol.1 (NRS 1953), p.125.

18. Augustus Phillimore, *The Life of Admiral of the Fleet Sir William Parker* (London 1876-80), cited in D A B Ronald, *Young Nelsons* (Oxford 2009), p.115.

19. Augustus Phillimore, *The Life of Admiral of the Fleet Sir William Parker* (London 1876-80), cited in D A B Ronald, *Young Nelsons* (Oxford 2009), p.120.

20. Talbot, *Life and Surprising Adventures of Mary Anne Talbot* (London 1809), reprinted in *The Lady Tars* (Tucson 2008), p.160.

21. Goodall, *Salt Water Sketches* (Inverness 1860), p.163.

22. Loyall Farragut, *The Life of David Glasgow Farragut* (New York 1879), cited in D A B Ronald, *Young Nelsons* (Oxford 2009), p.245. David served in the US Navy.

23. Equiano, *The Interesting Narrative of the Life of Olaudah Equiano* (Boston 1791, 1995, Bedford edition), pp.68-69.

24. Hay, *Landsman Hay* (London 1953), p.181.

25. Thomas Trotter, *Medicina Nautica* (London 1797), p.38.

26. Sir William Henry Dillon, *A Narrative of my Professional Adventures*, vol.1 (NRS 1953), p.125.

27. Leech, *A Voice from the Main Deck* (London 1857, 1999), p.74.

28. Leech, *A Voice from the Main Deck* (London 1857, 1999), p.75.

29. Leech, *A Voice from the Main Deck* (London 1857, 1999), pp.75-76.

30. Leech, *A Voice from the Main Deck* (London 1857, 1999), p.76.

31. Charles Pemberton, *The Autobiography of Pel. Verjuice* (London 1929), p.202.

32. Robinson, *Jack Nastyface* (London 1836, 1973), p.110.

33. Robinson, *Jack Nastyface* (London 1836, 1973), p.115.

34. Leech, *A Voice from the Main Deck* (London 1857, 1999), p.76.

35. Leech, *A Voice from the Main Deck* (London 1857, 1999), p.68.

36. Leech, *A Voice from the Main Deck* (London 1857, 1999), pp.73-74.

37. See Roy & Lesley Adkins, *Jack Tar* (London 2008), p.299.

38. Leech, *A Voice from the Main Deck* (London 1857, 1999), p.81.

39. Sir William Henry Dillon, *A Narrative of my Professional Adventures*, vol.1 (NRS 1953), p.130.

40. Leech, *A Voice from the Main Deck* (London 1857, 1999), pp.81, 83.

41. Leech, *A Voice from the Main Deck* (London 1857, 1999), pp.81-82.

42. For references to Navy and Marine Society sources see Roland Pietsch, 'Ships' Boys and Charity in the Mid-Eighteenth Century' (unpublished PhD thesis, University of London 2003), pp.236-237, 301-357.

43. *London Magazine*, May 1758, pp.246-247.

44. See Rodger, *The Command of the Ocean* (London 2004), p.319.

45. See Gilbert Blane, 'Statements of the Comparative Health of the British Navy, from the Year 1779 to the Year 1814, with Proposals for its Farther Improvement', in *Medico-Chirurgical Transactions*, vol.6 (1815), pp.561-563.

46. George's story is taken from Roy & Lesley Adkins, *Jack Tar* (London 2008), pp.245-246.

47. Leech, *A Voice from the Main Deck* (London 1857, 1999), pp.83-87.

48. Pietsch, 'Ships' Boys and Charity in the Mid-Eighteenth Century' (unpublished PhD thesis, University of London 2003), pp.240-248.

49. *Regulations and instructions Relating to His Majesty's service at sea* (1757, 9th ed.), pp. 29-30.

50. William Robinson, *Jack Nastyface* (London 1836, 1973), p.55.

51. Patrick O'Brian, *Master and Commander* (London 1970, 2002), p.144.

52. Hay, *Landsman Hay* (London 1953), p.93.

53. NMM, MSY/O/9, no.11142; MSY/P/4, no.11142; MSY/K/2, p.46, no.2538; MSY/B/8, 25-30/09/1809, 05-12/07/1810, 09/07/1812; MSY/D/3, 21/07/1812; MSY/G/1, p.8; and John Marshall, *The Royal Navy Biography: Supplement, Part IV* (London 1830), pp.407-418.

54. NMM, MSY/K/2, no.2538.

55. See NMM, MSY/B/8, 14-28/09/1809, 05-12/07/1810, 09/07/1812.

56. See Rodger, *The Command of the Ocean* (London 2004), pp.445, 508, 547. I am also indebted to Nicholas Rodger for discussions of social mobility in the Navy.

57. According to Anthony Lincoln & Robert McEwen, *Lord Eldon's Anecdote Book* (London 1960), p.20.

58. Charles Pemberton, *The Autobiography of Pel. Verjuice* (London 1929), p.148.

59. See Rodger, *The Command of the Ocean* (London 2004), p.508.

60. Samantha Cavell, 'A Social History of Midshipmen and Quarterdeck Boys in the Royal Navy, 1761-1831' (unpublished PhD thesis, University of Exeter 2010).

Chapter 8 Jim's Return from the Sea

1. M D Hay, *Landsman Hay* (London 1953), pp.171-172.

2. NMM, MSY/O/8 & MSY/P/4, no.10749.

3. Charles Robinson, *The British Tar in Fact and Fiction* (London & New York 1909), p.244.

4. Charles Pemberton, *The Autobiography of Pel. Verjuice* (London 1929).

5. Adam Smith, *An Inquiry into the Nature and Causes of the Wealth of Nations* (London 1776; Indiana 1994), p.470.

6. For all of the proposals see Isaac Land, *War, Nationalism, and the British Sailor* (New York 2009), p.86.

7. See Marcus Rediker, *Between the Devil and the Deep Blue Sea* (Cambridge 1987, 1998).

8. NMM, MSY/A/2, 12/07/1764.

9. See Peter Earle, 'English Sailors, 1570-1775', in Paul van Royen, Jaap Bruijn & Jan Lucassen (eds.), *'Those Emblems of Hell'?* (St. John's 1997), pp.75-83; also Peter Linebaugh, *The London Hanged* (London 1991, 1993), p.127; and Ralph Davis, *The Rise of the English Shipping Industry* (Newton Abbot 1962, 1972), pp.58-80, 137.

10. See acts 12 Charles II, c.16 (1660); 12 Anne, c.14 (1712); 3 George III, c.8 (1762).

11. John Bechervaise, *A Farewell to my Old Shipmates and Messmates* (Portsea 1847), pp.17-18.

12. Reprinted in Charles Robinson, *The British Tar in Fact and Fiction* (London & New York 1909), p.432.

13. NMM, MSY/A/2, 25/08/1763, also 16/12/1762.

14. Mary Lacy, *The History of the Female Shipwright* (London 1773), reprinted in *The Lady Tars* (Tucson 2008), pp.91, 93.

15. TNA, ADM 2/89, pp.443-445, 480-484; ADM 2/232, pp.71, 115; ADM 2/722, pp.140-142, 175; ADM 3/70, 23/12/1762, 20/01/1763.

16. NMM, MSY/A/2, 04/10/1764.

17. NMM, MSY/A/2, 01/12/1763.

18. John Fielding, *An Account of the Origin and Effects of a Police* (London 1758), p.25.

19. NMM, MSY/A/2, 20/12/1764; MSY/H/4, no.342.

20. NMM, MSY/A/2, 04/10/1764.

21. John Cremer, *Ramblin' Jack* (London 1936), pp.68-70.

22. NMM, MSY/A/2, 17/03/1763, 31/03/1763.

23. NMM, MSY/G/2, p.106, 21/06/1818.

24. John Fielding *An Account of the Receipts and Disbursements Relating to Sir John Fielding's Plan* (London 1769), p.15.

25. R. L. Stevenson, *Kidnapped* (London 1886, 1895), p.63.

26. Thomas Trotter, *Medicina Nautica* (London 1797), p.38.

27. Edward Ward, *The London Spy* (London 1709, East Lansing 1993), pp.245-246.

28. See Gilbert Blane, 'Statements of the Comparative Health of the British Navy, from the Year 1779 to the Year 1814, with Proposals for its Farther Improvement', in *Medico-Chirurgical Transactions*, vol.6 (1815), pp.564-565; and Michael Lewis, *A Social History of the Navy* (London 1960), pp.396-397.

29. Gilbert Blane, *Select Dissertations on Several Subjects of Medical Science*, vol.1 (London 1833), p.84.

30. See David Russel, *Scenes from Bedlam* (London 1997), p.55.

31. Isaac Land, *War, Nationalism, and the British Sailor* (New York 2009), pp.38-39.

32. I am indebted to Nikola Kern for our conversations on the possible psychological effects. The rounds of beer I paid for in the pub were not enough to express my gratitude. While we discussed the topic, a brick flew through the pub's side-window, narrowly missing the regulars sitting at the bar. As the attackers had immediately fled on scooters, the punters returned to the seats where they had sat before, next to the broken window and where the brick had hit the bar. Going home, or at least taking a seat further away from the window, would have been a sensible precaution to take, seeing that this seemed part of an ongoing dispute. Yet in their world this was not an option, even if one of them had quietly thought about it.

33. All testimonies of the sons of sailors are taken from Jane Humphries' forthcoming book *Childhood and Child Labour in the British Industrial Revolution* (Cambridge 2010). I am indebted to Jane Humphries for allowing me to read her manuscript.

34. Leech, *A Voice from the Main Deck* (London 1857, 1999), p.127-128.

35. Leech, *A Voice from the Main Deck* (London 1857, 1999), p.130.

36. Leech, *A Voice from the Main Deck* (London 1857, 1999), p.130.

37. Daniel Goodall, *Salt Water Sketches* (Inverness 1860), p.63.

38. Suzanne Stark, *Female Tars* (London 1996, 1998), p.125.

Epilogue

1. R L Stevenson, *Treasure Island* (London 1883, 1927), p.5. For Billy Bones' continuing presence in youth culture see The Pogues' song *Billy's Bones* (1985) and The Libertines' *Time for Heroes* (2002).

2. Samuel Johnson, by the way, defined youth in his first eighteenth-century English language dictionary as lasting from the age of fourteen to twenty-eight.

3. Nauticus (or The Sailors Advocate), *The Rights of the Sailors Vindicated* (London 1772), p.30,

calculates with 120,000 seamen to a total population of 8.5 million.

4. See also David J Starkey, 'War and the Market for Seafarers in Britain, 1736-1792', in Lewis R Fisher & Helge W Nordvik (eds.), *Shipping and Trade* (Pontefract 1990), p.39.

5. An explanation given by Glyn Williams in discussion with the sceptical author (2003).

6. NMM, MSY/B/8, 19/05/1810.

7. Based on estimates given in John Landers, *Death and the Metropolis* (Cambridge 1993), pp.99-100, 180.

8. Charles Pemberton, *The Autobiography of Pel. Verjuice* (London 1929), p.108.

9. From an advertisement copied in NMM, MSY/A/1, 08/01/1762.

10. Hanway, *A Letter from a Member of the Marine Society* (London 1757, 3rd ed.), p.4.

11. Walpole cited in Daniel Baugh, *British Naval Administration in the Age of Walpole* (Princeton 1965), p.1.

12. Leech, *A Voice from the Main Deck* (London 1857, 1999), p.81.

Bibliography

Primary Sources

Manuscript Sources — Royal Navy (Admiralty)
All held at The National Archives (TNA) in Kew, London.

ADM 1/655	The Downs Commander-in-Chief's Letters to Admiralty, 1758-1760
ADM 1/921-939	Portsmouth Commander-in-Chief's Letters to Admiralty, 1756-1763
ADM 1/1435-2738	Captains' Letters to Admiralty, 1698-1839
ADM 1/3681	Solicitor of the Admiralty, 1779-1783
ADM 1/4120-6	Letters from secretaries of state to Admiralty
ADM 1/4280	Letters from Societies, etc., to Admiralty, 1718-1810
ADM 1/5164-5179	Privy Council Office's Letters, 1755-1794
ADM 1/5295-5302	Courts Martial, 1755-1764
ADM 2/76-91	Lords' Letters: Orders and Instructions, 1754-1764
ADM 2/220-233	Lords' Personal Letters (to Navy Board), 1756-1764
ADM 2/371	Lords' Letters to Secretaries of State, 1756-1765
ADM 2/515-535	Secretary's Letters to Public Officers and Flag Officers, 1755-1763
ADM 2/705-722	Secretary's Common Letters, 1756-1763
ADM 2/1055-1057	Secretary's Legal Correspondence, 1747-1770
ADM 2/1331-1332	Secretary's Secret Letters, 1745-1778
ADM 3/65-70	Admiralty Board Minutes, 1756-1763
ADM 6/18-19	Commission and Warrant Books, 1751-1763
ADM 6/34-35	Commissions and Warrants (sent to outports/overseas), 1757-1777
ADM 6/61	Original Commissions and Warrants, 1755-1763
ADM 7/393-397	Registers of Protections from being pressed by the Pressgangs
ADM 7/567	Navy Progress, 1755-1805
ADM 8/30-39	List Books (disposition of ships, names of officers), 1755-1763
ADM 12/26	Analysis and Digest of Court Martial Convictions, 1755-1806, Si-W
ADM 25/51-64	Officers' Half Pay Registers, 1756-1763
ADM 33	Ships' Pay Books, 1715-1830
ADM 35/216	Pay Book of the *Bounty* (AS), 1787-1790
ADM 36	Ships' Muster Books, 1688-1808
ADM 51	Captains' Logs, 1669-1852
ADM 52	Masters' Logs, 1672-1840
ADM 67/266	Royal Greenwich Hospital, Digest of Minutes, 1694-1829
ADM 97	Sick and Hurt Board

ADM 102/37   Deaths of Seamen at Haslar Hospital, 1755-1765
ADM 305/1-2   Haslar Hospital: Minutes of Council, 1755-1763
At the National Maritime Museum (NMM), Greenwich:
Adm/B/153-72   Letters from Navy Board to Admiralty, 1756-1763
Adm/L   Lieutenants' Logs

Manuscript Sources – Marine Society
All held at the National Maritime Museum (NMM) in Greenwich, London.

MSY/A/1-5	Fair Minutes of the Committee of the Marine Society (1756-1774)
MSY/B/8	Fair Minutes of the Committee (1809-1814)
MSY/C/2	Index to Minutes Vol.8 (1809-1814)
MSY/D/3	Fair Minutes of the General & Extraordinary Court (1806-1825)
MSY/E/1-2	Indices to Fair Minutes (1756-1825)
MSY/F/1	Agenda Book of Business
MSY/G/1-2	Letter Book (1802-1824)
MSY/H/1-4	Entry Books of Boys admitted (1756-1763)
MSY/J/3	Miscellaneous Volumes and Papers
MSY/K/1-6	Boys Received & Discharged from Society's Ship (1786-1818)
MSY/O/1-15	Registers of Boys entered as Servants in the King's Ships (1770-1873)
MSY/P/4	Alphabetical Index to MSY/O (1794-1811)
MSY/Q/1-17	Registers of Apprentices sent to Merchant Ships (1772-1950)
MSY/Q/31	Eight Indentures for Boys apprenticed to Merchant Ships (1792)
MSY/S/1-5	Registers of Landmen Volunteers (1756-1814)
MSY/T/1-17	Registers of Girl Apprentices under Hick's Trust (1771-1978)
MSY/U/21	Donations and Legacies with alphabetical index (1756-1842)
MSY/X/1	Ledgers (1756-1807)

Printed Sources – Admiralty
'Additional Regulations and Instructions Relating to His Majesty's Service at Sea' (London 1756), in *Regulations and Instructions Relating to His Majesty's Service at Sea* (London 1757, 9th ed.), pp.191-232.
Regulations and Instructions Relating to His Majesty's Service at Sea (London 1731-1808, various editions).

Printed Sources – Marine Society
'Rules, Forms and Regulations of the Marine Society', published in Hanway, *Three Letters on the Subject of the Marine Society: Letter III* (London 1758).
'Rules, Forms and Regulations of the Marine Society', published in Hanway, *An Account of the Marine Society* (London 1759, 6th ed.), pp.67-144.
The Origin, Progress, and Present State of the Marine Society (London 1770).
The Bye-Laws and Regulations of the Marine Society (London 1772, 1775).
A Short History of the Society together with the Act of Incorporation and the Bye-Laws (London 1952).
The Marine Society (London 1981).

(Re-)Printed Primary Sources

Anonymous, *The Effects of Industry and Idleness Illustrated in the Life, Adventures, and Various Fortunes of Two Fellow-'Prentices of the City of London: Being an Explanation of the Moral of Twelve Celebrated Prints, Lately Published, and Designed by the Ingenious Mr. Hogarth* (London 1748).

Anonymous, *Facts, Records, Authorities and Arguments Concerning the Claims of Liberty and the Obligations of Military Service* (London 1758).

Anonymous, 'The Female Cabin Boy', in Castle, Terry (ed.), *The Literature of Lesbianism: A Historical Anthology from Ariosto to Stonewall* (New York 2003), pp.248-249.

Ashton, John, *Chap-Books of the Eighteenth Century* (London 1882, 1969).

Barker, Matthew Henry, *Greenwich Hospital: A Series of Naval Sketches, descriptive of the Life of a Man-Of-War's Man, by an Old Sailor, with illustrations by George Cruikshank* (London 1836).

Barlow, Edward, *Barlow's Journal of his Life at Sea in King's Ships, East & West Indiamen and other Merchantmen from 1659 to 1703*, transcribed from the original manuscript by Basil Lubbock, 2 vols (London 1934).

Bechervaise, John, *Thirty-Six Years of a Seafaring Life, by an old Quarter Master* (Portsea, London 1839).

Bechervaise, John, *A Farewell to my Old Shipmates and Messmates; with some Examples, and a few Hints of Advice, by the Old Quarter Master* (Portsea 1847).

Blane, Gilbert, 'Statements of the Comparative Health of the British Navy, from the Year 1779 to the Year 1814, with Proposals for its Farther Improvement', in *Medico-Chirurgical Transactions*, vol.6 (1815), pp.490-573.

Blane, Gilbert, *Select Dissertations on Several Subjects of Medical Science*, vol.1 (London 1833).

Butler, William (Charles), *An Essay on the Legality of Impressing Seamen* (London 1777).

Coxere, Edward, *Adventures by Sea of Edward Coxere*, edited by E H W Meyerstein (Oxford 1945).

Cremer, John, *Ramblin' Jack: The Journal of Captain John Cremer, 1700-1774*, transcribed by R Reynell Bellamy (London 1936).

Defoe, Daniel, *Robinson Crusoe* (London 1719, 1975).

Dibdin, Charles, *The Sea-Songs of Charles Dibdin* (London 1852?).

Dickens, Charles, *Oliver Twist* (London 1838, 1992, Wordsworth edition).

Dillon, Sir William Henry, *A Narrative of my Professional Adventures, 1790-1839*, edited by Michael A. Lewis, vol.1 (Navy Records Society 1953).

Dingley, Robert, *An Essay on the Pernicious Practice of Impressing Seamen into the King's Service* (London 1760).

Equiano, Olaudah, *The Interesting Narrative of the Life of Olaudah Equiano* (Boston 1791, 1995, Bedford edition).

Fielding, Henry, *An Enquiry into the Causes of the Late Increase of Robbers* (London 1751).

Fielding, Henry, *A Proposal for Making an Effectual Provision for the Poor, for Amending their Morals, and for Rendering them Useful Members of Society* (London 1753).

Fielding Henry, *The History of Tom Jones, a Foundling* (London 1749, 1997).

Fielding, John, *A Plan for Preventing Robberies Within Twenty Miles of London* (London 1755).

Fielding John, *An Account of the Origin and Effects of a Police Set on Foot by His Grace the Duke of Newcastle in the year 1753, upon a Plan Presented to His Grace by the Late Henry Fielding, Esqr, to which is added a Plan for Preserving those Deserted Girls in this Town, who Become Prostitutes from Necessity* (London 1758).

Fielding, John, *The Newgate Magazine; or Malefactors Monthly*, 2 vols. (London 1765-1766).

Fielding, John, *An Account of the Receipts and Disbursements Relating to Sir John Fielding's Plan, for the Preserving of Distressed Boys, by Sending them to Sea* (London 1769).

Fielding, John, *A Brief Description of the Cities of London and Westminster* (London 1776).

Foundling Hospital, *An Account of the Hospital for the Maintenance and Education of Exposed and Deserted Young Children* (London 1749).

Glasse, Samuel, *A Sermon Preached before the President, Vice-Presidents, and Governors, of the Marine Society . . . to which is added an Abstract of the Proceedings of the Marine Society, from its First Institution* (London 1778).

Goodall, Daniel, *Salt Water Sketches, being the Incidents in the Life of Daniel Goodall, Seaman and Marine* (Inverness 1860).

Grant, Gordon, *The Life and Adventures of John Nicol, Mariner* (London 1822, 1937).

Greenwich Hospital, *Establishment for Admitting, Maintaining and Educating of Poor Boys, in the Royal Hospital for Seamen at Greenwich, and for Binding them out Apprentices to sea Sea-Service* (London 1732).

Hanway, Jonas, *A Letter from a Gentleman to his Friend Concerning the Naturalization of the Jews* (London 1753).

Hanway, Jonas, *A Review of the Proposed Naturalization of the Jews* (London 1753).

Hanway, Jonas, *A Journal of Eight Days' Journey from Portsmouth to Kingston upon Thames . . . an Essay on Tea* (London 1756).

Hanway, Jonas, *Thoughts on the Duty of a Good Citizen, with Regard to War and Invasion* (London 1756).

Hanway, Jonas, *A Letter from a Member of the Marine Society* (London 1757, 1st, 3rd & 4th ed.).

Hanway, Jonas, *Motives for the Establishment of the Marine Society* (London 1757).

Hanway, Jonas, *To the Marine Society, in Praise of the Great and Good Work they have done* (London 1757).

Hanway, Jonas, *A Plan for Establishing a Charity-House, or Charity-Houses, for the Reception of Repenting Prostitutes* (London 1758).

Hanway, Jonas, *Thoughts on the Plan for a Magdalen-House for Repentant Prostitutes* (London 1758).

Hanway, Jonas, *Three Letters on the Subject of the Marine Society: Letter I – On Occasion of their Clothing for the Sea 3097 Men, and 2045 Boys, to the End of Dec. 1757; Letter II – Pointing Out Several Advantages Accruing to the Nation from this Institution; Letter III – Being a Full Detail of the Rules and Forms of the Marine Society . . . To which is prefixed, a General View of the Motives for Establishing this Society* (prefix co-authored by John Thornton) (London 1758).

Hanway, Jonas, *Two Letters: Letter IV – Being Thoughts on the Means of Augmenting the Number of Mariners in these Kingdoms, upon Principles of Liberty; Letter V – To Robert Dingley Esq., containing Moral and Political Reasons for Relieving Prostitutes who are Inclined to Forsake their Evil Course of Life* (London 1758).

Hanway, Jonas, *An Account of the Marine Society, Recommending the Piety and Policy of the Institution, and Pointing Out the Advantages Accruing to the Nation* (London 1759, 6th ed.).

Hanway, Jonas, *Reasons for an Augmentation of at least Twelve Thousand Mariners* (London 1759).

Hanway, Jonas, *An Account of the Society for the Encouragement of British Troops in Germany and North America* (London 1760).

Hanway, Jonas, *Serious Considerations on the Salutary Design of the Act of Parliament for a Regular, Uniform Register of the Parish Poor in all the Parishes within the Bills of Mortality* (London 1762).

Hanway, Jonas, *Christian Knowledge Made Easy: with a Plain Account of the Lord's-Supper. To which is added, The Seaman's faithful Companion, with an Historical Account of the Late War* (London 1763).

Hanway, Jonas, *Instructions, Religious and Prudential, to Apprentices, and Servants in General, Placed Out by the Marine Society* (London 1763).

Hanway, Jonas, *The Seaman's Faithful Companion* (London 1763).

Hanway, Jonas, *The Case of the Parish Infant Poor within the Bills of Mortality* (London 1766).

Hanway, Jonas, *An Earnest Appeal for Mercy to the Children of the Poor* (London 1766).

Hanway, Jonas, *Letters to the Guardians of the Infant Poor* (London 1767).

Hanway, Jonas, *Moral and Religious Instructions, intended for Apprentices, and also for the Parish Poor* (London 1767).

Hanway, Jonas, *Observations on the Causes of the Dissoluteness which Reigns Among the Lower Classes of the People* (London 1772).

Hanway, Jonas, *The State of Chimney-Sweepers' Young Apprentices* (London 1773).

Hanway, Jonas, *The Defects of Police: The Cause of Immorality, and the Continual Robberies Committed, Particularly in and about the Metropolis* (London 1775).

Hanway, Jonas, *The State of Master Chimney-Sweepers, and their Journeymen, Particularly of the Distressed Boys* (London 1779).

Hanway, Jonas, *Rules and Regulations of the Maritime School* (London 1781).

Hanway, Jonas, *Abstract of the Proposal for County Naval Free Schools* (London 1783).

Hanway, Jonas, *Letters to the Governors of the Maritime-School* (London 1783).

Hanway, Jonas, *Proposal for County Naval Free Schools to be built on Waste Lands* (London 1783).

Hanway, Jonas, *Prudential Instructions to the Poor Boys Fitted Out by the Corporation of the Marine Society* (London 1783).

Hanway, Jonas, *Reasons for Pursuing the Plan Proposed by the Marine Society for the Establishment of County Free Schools on Waste Lands* (London 1784).

Hanway, Jonas, *Papers Recommended to the Mature Consideration of the Governors of the Marine Society* (London 1785).

Hanway, Jonas, *A Sentimental History of Chimney Sweepers* (London 1785).

Hay, M D (ed.), *Landsman Hay: The Memoirs of Robert Hay, 1789-1847* (London 1953).

Hayley, W, *Epistle to a Friend, on the Death of J Thornton* (London 1780).

Johnson, Samuel, *A Dictionary of the English Language* (London 1755, 1831).

King, Edward, *Proposals for Establishing at Sea a Marine School ... Written in Consequence of the Report Made by J. Hanway* (London 1785).

Kingston, W H G, *From Powder Monkey to Admiral* (London 1870, 1910).

Lacy, Mary, *The History of the Female Shipwright to whom the Government has granted a Superannuated Pension of Twenty Pounds per Annum, during her life* (London 1773), reprinted in *The Lady Tars: The Autobiographies of Hannah Snell, Mary Lacy and Mary Anne Talbot* (Tucson 2008), pp.56-140.

Leech, Samuel, *A Voice from the Main Deck: Being a Record of the Thirty Years Adventures of Samuel Leech* (London 1857, 1999).

Lind, James, *An Essay on the Most Effectual Means of Preserving Seamen in the Royal Navy* (London 1757, 1762).

Lind, James, *Two Papers on Fevers and Infection* (London 1761, 1763).

McPherson, Charles, *Life on Board a Man-of-War* (Glasgow 1829).

Marryat, Captain Frederick, *Peter Simple* (1834, New York 1998).

Marryat, Captain Frederick, *Mr Midshipman Easy* (1836, Stroud 2007).

Massie, J, *Further Observations Concerning the Foundling Hospital* (London 1759).

Massie, J (presumably), *Six Concluding Letters to a Senator on the Tendencies of the Foundling Hospital in its Boundless Extent* (London 1760).

Melville, Herman, *Billy Budd, Foretopman* (London 1924, 1946, John Lehmann edition).

A Merchant of the City of London, *A Plea for the Poor* (London 1759).

Mortimer, K, *The Universal Director; or, the Nobleman and Gentleman's True Guide to the Masters and Professors of the Liberal and Polite Arts and Sciences; and of the Mechanic Arts, Manufactures, and Trades, Established in London and Westminster, and their Environs* (London 1763).

Moss, William, *A Familiar Medical Survey of Liverpool: Addressed to the Inhabitants at Large* (Liverpool/London 1784).

Nauticus (or The Sailors Advocate), *The Rights of the Sailors Vindicated* (London 1772).

Parsons, George Samuel, *I sailed with Nelson* (London 1843, 1973).

Pemberton, Charles Reece, *The Autobiography of Pel. Verjuice, with an introduction on his life and work* (London 1929).

Pugh, John, *Remarkable Occurrences in the Life of Jonas Hanway* (London 1787, 1788).

Richardson, Samuel (presumably), *Apprentice's Vade Mecum: or, Young Man's Pocket-Companion* (1734), ed. by Augustan Reprint Society, nos.169-170 (Los Angeles 1975).

Robinson, William, *Jack Nastyface: Memoirs of an English Seaman* (London 1836, 1973).

Scott, Thomas, *A Discourse on ii Cor. Chap.V. Ver. 14, 15: Occasioned by the Death of John Thornton* (London 1791).

A Sea-Officer, 'Some Hints for the More Effectually Regulating and Disciplining His Majesty's Navy' (1758), in J S Bromley (ed.), *The Manning of the Royal Navy: Selected Public Pamphlets, 1693-1873* (Navy Records Society, vol.119, 1974/6), pp.114-123.

Sharp, William, *The Amiableness and Advantage of Making Suitable Provision for the Education and Employment of poor Children* (Oxford 1755).

Smith, Adam, *An Inquiry into the Nature and Causes of the Wealth of Nations* (London 1776; Indiana 1994).

Smollett, Tobias, *The Adventures of Roderick Random* (London 1748; Oxford 1999).

Spavens, William, *The Narrative of William Spavens, a Chatham Pensioner* (Louth 1796; London 1998).

Stepney Society (possibly Jonas Hanway), *Instructions to Apprentices Placed out by the Stepney-Society to Marine Trades* (London 1759).

Stevenson, Robert Louis, *Treasure Island* (London 1883, 1927).

Stevenson, Robert Louis, *Kidnapped, being the Adventures of David Balfour* (London 1886, 1895).

Swift, Butler, *Tyburn to the Marine Society: a Poem* (1759).

Talbot, Mary Anne, *Life and Surprising Adventures of Mary Anne Talbot, in the Name of John Taylor, a Natural Daughter of the Late Earl Talbot* (London 1809), reprinted in *The Lady Tars: The Autobiographies of Hannah Snell, Mary Lacy and Mary Anne Talbot* (Tucson 2008), pp.147-186.

Témeraire Mutiny: *The Trial of the Mutineers, late of his Majesty's Ship Témeraire, held on board the Gladiator, in Portsmouth Harbour, January 6, 1802* (London 1802).

Thomas, Aaron, *The Caribbean Journal of a Royal Navy Seaman, 1798-1799* (http://scholar.library.miami.edu/thomas, accessed 22/11/2009).

Trotter, Thomas, *Medicina Nautica: An Essay on the Diseases of Seamen, comprehending the History of Health in His Majesty's Fleet, under the command of Richard Earl Howe, Admiral* (London 1797).

Ward, Edward (Ned), *The Wooden World dissected: in the Character of a Ship of War* (Edinburgh 1707, 1779).

Ward, Edward (Ned), *The London Spy: Ned Ward's classic account of underworld life in eighteenth-century London*, edited by Paul Hyland (London 1709, East Lansing 1993).

Welch, Saunders, *Observations on the Office of Constable* (London 1754).

Welch, Saunders, *A Proposal to Render Effectual a Plan to Remove the Nuisance of Common Prostitutes from the Streets of this Metropolis; . . . To which is annexd, a Letter upon the Subject of Robberies, wrote in the year 1753* (London 1758).

Wheeler, *The Letters of Private Wheeler, 1809-1828*, edited by B H Liddell Hart (Adlestrop, Gloucestershire 1951).

Woodward, Josiah, *The Great Charity of Instructing poor Children* (London 1700).

Woodward, Josiah, *The Seaman's Monitor* (London 1705, 1767).

Contemporary Newspapers and Magazines

The Annual Register, The General Evening Post, The Gentleman's Magazine, The London Magazine: or Gentleman's Monthly Intelligencer, Public Advertiser.

Databases

Floud, Roderick, *Long-Term Changes in Nutrition, Welfare and Productivity in Britain* [computer file]. Colchester, Essex: UK Data Archive [distributor], 7 July 1986. SN: 2132.[1]

Floud, Roderick, *Long-Term Changes in Nutrition, Welfare and Productivity in Britain* [computer file]. Colchester, Essex: UK Data Archive [distributor], 7 July 1986. SN: 2134. [2]

Hitchcock, Tim, & Shoemaker, Robert B, *The Proceedings of the Old Bailey* (http://www.OldBaileyOnline.Org, accessed August 2008).

Payne, Dianne, *Marine Society Registers of Boys, MSY/O/1-4.*[3]

Pietsch, Roland, *Marine Society Registers of Boys, MSY/H/1-2.*[4]

Secondary Sources

Adkins, Roy & Lesley, *Jack Tar: Life in Nelson's Navy* (London 2008).

Allan, D G C, *William Shipley: Founder of the Royal Society of Arts* (London 1979).

Allan, D G C, 'Jonas Hanway and the Society of Arts', *Journal of the Royal Society of Arts*, vol.134 (1986), pp.650-653.

---

1. Contains data of Marine Society's landsmen, 1756-1812, no names though.
2. Contains data of Marine Society's boys, 1770-1873, no names though.
3. I am indebted to Dianne Payne for allowing me to use the database she compiled of the Marine Society's boy registers for the period 1770-1780. The database is not publicly available.
4. Contains the Society's boy recruits 1756-1762; included on CD attached to Pietsch, 'Ships' Boys and Charity in the Mid-Eighteenth Century' (unpublished PhD thesis, University of London 2003).

Allan, D G C & Abbott, John L, '"Compassion and Horror in Every Human Mind": Samuel Johnson, The Society of Arts, and Eighteenth-Century Prostitution', in Allan & Abbott (eds.), *The Virtuoso Tribe of Arts & Sciences: Studies in the Eighteenth-Century Work and Membership of the London Society of Arts* (Athens [Georgia] 1992), pp.18-37.

Andrew, Donna T, *Philanthropy and Police: London Charity in the Eighteenth Century* (Princeton 1989).

Ariès, Philippe, *Centuries of Childhood* (Paris 1960; London 1996).

Baacke, Dieter, *Jugend und Jugendkulturen: Darstellung und Deutung* (Weinheim 1987, 1993).

Babington, Anthony, *A House in Bow Street: Crime and the Magistracy, London 1740-1881* (London 1969).

Baugh, Daniel A, *British Naval Administration in the Age of Walpole* (Princeton 1965).

Baynham, Henry W F, *From the Lower Deck: the Old Navy, 1780-1840* (Hutchinson 1969).

Beaglehole, J C (ed.), *The Journals of Captain James Cook on His Voyages of Discovery: The Voyage of the Endeavour, 1768-1771* (Cambridge 1955).

Beaglehole, J C, *The Life of Captain James Cook* (London 1974).

Beattie, J M, *Crime and the Courts in England, 1660-1800* (Oxford 1986).

Black, J, *The English Press in the Eighteenth Century* (London 1987).

Bligh, John, *Vice Admiral William Bligh FRS* (Rochester 2001).

Bosanquet, Henry, *Annals of the Marine Society* (London 1955).

Bowen, H V, 'British Conceptions of Global Empire, 1756-83', *Journal of Imperial and Commonwealth History*, vol.26 (1998), pp.1-27.

Bromley, J S (ed.), *The Manning of the Royal Navy: Selected Pamphlets, 1693-1873* (Navy Records Society, vol.119, 1974/6).

Bromley, J S, 'The British Navy and its Seamen after 1688: Notes for an Unwritten History', in S Palmer & G Williams (eds.), *Charted and Uncharted Waters: Proceedings of a Conference on the Study of British Maritime History* (London 1981), pp.148-163.

Burg, B R, *Sodomy and the Pirate Tradition: English Sea Rovers in the Seventeenth-Century Caribbean* (New York, London 1983, 1995).

Burg, B R, *Boys at Sea: Sodomy, Indecency, and Courts Martial in Nelson's Navy* (Houndmills & New York 2007).

Burke, Peter, *Popular Culture in Early Modern Europe* (Aldershot, Cambridge 1978, 1994).

Caplan, Jane (ed.), *Written on the Body: The Tattoo in European and American History* (London 2000).

Carretta, Vincent, *Equiano, the African: Biography of a Self Made Man* (Athens, Georgia 2005).

Cavell, Samantha, 'A Social History of Midshipmen and Quarterdeck Boys in the Royal Navy, 1761-1831' (unpublished PhD thesis, University of Exeter 2010).

Clark, Peter, *British Clubs and Societies, 1580-1800: The Origins of an Associational World* (Oxford 2000).

Clayton, Tim, *Tars: The Men who made Britain rule the Waves* (London 2007).

Clifton, Gloria, *Directory of British Scientific Instrument Makers, 1550-1851* (London 1995).

Clowes, William Laird, *The Royal Navy: a History from the Earliest Times to Present: Vol. III* (London 1898; New York 1966).

Cock, Randolph, & Rodger, N A M (eds.), *A Guide to the Naval Records in the National Archives of the UK* (London 2006, 2008).

Cohen, M, *Fashioning Masculinity: National Identity and Language in the Eighteenth Century*

(London 1996).

Colley, Linda, *Britons: Forging the Nation, 1707-1837* (London 1992, 1994).

Compstone, H F B, *The Magdalen Hospital: The Story of a Great Charity* (London 1917).

Cooper, Janet (ed.), *A History of the County of Essex: Vol. IX* (Oxford 1994).

Cordingly, David, *Life Among the Pirates: The Romance and the Reality* (London 1995, 1996).

Corfield, P J, 'Class by Name and Number in Eighteenth-Century Britain', *History*, vol.72 (1987), pp.38-61.

Cowherd, Raymond G, *Political Economists and the English Poor Laws: a Historical Study of the Influence of Classical Economics on the Formation of Social Welfare Policy* (Athens [Georgia], 1977).

Crimmin, Patricia K, 'The Sick and Hurt Board and the Health of Seamen, c.1700-1806', *Journal for Maritime Research* (December 1999).

Cunningham, Hugh, & Innes, Joanna (eds.), *Charity, Philanthropy and Reform: from the 1690s to 1850* (Basingstoke 1998).

Daunton, Martin J, *An Economic and Social History of Britain, 1700-1850* (Oxford 1995).

Daunton, Martin J (ed.), *Charity, Self-Interest and Welfare in the English Past* (London 1996).

Davis, Natalie Zemon, 'The Reasons of Misrule: Youth Groups and Charivaris in Sixteenth-Century France', *Past and Present*, vol.50 (1971), pp.41-75.

Davis, Ralph, *The Rise of the English Shipping Industry in the Seventeenth and Eighteenth Centuries* (Newton Abbot 1962, 1972).

Davison, Lee, Hitchcock, Tim, Keirn, Tim, & Shoemaker, Robert B (eds.), *Stilling the Grumbling Hive: The Response to Social and Economic Problems in England, 1689-1750* (New York/Stroud 1992).

Deane, Phyllis, & Cole, William A, *British Economic Growth, 1688-1859: Trends and Structure* (Cambridge 1967).

deMause, Lloyd, 'On Writing Child History', *Journal of Psychohistory*, vol.16, (http://www.geocities.com/kidhistory/writech1.htm, 1988, accessed 20/11/2002).

Dening, Greg, *Mr Bligh's Bad Language: Passion, Power and Theatre on the Bounty* (Cambridge 1992).

Distad, N Merrill, 'Jonas Hanway and the Marine Society', *History Today*, vol.33 (1973), pp.434-440.

Donald, Diana, *The Age of Caricature: Satirical Prints in the Age of George III* (New Haven 1996).

Dull, Jonathan R, *The French Navy and the Seven Years' War* (Lincoln-Nebraska 2005).

Earle, Peter, *The Making of the English Middle Class: Business, Society and Family Life in London, 1660-1730* (London 1989).

Earle, Peter, 'English Sailors, 1570-1775', in Paul van Royen, Jaap Bruijn & Jan Lucassen (eds.), *'Those Emblems of Hell'?: European Sailors and the Maritime Labour Market, 1570-1870* (St John's, Newfoundland 1997), pp.73-92.

Earle, Peter, *Sailors: English Merchant Seamen, 1650-1775* (London 1998).

Eder, Markus, *Crime and Punishment in the Royal Navy of the Seven Years War, 1755-1763* (Aldershot 2004).

Endelman, Todd M, *The Jews of Georgian England, 1714-1830: Tradition and Change in a Liberal Society* (1979, Michigan 1999).

Fahrner, Robert, *The Theatre Career of Charles Dibdin the Elder, 1745-1814* (New York 1989).

Floud, Roderick, & Wachter, Kenneth, 'Poverty and Physical Stature: Evidence on the

Standard of Living of London Boys, 1770-1870', *Social Science History*, vol.6 (1982), pp.422-452.

Floud, Roderick, Wachter, Kenneth, & Gregory, Annabel, *Height, Health and History: Nutritional Status in the United Kingdom, 1750-1980* (Cambridge 1990).

Frampton, Richard, 'The Emblems of the Marine Society "Charity and Policy United"', *Journal of the Royal Society of Arts*, vol.134 (1986), pp.659-62.

Friedenberg, Zachary B, *Medicine under Sail* (Annapolis 2002).

Fury, Cheryl A, 'Training and Education in the Elizabethan Maritime Community, 1585-1603', *The Mariner's Mirror*, vol.85, no.2 (May 1999), pp.147-161.

Fury, Cheryl A, *Tides in the Affairs of Men: The Social History of Elizabethan Seamen, 1580-1603* (Westport 2002).

George, M Dorothy, *London Life in the Eighteenth Century* (London, 1925, 1992).

Gilbert, Arthur N, 'Buggery and the British Navy, 1700-1861', *Journal of Social History*, vol.10 (1976), pp.72-98.

Gillis, John R, *Youth and History: Tradition and Change in European Age Relations, 1770-Present* (London 1974, 1981).

Glennie, Paul, *'Distinguishing Men's Trades': Occupational Sources and Debates for Pre-Census England* (Bristol 1990).

Goldberg, Angus E, 'The Somers' Mutiny of 1842' (unpublished PhD thesis, St. Andrew's University 2000).

Gradish, Stephen F, *The Manning of the British Navy During the Seven Years' War* (London 1980).

Green, David, *From Artisans to Paupers: Economic Change and Poverty in London, 1790-1870* (Aldershot 1995).

Hackman, W Kent, 'The British Raid on Rochefort, 1757', *Mariner's Mirror*, vol.64 (1978), pp.263-275.

Hancock, David, *Citizens of the World: London Merchants and the Integration of the British Atlantic Community, 1735-1785* (Cambridge 1995).

Harris, Bob, 'Patriotic Commerce and National Revival: The Free British Fishery Society and British Politics, c.1749-58', *English Historical Review*, vol.114 (1999), pp.285-313.

Hebdige, Dick, *Subculture: The Meaning of Style* (London 1979).

Heintel, Markus, & Baten, Jörg, 'Smallpox and Nutritional Status in England, 1770-1873: on the Difficulties of Estimating Historical Heights', *Economic History Review*, vol.51 (1998), pp.360-371.

Hellmuth, Eckhart (ed.), *The Transformation of Political Culture: England and Germany in the Late Eighteenth Century* (Oxford, London 1990).

Heywood, Colin, *A History of Childhood: Children and Childhood in the West from Medieval to Modern Times* (Cambridge 2001).

Himmelfarb, Gertrude, *The Idea of Poverty: England in the Early Industrial Age* (Trowbridge 1984, 1985).

Hitchcock, Tim, *Down and Out in Eighteenth-Century London* (New York 2004).

Hope, Ronald, 'The Blind Beak of Bow Street and the Marine Society', *Sea History*, vol.24 (1982), p.26.

Hope, Ronald, *A New History of British Shipping* (London 1990).

Hope, Ronald, *Poor Jack: The Perilous History of the Merchant Seaman* (London 2001).

Hubrig, Hans, *Die Patriotischen Gesellschaften des 18. Jahrhunderts* (Weinheim 1957).

Humphries, Jane, *Childhood and Child Labour in the British Industrial Revolution* (Cambridge 2010).

Hutchins, John H, *Jonas Hanway, 1712-1786* (London, New York 1940).

Hutchinson, John R, *The Press-Gang Afloat and Ashore* (London 1913).

Innes, Joanna, 'The "Mixed Economy of Welfare" in Early Modern England: Assessments of the Options from Hale to Malthus (*c.* 1683-1803)', in M J Daunton (ed.), *Charity, Self-Interest and Welfare in the English Past* (London 1996), pp.139-180.

Jarrett, Dudley, *British Naval Dress* (London 1960).

Jayne, R Everett, *Jonas Hanway: Philanthropist, Politician, Author, 1712-1786* (London 1929).

Jenks, Timothy, *Naval Engagements: Patriotism, Cultural Politics, and the Royal Navy, 1793-1815* (Oxford 2006).

Jones, Mary G, *The Charity School Movement: a Study of Eighteenth Century Puritanism in Action* (London 1938, 1964).

Kemp, Peter, *The British Sailor: a Social History of the Lower Deck* (London 1970).

Kennedy, Paul M, *The Rise and Fall of British Naval Mastery* (London 1976, 1983).

Kindleberger, Charles P, *Mariners and Markets* (New York 1992).

King, Peter, *Crime, Justice, and Discretion in England, 1740-1820* (Oxford 2000).

King, Peter, *Crime and Law in England, 1750-1840* (Cambridge 2006).

Kirkman Gray, Benjamin, *A History of English Philanthropy: from the Dissolution of the Monasteries to the Taking of the First Census* (London 1905).

Kish, Leslie, *Survey Sampling* (New York, London, Sidney 1965).

Kocka, Jürgen, *Weder Stand noch Klasse: Unterschichten um 1800* (Bonn 1990).

Knight, Roger, *The Pursuit of Victory: The Life and Achievement of Horatio Nelson* (London 2005).

Krausman Ben-Amos, Ilana, *Adolescence and Youth in Early Modern England* (New Haven & London 1994).

Laird Clowes, William, *The Royal Navy: A History from the Earliest Times to the Present*, vol.3 (London 1898).

Lamb, Jonathan, *Preserving the Self in the South Seas, 1680-1840* (Chicago and London 2001).

Lamb, Jonathan, *The Evolution of Sympathy in the Long Eighteenth Century* (London 2009).

Lambert, Andrew, *Nelson: Britannia's God of War* (London 2004).

Land, Isaac E, 'Domesticating the Maritime: Culture, Masculinity, and Empire in Britain, 1770-1820' (unpublished PhD thesis, University of Michigan 1999).

Land, Isaac, 'The Many-Tongued Hydra: Sea Talk, Maritime Culture, and Atlantic Identities, 1700-1850,' in *Journal of American and Comparative Cultures*, vol.25, nos.3-4 (December 2002), pp.412-417.

Land, Isaac, *War, Nationalism, and the British Sailor, 1750-1850* (New York 2009).

Land, Isaac, 'The Humours of Sailortown: Atlantic History Meets Subculture Theory', in Glenn Clark, Judith Owens & Greg Smith (eds.), *City Limits: Perspectives on the Historical European City* (Montreal, 2010), (to be published).

Landers, John, *Death and the Metropolis: Studies in the Demographic History of London, 1670-1830* (Cambridge 1993).

Langford, Paul, *A Polite and Commercial People: England, 1727-1783* (Oxford 1989, 1998).

Langford, Paul, *Public Life and the Propertied Englishman, 1689-1798* (Oxford 1991).

Lavery, Brian (ed.), *Shipboard Life and Organisation, 1731-1815* (Navy Records Society, vol. 138, 1998).

Lawrence, Christopher, 'Disciplining Disease: Scurvy, the Navy, and Imperial Expansion, 1750-1825', in David Philip Miller & Peter Hanns Reill (eds.), *Visions of Empire: Voyages, Botany, and Representation of Nature* (Cambridge 1996, 1998), pp.80-106.

Lawson, John & Silver, Harold, *A Social History of Education in England* (London 1973).

Lees, Lyn Hollen, *The Solidarity of Strangers: The English Poor Laws and the People, 1700-1948* (Cambridge 1998).

Lemisch, Jesse, 'Jack Tar in the Streets: Merchant Seamen in the Politics of Revolutionary America', *William and Mary Quarterly*, 3rd Series, vol.25 (1968), pp.371-407.

Leslie-Melville, Ronald, *The Life and Work of Sir John Fielding* (London 1934).

Lewis, Michael A, *A Social History of the Navy, 1793-1815* (London 1960).

Lincoln, Anthony L J, & McEwen, Robert Lindley (eds.), *Lord Eldon's Anecdote Book* (London 1960).

Linebaugh, Peter, *The London Hanged: Crime and Civil Society in the Eighteenth Century* (London 1991, 1993).

Linebaugh, Peter, & Rediker, Marcus, *The Many-Headed Hydra: Sailors, Slaves, Commoners, and the Hidden History of the Revolutionary Atlantic* (London 2000).

Lloyd, Christopher, *The British Seaman, 1200-1860: a Social Survey* (London 1968, 1970).

Lloyd, Christopher (ed.), *The Health of Seamen: Selections from the Works of Dr James Lind, Sir Gilbert Lane and Thomas Trotter* (Navy Records Society, vol.57, 1965).

Lloyd, Christopher, & Coulter, Jack L S, *Medicine and the Navy*, vol.3 (Edinburgh, London 1961).

Lyon, David, *The Sailing Navy List: all the Ships of the Royal Navy – Built, Purchased and Captured – 1688-1860* (London 1993).

Macmillan, David S, 'The Russia Company of London in the Eighteenth Century: the Effective Survival of a "Regulated" Chartered Company', *Guildhall Miscellany*, vol.4 (1971/3), pp.222-236.

Marshall, Dorothy, *The English Poor in the Eighteenth Century: a Study in Social and Administrative History* (London 1926, 1969).

Marshall, John, *Royal Navy Biography, or Memoirs of the Services of all the Flag-Officers, Superannuated Rear-Admirals, Retired-Captains, Post-Captains, and Commanders, Supplement, Part IV* (London 1830).

Masefield, John, *Sea Life in Nelson's Time* (Barnsley 1905, 2002).

McClure, Ruth K, *Coram's Children: The London Foundling Hospital in the Eighteenth Century* (New Haven 1981).

McCreery, Cindy, 'True Blue and Black, Brown and Fair: Prints of British Sailors and their Women During the Revolutionary and Napoleonic Wars', *British Journal for Eighteenth-Century Studies*, vol.23 (2000), pp.135-152.

McNaught, Charles, 'Roundabout Old East London', series in *East London Observer* (15/04/1911 & 10/08/1912, for Stepney Society).

Miller, Amy, *Dressed to Kill: British Naval Uniform, Masculinity and Contemporary Fashions, 1748-1857* (London 2007).

Miller Lydenberg, Harry, *Crossing the Line: Tales of the Ceremony During Four Centuries* (New York 1957).

Mitchell, Brian R, *Abstract of British Historical Statistics* (Cambridge 1988).

Mitterauer, Michael, *Sozialgeschichte der Jugend* (Frankfurt 1986).

Mollison, James, & Morris, Desmond, *The Disciples* (London 2008).

Moore, Lucy, *The Thieves' Opera: The Remarkable Lives of Jonathan Wild, Thief-Taker, and Jack Sheppard, House-Breaker* (London 1997).

Morris, R J, 'Civil Society and the Nature of Urbanism: Britain, 1750-1850', *Urban History*, vol.25 (1998), pp.289-301.

Morris, R J, 'Fuller Values, Questions and Contexts: Occupational Coding and the Historian', in K Schürer & H Diedericks (eds.), *The Use of Occupations in Historical Analysis* (St Katherinen, 1993), pp.5-21.

Namier, Sir Lewis, & Brooke, John, *The History of Parliament: The House of Commons, 1754-1790* (London 1964).

Nash, Stanley, 'Prostitution and Charity: The Magdalen Hospital, a Case Study', *Journal of Social History*, vol.17 (1984), pp.617-628.

Neale, Jonathan, *The Cutlass and the Lash: Mutiny and Discipline in Nelson's Navy* (London, Sidney 1985).

Neuberg, Victor, *Popular Education in Eighteenth Century England* (London 1971).

Newell, Philip, *Greenwich Hospital, a Royal Foundation, 1692-1983* (London 1984).

Newman, Gerald, *The Rise of English Nationalism: a Cultural History, 1740-1830* (London 1997).

Nicholls, Sir George, *A History of the English Poor Law in Connection with the State of the Country and the Condition of the People* (London 1898).

Nichols, Reginald H, & Wray, F A, *The History of the Foundling Hospital* (London 1935).

Norton, Rictor (ed.), 'A Robber Swears Sodomy against his Victim, 1759', *Homosexuality in Eighteenth-century England: a Sourcebook*, (http://www.infopt.demon.co.uk/1759browhtm, upd. 25/04/2000, accessed 12/09/2002).

Norton, Rictor (ed.), 'Madge Culls, 1781', *Homosexuality in Eighteenth-century England: a Sourcebook* (http://www.infopt.demon.co.uk/1781parkhtm, upd. 26/02/2002, accessed 12/09/1002).

Ogborn, Miles, *Spaces of Modernity: London's Geographies, 1680-1780* (New York, London 1998).

Owen, David, *English Philanthropy, 1660-1960* (Cambridge, Mass. 1964).

Palmer, Sarah, & Williams, David M, 'British Sailors, 1775-1870', in Paul van Royen, Jaap Bruijn, & Jan Lucassen (eds.), *'Those Emblems of Hell'?: European Sailors and the Maritime Labour Market, 1570-1870* (St John's, Newfoundland 1997), pp.93-118.

Palmer, Sarah, & Williams, Glyn (eds.), *Charted and Uncharted Waters: Proceedings of a Conference on the Study of British Maritime History* (London 1981).

Patten, J, 'Urban Occupations', *Transactions of Institute for British Geographers*, vol.2 (1997), pp.296-313.

Paulson, Ronald, *Emblem and Expression: Meaning in English Art of the Eighteenth Century* (London 1975).

Paulson, Ronald, *Popular and Polite Art in the Age of Hogarth and Fielding* (Notre Dame, London 1979).

Payne, Dianne, 'Rhetoric, Reality and the Marine Society', in *The London Journal*, vol.30, no.2 (2005), pp 66-84.

Payne, Dianne Elizabeth, 'Children of the Poor in London, 1700-1780' (unpublished PhD thesis, University of Hertfordshire 2008).

Pearsall, A W H, 'Jonas Hanway and Naval Victualling', *Journal of the Royal Society of Arts*, vol.134 (1986), pp.656-658.

Phillips, Carla Rahn, '"The Life Blood of the Navy": Recruiting Sailors in Eighteenth-Century

Spain', *Mariner's Mirror*, vol.87 (2000), pp.420-445.

Phillipson, David, *Band of Brothers: Boy Seamen in the Royal Navy, 1800-1956* (Stroud 1996).

Pietsch, Roland, *Dialog mit Niccolò Machiavelli: ein Versuch* (Marburg 1995).

Pietsch, Roland, 'Die Bankrestriktion in England um die Zeit der Kriege gegen Frankreich, 1797-1815: Ein Anlaß für Geldtheoretische und Politische Kontroversen' (unpublished MA thesis, TU Berlin 1996).

Pietsch, Roland, 'A Boyhood at Sea: The Records of the Marine Society at the National Maritime Museum, Greenwich', *Genealogists' Magazine*, vol.27 (2001), pp.3-8.

Pietsch, Roland W W, 'Ships' Boys and Charity in the Mid-Eighteenth Century: The London Marine Society, 1756-1772' (unpublished PhD thesis, University of London 2003).

Pietsch, Roland, 'Ship's Boys and Youth Culture in Eighteenth-Century Britain: The Navy Recruits of the London Marine Society', *The Northern Mariner/Le Marin du Nord*, vol.14, no.4 (October 2004), pp.11-24.

Pietsch, Roland, '"The Idle Apprentice sent to Sea": Sailors and Urban Youth Culture in the Eighteenth Century', *Trafalgar Chronicle*, no.19 (2009), pp.174-189.

Pinchbeck, Ivy, & Hewitt, Margaret, *Children in English Society: Vol. 1* (London, Toronto 1969).

Pitcairn Jones, A G, 'Midshipmen', *Mariner's Mirror*, vol.40 (1954), pp.212-219.

Plumb, J H, 'The New World of Children in Eighteenth-Century England', *Past and Present*, vol.67 (1975), pp.64-95.

Pope, Dudley, *The Black Ship* (London 1963).

Pope, Steve, *Hornblower's Navy: Life at Sea in the Age of Nelson* (London 1998).

Prentice, Rina, 'Ragged Boys: Jonas Hanway and the Origins of the Marine Society' (unpublished paper, National Maritime Museum, London 1998).

Pringle, Patrick, *Hue and Cry: The Birth of the British Police* (London 1955).

Pringle, Patrick, *Henry and Sir John Fielding: The Thief-Catchers* (London 1968).

Pullan, Brian, 'Charity and Poor Relief in Early Modern Italy', in M J Daunton (ed.), *Charity, Self-Interest and Welfare in the English Past* (London 1996), pp.65-89.

Quilley, Geoff, 'Duty and mutiny: the aesthetics of loyalty and the representation of the British sailor *c.*1798-1800', in Philip Shaw (ed.), *Romantic Wars: Studies in Culture and Conflict, 1793-1822* (Aldershot 2000), pp.80-109.

Rauh, Nicholas K, *Merchants, Sailors, and Pirates in the Roman World* (Stroud 2003).

Razzell, Peter, *The Conquest of Smallpox: The Impact of Inoculation on Smallpox Mortality in Eighteenth Century Britain* (Sussex 1977).

Razzell, Peter, 'Did Smallpox reduce Height?', *Economic History Review*, vol.51 (1998), pp.351-359.

Razzell, Peter, 'Did Smallpox reduce Height? A final Comment', *Economic History Review*, vol.54 (2001), pp.108-109.

Razzell, Peter, *Population and Disease: Transforming English Society, 1550-1850* (Sussex 2007).

Rediker, Marcus, *Between the Devil and the Deep Blue Sea: Merchant Seamen, Pirates, and the Anglo-American Maritime World, 1700-1750* (Cambridge 1987, 1998).

Regan, Shaun, 'Slavery, Service and the Sea: Olaudah Equiano and the Seven Years' War,' in Frans de Bruyn & Shaun Regan (eds.), *The Culture of the Seven Years' War: Empire, Identity and the Arts* (forthcoming publication).

Ribeiro, Aileen, 'Men and Umbrellas in the Eighteenth Century', *Journal of the Royal Society of Arts*, vol.134 (1986), pp.653-656.

Roberts, Michael J D, 'Head versus Heart? Voluntary Associations and Charity Organization in England, *c.* 1700-1850', in Hugh Cunningham & Joanna Innes (eds.), *Charity, Philanthropy and Reform: From the 1690s to 1850* (Basingstoke 1998), pp.66-86.

Robinson, Charles Napier, *The British Tar in Fact and Fiction: The Poetry, Pathos, and Humour of the Sailor's Life* (London & New York 1909).

Rodger, N A M, *Naval Records for Genealogists* (London 1984, 1998).

Rodger, N A M, 'Stragglers and Deserters from the Royal Navy during the Seven Years War', *Bulletin of the Institute of Historical Research*, vol.57 (1984), pp.56-79.

Rodger, N A M, *The Wooden World: an Anatomy of the Georgian Navy* (London 1986, 1988).

Rodger, N A M, *The Command of the Ocean: A Naval History of Britain, 1649-1815* (London 2004).

Rodgers, Betsy, *The Cloak of Charity: Studies in Eighteenth-Century Philanthropy* (London 1949).

Rogers, Nicholas, *Crowds, Culture and Politics in Georgian Britain* (Oxford 1998).

Rogers, Nicholas, *The Press Gang: Naval Impressment and its Opponents in Georgian Britain* (London 2007).

Ronald, D A B, *Young Nelsons: Boy Sailors during the Napoleonic Wars* (Oxford 2009).

Russell, David, *Scenes from Bedlam: A History of Caring for the Mentally Disordered at the Bethlem Royal Hospital and The Maudsley* (London 1997).

Schürer, Kevin, & Diederiks, Herman (eds.), *The Use of Occupations in Historical Analysis* (St Katharinen 1993).

Schwarz, L D, *London in the Age of Industrialisation: Entrepreneurs, Labour Force and Living Conditions, 1700-1850* (Cambridge 1992).

Sedgwick, T E, 'Jonas Hanway, Founder of the Marine Society', *Marine Magazine*, vol.6 (1916), pp.1-5, 13-16.

Shoemaker, Robert B, *London Mob: Violence and Disorder in Eighteenth-Century England* (London 2004).

Shore, Heather, *Artful Dodgers: Youth and Crime in Early Nineteenth-Century London* (Suffolk 1999).

Slack, Paul, *The English Poor Law, 1531-1782* (Cambridge 1990, 1995).

Smith, Steven R, 'The London Apprentices as Seventeenth Century Adolescents', *Past and Present*, vol.61 (1973), pp.149-161.

Stark, Suzanne J, *Female Tars: Women Aboard Ship in the Age of Sail* (London 1996, 1998).

Starkey, David J, *British Privateering Enterprise in the Eighteenth Century* (Exeter 1990).

Starkey, David J, 'War and the Market for Seafarers in Britain, 1736-1792', in Lewis R Fisher & Helge W Nordvik (eds.), *Shipping and Trade, 1750-1950: Essays in International Maritime Economic History* (Pontefract 1990), pp.25-42.

Stone, Lawrence, *The Family, Sex and Marriage in England 1500-1800* (London 1977).

Sugden, John, *Nelson: A Dream of Glory* (London 2004, 2005).

Syrett, David, & Di Nardo, R L (eds.), *The Commissioned Sea Officers of the Royal Navy, 1660-1815* (Aldershot 1994).

Taylor, James S, 'Philanthropy and Empire: Jonas Hanway and the Infant Poor of London', *Eighteenth-Century Studies*, vol.12 (1978-9), pp.285-305.

Taylor, James S, *Jonas Hanway, Founder of the Marine Society: Charity and Policy in Eighteenth-Century Britain* (London 1985).

Taylor, James S, 'Jonas Hanway: Christian Mercantilist', *Journal of the Royal Society of Arts*, vol.134 (1986), pp.641-645.

Tawney, A J & R H, 'An Occupational Census of the Seventeenth Century', *Economic History Review*, vol.5 (1934), pp.25-64.

Thomas, E G, 'The Old Poor Law and Maritime Apprenticeship', *Mariner's Mirror*, vol.63 (1977), pp.153-161.

Thompson, Roger, 'Adolescent Culture in Colonial Massachusetts', *Journal of Family History*, vol.9 (1984), pp.127-144.

Turley, Hans, *Rum, Sodomy, and the Lash: Piracy, Sexuality, and Masculine Identity* (New York, London 1999).

Turner, H D T, *The Royal Hospital School, Greenwich* (London & Chichester 1980).

Turner, H D, *The Cradle of the Navy: The Story of the Royal Hospital School at Greenwich and at Holbrook, 1694-1988* (York 1990).

Van der Merwe, Pieter, *'A Refuge for All': Greenwich Hospital, 1694-1994* (London 1994).

Voth, Hans-Joachim, & Leunig, Timothy, 'Did Smallpox reduce Height? Stature and the Standard of Living in London, 1770-1873', *Economic History Review*, vol.49 (1996), pp.541-60.

Voth, Hans-Joachim, & Leunig, Timothy, 'Did Smallpox reduce Height: a Reply to our Critics', *Economic History Review*, vol.51 (1998), pp.372-381.

Voth, Hans-Joachim, & Leunig, Timothy, 'Smallpox really did reduce Height: a Reply to Razzell', *Economic History Review*, vol.54 (2001), pp.110-114.

Watson, Harold Francis, *Coasts of Treasure Island: A Study of the Backgrounds and Sources for Robert Louis Stevenson's Romance of the Sea* (San Antonio 1969).

Willan, Thomas S, *The Early History of the Russia Company* (New York 1968).

Williams, Glyn, *The Prize of all the Oceans: The Triumph and Tragedy of Anson's Voyage Round the World* (London 1999).

Wilson, Kathleen, 'Urban Culture and Political Activism in Hanoverian England: The Example of Voluntary Hospitals', in Eckhart Hellmuth (ed.), *The Transformation of Political Culture: England and Germany in the Late Eighteenth Century* (Oxford/London 1990), pp.165-184.

Wilson, Kathleen, *The Sense of the People: Politics, Culture and Imperialism in England, 1715-1785* (Cambridge 1995).

Wilson, Kathleen, *The Island Race: Englishness, Empire and Gender in the Eighteenth Century* (London & New York 2003).

Woodman, Richard, . . .*of Daring Temper: 250 Years of the Marine Society* (London 2006).

Wrigley, E Anthony (ed.), *An Introduction to English Historical Demography: From the Sixteenth to the Nineteenth Century* (London 1996).

Wrigley, E Anthony, & Schofield, Roger S., *The Population History of England, 1541-1871: a Reconstruction* (Cambridge 1981, 1989).

Wrigley, E A, Davies, R S, Oeppen, J E, Schofield, R S (eds.), *English Population History from Family Reconstitution, 1580-1837* (Cambridge 1997).

Yarbrough, Anne, 'Apprentices as Adolescents in Sixteenth-Century Bristol', *Journal of Social History*, vol.13 (1979), pp.67-82.

Zinsser, Hans, *Rats, Lice and History* (New York 1935, 1965).

Index

References to illustrations are given in *italic*.